A MILITARY ATTACHÉ
IN THE BALKANS.

Military Attaché A.

KING BORIS III.

(Presented to the Author).

The Experiences of a Military Attaché in the Balkans

BY

Lt.-Col. The HONBLE. H. D. NAPIER, C.M.G.

The Naval & Military Press Ltd

Reproduced by kind permission of the Central Library,
Royal Military Academy, Sandhurst

Published by
The Naval & Military Press Ltd
Unit 10, Ridgewood Industrial Park,
Uckfield, East Sussex,
TN22 5QE England
Tel: +44 (0) 1825 749494
Fax: +44 (0) 1825 765701
www.naval-military-press.com
www.military-genealogy.com

© The Naval & Military Press Ltd 2010

The Naval & Military Press ...

...offer specialist books for the serious student of conflict. The range of titles stocked covers the whole spectrum of military history with titles on uniforms, battles, official histories, specialist works containing Medal Rolls and Casualties Lists, and numismatic titles for medal collectors and researchers.

The innovative approach they have to military bookselling and their commitment to publishing have made them Britain's leading independent military bookseller.

In reprinting in facsimile from the original, any imperfections are inevitably reproduced and the quality may fall short of modern type and cartographic standards.

ERRATA ET ADDENDA.

For reference to Frontispiece, see page 241.
Page 11, lines 29, and 30, "?" read page 173.
Page 31, line 19, for " day " read " days."
Page 191, line 23, for " up to the " read " up the."
Page 233, line 35, for " behaviours " read " behaviour."
Page 238, line 7, for " been " read " gone."
Page 245, lines 17-31, omit inverted commas.
Page 272, at foot, read signature " H. D. Napier."
Index—Thompson, " Col. C. B.," read " Thomson, Lord "; " Wemyss, Admiral," read "Wester Wemyss, Lord."

Contents.

PREFACE.

CHAPTER I.

Appointed Military Attaché Bulgaria—Journey to Sofia—Pro-German sentiments of Bulgarian General—Bulgarian War Strength—Union Club—Result of Balkan War—General Boyadjiew—First conclusions as to necessity of winning Bulgaria for Entente—Co-operation of Roumania also necessary—Visit of Brothers Buxton 17

CHAPTER II.

At Bukarest—Ovation to Filipescu—Take Yonescu—Revolutionary condition of Roumania—Likelihood of War with Austria—General Fitcheff replaces Boyadjiew as Minister of War—Suggestion of Co-operation with Roumania 30

CHAPTER III.

Serbian Views on Bulgarian Co-operation—Daneff explains Outbreak of Second Balkan War—Diamandi's visit to Rome—Critical state of affairs in Turkey—Death of King of Roumania—Attempted Assassination of Buxtons—General Savoff, late Commander-in-Chief—Fall of Antwerp—The Bulgarian peasant 38

CHAPTER IV.

Second Visit to Roumania—Buxtons in Hospital—Explanation of Roumania's inaction—Interviews with Filipescu, Také Yonescu and Bratiano—Suggestion of proposals to emanate from London—State of Germany and Austria—Letter to Crown Prince of Serbia—Buxton's interview with Turkish assassin—General Iliescu—Buxtons audience with Queen—Inspection of Roumanian Troops, etc.—Lunch with General Iliescu—Interviews with French and Russian Ministers—Bulgaria declines offer of Line of the Vardar and Enos Midia—Take Yonescu in correspondence with Venizelos 52

CONTENTS.

CHAPTER V.

Return to Sofia—Offer of Resignation—Reply—Assertion of right to telegraph Military Attaché's views to London—Interview with Diamandi—Dubious attitude of Bulgaria—War Minister neutral—Turkish Expeditionary Force—Rumours of Agreement between Italy and Balkan States—Bulgarian General's views on Russian strategy—Minister of War defines Bulgaria's wants in Macedonia ... 85

CHAPTER VI.

Third visit to Roumania—Roumanian preparations for War—Certain that Italy will fight Austria—Number of men available for Roumanian army—Ghenadieff's special mission to Rome—Bourchier optimistic regarding Bulgaro-Roumanian alliance—Visit of Trevelyan and Seton Watson—Iliescu suggests making use of Bulgars—Concentration of German troops on Roumanian borders—Consequent reluctance of Roumaia and Bulgaria to fight—Unfriendly attitude of General Fitcheff—Serbian attitude to Bulgars explained—German loan to Bulgaria—Favourable time for getting Bulgaria in, now past—Bulgarian officers of Reserve to be called out—Advisability of acquainting Bulgarian Opposition Parties with Entente's offer 99

CHAPTER VII.

Visit to Nisch—Lunch with Crown Prince of Serbia—Conversations with Passitch, Prince Troubetzkoi and Tchapraschikoff—Dinner with Crown Prince and political discussion—Return to Sofia—Sir A. Paget to visit Sofia—General Pau—Bulgaro-Greek relations 112

CHAPTER VIII.

Fourth visit to Roumania — Thompson appointed Military Attaché in Roumania—Suez Canal expedition—Austro-German troops near Roumanian front—Experiments with bullet proof shield—Progress in forcing Dardanelles—Result on Bulgaria—Arrival of Colonel Thompson—Farewell audience with King of Roumania—Conversation with Filipescu—Arrival of General Sir A. Paget—Dinner at Russian Legation—Farewell audience with Queen of Roumania—Crown Prince 122

CHAPTER IX.

Return to Sofia—Effect of storm on river Danube—Paget arrives Sofia—His audience with King of Bulgaria—Probability of Bulgaria speedily joining Entente annulled by loss of three British ships in Dardanelles—Contraband of War—Departure of O'Reilly—Pourparlers in London—War Office rejects inventor's offer re bullet proof shields—Greek suggestion for Entente to seize Dedeagatch—British Minister's reply—Necessity of granting Russia Constantinople—Sir E. Grey suggests offer of 1912 Line—Opposition of French—Interview with Savinsky—War Minister approves 1912 Line and plans co-operation 131

CONTENTS.

CHAPTER X.

Visit to Lemnos—Interview with Sir Ian Hamilton—Conference on board Staff transport—Suggestion for landing in Gulf of Saros—Return to Sofia—War Minister ready to co-operate if political negotiations succeed—News of landing on Gallipoli Peninsula—Greeks endeavour to quarrel with Bulgaria — News from Gallipoli points to a long campaign — Bulgarian Cabinet ignores advice of War Minister and prefers to remain neutral—Russian defeat in Galicia—Fitzmaurice advises offer of 1912 Line—Italy declares war on Austria—Offer of 1912 Line again delayed by French—Bulgarian army recovers its spirit—Consequent danger of war with Serbia—Bad news from Gallipoli—Formal offer of 1912 Line by Entente Ministers—Fall of Pshemysl—Russian Military Attaché despondent and Italian Minister depressed—Visit of Captain Amery—Fitzmaurice's interview with War Minister—Friction between Bulgaria and Turkey—Visit of Sir Mark Sykes—Improbability of now securing Bulgaria's aid 146

CHAPTER XI.

Chief of Staff's views regarding point of attack on Gallipoli repeated—Bulgaria's non-committal reply to Entente offer—Arrival of O'Beirne—Departure of Sir H. Bax Ironside—Entente Ministers suggest occupation of Macedonia by Bulgarian or by Entente troops—Arrival of Sir V. Chirol—I advise despatch of 100,000 Entente troops based on Salonika in preference to O'Beirne and Chirol's plan for occupation of part promised to Bulgaria—Sazonoff objects to occupation of Macedonia—O'Beirne persists—Chirol goes to Nisch—Gantcheff's mission to Berlin—Chirol goes to Bukarest—Rumours of General Fitcheff's resignation—Interview with Daneff—Entente request to Serbia—Serbia summons special Council to consider request—General Jekoff replaces Fitcheff as War Minister 166

CHAPTER XII.

Interview with Jekoff—Serbian reply to Entente Note—Disgust of O'Beirne—Interview with Boyadjiew—O'Beirne's audience with the King of Bulgaria—Further details of Serbian reply—Visit to Vratza for Bulgarian manoeuvres—O'Beirne takes up suggestion of landing force at Salonika—Final offer of 1912 Line by Entente—Visit of Duke of Mecklenburg to Sofia—Bourchier sanguine as to attitude of opposition—Russian officers report on Gallipoli—Opposition leaders interview with King—Interview with Gueschoff—Second Visit of Sir Ian Hamilton—Bulgars commence mobilization—Journey to Imbros and Anzac—Conversation with Sir Ian Hamilton—Return to Sofia 185

CONTENTS.

CHAPTER XIII.

Page.

British Legation thinks of offering more concessions to Bulgaria—French and Russian Military Attachés not of that opinion—Serbs suggest attacking Bulgaria before her mobilization is completed—Interview with Minster of War—Serbs refusal of Entente offer very damaging to our prestige—Progress of mobilization—Entente Ministers equally divided for or against an ultimatum to Bulgaria—Russians issue ultimatum and we follow suit—O'Beirne is of opinion that we should have remained and considers war with Bulgaria due to Russian Military Attaché—Departure of Entente Missions—Arrival at Athens—Attached to Legation—Necessity of making Greeks join Entente—Interview with Venizelos—Colonel Cunningham leaves for London—Greek harvest—Interview with General Duzmanis, Chief of Greek Staff—Endeavour to force hand of Greece—Resignation of Greek Premier—Lord Kitchener visits the Dardanelles ... 205

CHAPTER XIV.

New Premier, M. Skouloudis warns French Minister that he will intern Entente troops if driven over Greek frontier—Suggestion of ultimatum to Greece and threat of bombardment—Admiral de Robeck approves of taking Fleet to Piræus—Sir Francis Elliot visits Lord Kitchener at Mudros—I accompany him—Council meeting on board—Lord Kitchener's views—Lord Kitchener visits King of Greece—Colonel Buckley suggests my returning to Roumania—Ordered home—Captured by submarine—Experiences on submarine voyage to Castel Nuovo—Journey to Vienna—Prisoner of war camp at Salzerbad—Exchanged—Appointed British Military Representative at Sofia—Demobilized ... 228

MAP OF THE BALKANS.

Appendices—Appendix A, B and C 246

Preface.

IN this world nothing succeeds like success. To most people it is sufficient that Bulgaria went against us in the late war to prove that Lord Grey's policy in endeavouring to secure her assistance was a mistaken policy, and was bound to fail, owing to the innate wickedness and treachery of Bulgaria.

In presenting to the public the following pages taken from my diary during 1914-15, I have endeavoured to show that the policy itself was sound, but the execution of it was tardily commenced and was carried out intermittently and with indecision.

It is true that, owing to the events of the second Balkan war and the treaty of Bukarest, the support of Bulgaria who had been both Russo-phil and Anglo-phil was half lost to us before the war began. Bulgaria had certainly been to blame for having actually attacked her allies during the war with Turkey, but there is no doubt that she had received severe provocation, and was led thereto by belief in the existence of a plot between Serbia and Greece to rob her of the territory in Macedonia which had been allotted to her in the original treaty between Bulgaria and Serbia. This treaty had formed the basis of an alliance of the Christian Powers in the war of liberation from the Turks. There were doubtless faults on both sides. Bulgaria should have treated the Serbs with greater liberality, seeing that the latter, through Austrian influence, had been denied access to the Adriatic. On the other hand, to the Bulgars it was maddening to think that while they were bearing the brunt of the campaign in Thrace and were besieging Adrianople, their allies were plotting to deprive them of the fruits of victory. The result was a feeling of rancour against Russia, who had, they thought, unduly favoured Serbia, and a fierce spirit of revenge that inclined them to take the side of Serbia's enemies.

PREFACE.

The Germans had laid their plans early in the day. By means of propaganda and unstinted bribery in the Press and in Government circles, before the war began, they had won a position which was non-existent prior to the Balkan war. Nevertheless, with the goodwill of Roumania and Serbia and by a rectification of the treaty of Bukarest, it would have been quite possible to have reconstituted the Balkan "bloc" during the first few months of the war and this would, in all human probability have prevented or have put an end to the defection of Turkey, the fiasco of the Dardanelles would not have taken place, Russia would have been saved by a liberal supply of guns and ammunition, and the war would have been very much shortened. But the Balkan States declined to play the game, and sink their quarrels for the common good. They regarded the war from a purely Balkan standpoint, and each Power hoped by conserving its forces intact to be in a position to dictate terms to its neighbours exhausted by a long war. Had the Entente been resolute and unanimous at any time during the first eight months of the war, there would still have been time to smooth over these differences. But in April it became known that Russia was to have Constantinople, and the fear of absorption was present both in Roumania and Bulgaria. Then the military situation grew less and less favourable as time went on. Already in February the Germans had scored a success by their loan of half a million francs, a loan which might have been secured in Paris a year before, had not the Russians insisted on political conditions. This success was nearly wiped out by the action of the allied fleets in sweeping up the Straits of the Dardanelles in March, but unfortunately the loss of three ships caused us to abandon the attempt, and another opportunity of gaining Bulgaria was lost. Then came the severe defeat of the Russians in Galicia in the month of June, followed by another German success in the diplomatic field, namely the conclusion of the Turko-Bulgarian negotiations resulting in a concession of territory by Turkey to Bulgaria, and the removal

PREFACE.

of a serious point of friction between these two countries, which might have proved very advantageous to the Entente. Finally the refusal of the Serbs, at the beginning of September, to give up the Macedonian territory demanded by the Entente led directly to the Bulgarian mobilization, and to the rupture of our relations with Bulgaria.

With regard to Greece, Lord Grey has been reproached for not having accepted the offer of her fleet at the commencement of the war for operations against Turkey. But at that time it was by no means certain that Turkey would enter the war against us, and it would have been contrary to our high moral code to have initiated an aggressive war against Turkey, even with the provocation received by their harbouring the "Goëben" and the "Breslau," however profitable it would doubtless have proved.

There is little doubt, however, that had this incident been handled diplomatically with firmness the Turks would have surrendered these two German vessels and have remained neutral.

Later on in 1915 when Greece renewed her offer of assistance, it was linked with the proposal to march through Bulgarian territory in company with Entente troops to the Dardanelles. This would undoubtedly have brought the Bulgarian army in full strength—at that time much superior to the Greek army—on the enemy's side (vide page ?, chapter ?). It does not need a great stategist to perceive that the prospect of a long land march with a powerful enemy situated on the flank, in its own territory, was hardly an alluring one to the Entente. Nor would it have been necessary to traverse Bulgarian territory in view of the fact that we had command of the sea, and might have disembarked a Greek army at Enos or elsewhere in the Gulf of Saros without incurring Bulgarian hostility. But that would not have suited the Greek strategists who evidently had their eye on the absorption of the entire Thracian littoral, which, thanks to the skill of M. Venizelos, they subsequently attained by diplomatic means.

PREFACE.

Lastly, Lord Grey has been blamed for not having permitted the Serbs to attack Bulgaria when the latter was in the act of mobilizing. Considering that Serbia was fighting for her life on the Danube, a raid on Bulgaria could not have been decisive. Serbia might have destroyed one division, and have seriously delayed the Bulgarian mobilization, but there was no possibility of a knock-out blow. The evidence given by the late Bulgarian Commander-in-Chief (vide Appendix) when on his recent trial at Sofia, shows that even at this stage, Bulgaria's assistance was not absolutely certain, but was conditional on the Germans' successful passage of the Danube. The late deeply-lamented Mr. O'Beirne at that time British Minister in Sofia, and one of the ablest diplomats of the day, held the opinion that even at this stage Bulgaria might have been kept neutral had not the Russians lost patience and demanded the immediate march of Bulgaria against Turkey in a 48 hours' ultimatum. Mr. O'Beirne may have been right, or he may have been wrong, but it is evident that Lord Grey's policy was not entirely misplaced. The Entente erred in not pushing its policy of bringing in Bulgaria sufficiently early or with sufficient vigour. Had the Entente done so, and found it of no avail, there would still have been time to have had recourse to Greece before that Power became intimidated by the threats of the Kaiser, and by the continuous successes of the Central Powers. When one thinks of the enormous prestige that Lord Grey enjoyed both in Russia and in France, one may regret that he did not over-rule, and no one but he could have done so, the discordant opinions of our allies in time to be of use. Unity of command in the diplomatic field was quite as urgent as in the strategic conduct of the war.

The recent issue in June (1923) of Sir George Buchanan's Memoirs affords another striking proof that I had been right from the very commencement of my mission to Bulgaria in 1914, when on the 9th September (vide page 90 of my memoirs) I expressed the view, not shared at the time by my Chief, nor by the various Governments of the Entente, that it was "an affair of the most urgent necessity to get Bulgaria in on our side at any price," and that the co-operation of Roumania, and the more or less voluntary compliance of Serbia were essential means to that end. I was never a believer in securing Bulgaria's neutrality. In Chapter 17 of his first volume, Sir George describes his audience with the Emperor in March, 1915, during which he announced the British Government's assent to the Russian demand for Constantinople, and discussed the conditions of Italy's entry into the war. He then goes on to say :— " Negotiations had at the same time been proceeding with Roumania, Greece and Bulgaria, and, from the language originally held by M. Bratiano, we had reason to hope that Roumania would at once follow Italy's example. Though aware that Italy was on the point of declaring war on Austria, she let slip the favourable moment in the spring of 1915, when the Russians held the more important of the Carpathian heights, and when her co-operation with the Russian army might have saved the situation."

Further on, Sir George continues :— " The military situation indeed, at the end of July (1915) was such that Bratiano was probably right in saying that for Roumania to march at that moment would be to court certain disaster. It would have been different had we won over Bulgaria to our side, for her intervention would have so improved matters that Roumania could have afforded to run the risk. On the other hand a definite assurance of Roumania's co-operation would have greatly facilitated our negotiations with Bulgaria."

A reference to my memoirs will show how earnestly I worked towards this end. My greatest regret was that my official position was not of sufficient importance to lend more weight to my views.

As regards the proper attitude to have adopted with Serbia, Sir George says :—"O'Beirne, who had been with me at Petrograd as Councillor of

Embassy, and who afterwards lost his life when travelling with Lord Kitchener to Russia, had been sent as Minister to Sofia, but unfortunately too late to retrieve the mistakes of his predecessor. He had early in September (1915) expressed the opinion that though Serbia might reject some of our demands, she would acquiesce were they imposed on her, and he was, in my opinion, right. I had myself, in the conversation which I and my French colleague had daily with Sazonoff, spoken in a very similar sense. Paléologue, on the contrary, protested that we could not hold such language or inflict such humiliation on an ally. The stakes, however, for which we were playing, were too high to allow considerations for the feelings of any Government to influence our policy. Could we but have won over Bulgaria to our side, Roumania would almost certainly have cast in her lot with us in the autumn of 1915. Turkey's fate would then have been sealed and the whole course of the war would have been changed. It was perhaps natural that Serbia should hesitate to cede what she regarded as her national territory, but it would have been different had the allied governments dictated such a course to her. Had they insisted on her allowing Bulgaria to occupy the uncontested zone then and there, it is doubtful whether Bulgaria, no matter how far King Ferdinand had committed himself in the negotiations with the Central Powers would, even at the eleventh hour, have marched against us. She certainly would not have done so had we taken action earlier in the year. Sazonoff did all that it was possible to do under the circumstances, but he was not empowered to hold the only language that would have turned the scales at Belgrade. But had they done so, the war would have been considerably shortened and Russia might have been spared the horrors of the Bolshevik revolution."

In the following chapters may be traced the various efforts made from time to time by the Entente Powers, more or less at the instigation of their representatives in Sofia, to gain Bulgaria as an ally.

PREFACE.

When, as Military Attaché, I first urged upon Sir Henry Bax Ironside the necessity of granting Bulgaria a concession of territory in Macedonia in exchange for her active support, early in September 1914, he did not approve. Later, when the Foreign Office had sanctioned such procedure, and the need of Bulgaria's help became more and more evident, Sir Henry told me that the real obstacle to making demands on Serbia was the Emperor of Russia, and this he knew from M. Spalaikovitch, the Serbian Minister in Petrograd, with whom he was in correspondence. I had known the latter as long ago as 1908 and could well imagine the kind of influence his fiery eloquence might have upon the Emperor and that it would be very hostile to any pretensions of Bulgaria.

But I did not cease from recommending that course in consequence. Sir George Buchanan's Memoirs now confirm the attitude of the Emperor and also inform us that M. Paléologue, the French Ambassador, was adverse to our making any demands on our Serbian ally. This, no doubt, explains why Sir George Buchanan was not able to influence either M. Sazonoff or the Emperor in that direction until Mr. O'Beirne, fresh from Petrograd, and intimately acquainted with the Russian authorities, took over the Legation in July, 1915, and realized the extreme urgency of the problem.

But by that time the situation of the Entente had so disimproved militarily that nothing would then have satisfied the Bulgars but actual and immediate occupation of Serbian Macedonia.

This the Serbs refused to grant, and thereby deprived the Entente of the last chance of winning Bulgaria, of shortening the war, and of saving Russia from anarchy.

I take this opportunity to offer my thanks to Sir George Buchanan for his courtesy in permitting me to make the above quotations; to Mr. Stancioff, Bulgarian Minister in London, for kind assistance in the preparation of a map, and to Miss Nadejda Stancioff, late Secretary of Legation at Washington, for the loan of photographs. I am also indebted to Mr. Charles Bentinck, Chargé d'Affaires at Athens, to Colonel Douglas Capitaneanu, late Military Atttaché of the Roumanian Legation, to Mr. Maclean, H.M. Consul at Zagreb, and to Mr. Keyser, H.M. Consul at Bucharest, for their kind assistance in collecting photographs.

H. D. NAPIER.

Experiences of a Military Attaché in the Balkans

Chapter One.

APPOINTED MILITARY ATTACHE BULGARIA—JOURNEY TO SOFIA—PRO-GERMAN SENTIMENTS OF BULGARIAN GENERAL—BULGARIAN WAR STRENGTH—UNION CLUB—RESULT OF BALKAN WAR—GENERAL BOYADJIEW—FIRST CONCLUSIONS AS TO NECESSITY OF WINNING BULGARIA FOR ENTENTE—CO-OPERATION OF ROUMANIA ALSO NECESSARY—VISIT OF BROTHERS BUXTON.

ON the outbreak of war at the beginning of August, 1914, having retired from the Army some two years previously, I volunteered, like everybody else, for active service. As I had already been a Military Attaché for several years in various countries, namely Persia, Russia, Serbia, and Bulgaria, I was at once selected to proceed to the latter country, and resume my last post as Military Attaché to our Legation at Sofia.

My journey out was uneventful. France at that time looked like the enchanted land when everyone suddenly fell asleep in whatever occupation he was engaged, only the sleepers were absent. Villages stood deserted except for some children here and there, and a few old people. Doors of houses were wide open, and carts left in the fields where they stood, when their horses were taken away for mobilization. The corn in many places had not been cut; in others it was in stooks and no one was at work.

Paris looked like a city of the dead. After delivering my Foreign Office bags at the Embassy, I was able, with some difficulty, to find a room in a half dismantled hotel, but recently one of the smartest of the once gay capital. Dinner at 9 o'clock was unobtainable, and I was thankful to get a cup of tea and dry bread.

On the following day, thanks to the good offices of the Embassy, I was able to secure a compartment as far as Marseilles. There, when walking about the streets, I saw the first trainload of wounded men being conveyed by trams to the Hospital. The women in the street got very excited and shouted abuse of " les sales Prussiens."

From Marseilles the train was crowded with Italians returning home, and I had a hard fight for a seat. Having to look after half a dozen bulky F.O. Bags as well, was no easy task, but somehow or other I managed to convey them in safety. A French regiment passed us in great spirits shouting " A Berlin." It was then about 9 p.m. Twelve hours later we passed the frontier at Ventimiglia, and reached Genoa in the afternoon. Here I was obliged to stay the night, and it was not until the following evening that I reached Rome.

The next day, August 23rd, after a hasty glimpse at the principal sights of Rome, I lunched at the Embassy with Sir Rennell Rodd who told me that the Austrian Ambassador here had misled his Government into believing that the Italians would come in on their side, although it would be with great reluctance. Colonel Granet, the Military Attaché, came to see me at the hotel, and said that the Italians were quite good enough to pit against the Austrians, but that their army was not yet ready, and they were greatly lacking in good non-commissioned officers. He also mentioned that the Serbs were very short of ammunition.

In the evening I left for Brindisi where I was met the following day at noon by our Consul, Mr. Sinclair, who kindly helped me to secure a cabin on a Greek steamer leaving that afternoon for Athens. Next morning by 6 o'clock we found ourselves at anchor in front of Corfu, a lovely place with a most attractive looking old Venetian fort built on a sort of miniature rock of Gibraltar with a draw-bridge to the mainland. The steamer was crowded with Greek and Russian merchants returning to their own countries. One of the latter had been in Sofia for some years, and told me that the Bulgars were much broken in spirit after their last war against their former allies. King Ferdinand, he said, had made the mistake of listening to Austria, who doubtless promised him all manner of things to induce him to attack the Serbs. The King was, of course, very bitter against the Czar who refused to back him up, but the people did not share that sentiment.

After leaving Corfu, we steamed towards the Gulf of Corinth, and by evening reached the beautifully situated town of Patras. The sun was setting and lit up the mountain behind the town into rich greens and browns. To make the scene still more theatrical, as the sun set summer lightning began to play beyond the mountains. The next morning we reached the mouth of the canal cut through the Isthmus of Corinth, and passed through between lofty perpendicular cliffs of sandstone, revetted near the water's edge by stone masonry. A strong current was running westward. A suspension bridge spanned the cutting far above us. The canal is only six kilometres long, in 20 minutes we were through, and by 10 o'clock reached the Pireus, the harbour of Athens.

My first visit was to Sir Francis Elliot, at the British Legation. He kindly put me in touch with the Military Attachés of our Allies. The Russian, a nice fellow, called Colonel Goudine Levkovitch, invited me to lunch, where I met Prince Lobanoff and another Secretary of Legation. They declared that our action was being much criticised with regard to Turkey and the Goëben and Breslau incident, and that we ought to declare war on her regardless of our Indian Mahomedans. We then went to see Colonel Braquet, the French M.A. He also was very vehement about the weakness that we were displaying towards Turkey, which would have "very serious consequences." He had commanded Mahomedan troops in Algeria and said that any sign of weakness was especially fatal with Mahomedans. I thoroughly agreed with him. Did I not know it, having served with Mahomedan troops myself in India? In England the Government was making too much of this Mahomedan feeling in India.

The same evening I went to see M. Venizelos, Prime Minister and Minister of War. He received me with great civility, and seemed a most agreeable and cheery person. He told me, in confirmation of my assertion that we, as a nation, were going to see this war through ; that the moment he heard that we had joined with France and Russia, he made up his mind that Germany would be beaten, and the Greeks at once inclined to our side. I asked him what prospect there would be of Bulgaria joining in with another Balkan Alliance against Austria and Germany, and he replied that he did not think it possible. The recollections of the last war were too recent. Perhaps in 5 years' time they might, but not now.

That evening I received my orders to continue my journey direct to Sofia, and, finding that a Greek steamer was leaving for Salonika the next day, I managed to secure a cabin by paying double fare, and embarked on the evening of the 28th. The ship was full of Russians, mostly Jews, but there was also an elderly Serbian Prince, Alexis Kara-Georgeeovitch, a cousin of King Peter, with his wife, the Princess, an American lady. They were both very interesting and most kind, sparing no pains to look after all sorts of Russian travellers. The Prince was bound for Nisch, where he intended to take up work on the Red Cross. The Princess amused me by saying she had no patience with these footling little countries. All of them should be made into one State, as they were really inhabited by the same kind of people. I was inclined to agree. What a vast amount of trouble this would save!

Arrived at Salonika harbour we were met by a steam-launch containing the harbour-master who had put off to meet the Prince and carry out the landing with full ceremony. I afterwards ascertained that they believed him to be a Russian Grand Duke, which accounted for all this fuss. We lunched together at the hotel, and then put off to look at the Greek fleet. There were 8 destroyers and 4 torpedo boats just getting ready to put to sea. We saw over a torpedo boat and a destroyer, and had tea with the British naval officer in charge. The Prince had confided to me secretly that the Greek army had been ordered to mobilize, and that the British Fleet was going to the Dardanelles, but I could get no confirmation of either from our Captain, who would have been informed had either been the case. Meanwhile the Greek ships were steaming away to Mitelene, followed in half an hour by their Commander, and we returned to Salonika.

On the 1st September, after a 24 hours' journey along a single line of railway, which passed through some magnificent scenery of narrow rocky gorges in the mountains up the valley of the Vardar, past the picturesque Turkish-built town of Veles, I arrived at Nisch. Here I met several old friends including Des Graz, the British Minister, M. Grouitch, lately Serbian Minister in London, and the First Secretaries of the Russian and Serbian Legations, formerly at Sofia. I found the Serbs very pleased at the result of the battle of Shabatz, where they had just taken 70 field guns, 12 howitzers, and some thousands of prisoners. The Prime Minister M. Pashitch, was unfortunately too unwell to receive me, but I saw Prince Paul, so well-known in London society, who was in charge of the Red Cross, and very sad at having heard of the loss of so many of his English friends. I left that night for Sofia, and put up at the Legation where I received a cordial welcome from Sir Henry Bax-Ironside.

During the next few days I was occupied with social duties. I wrote my name in the King's Book at the Palace and ascertained that he very rarely saw members of the Diplomatic Corps now. Dobrovitch, his private secretary, was in Vienna, so I did not press for an audience. I called on the principal Diplomats and Bulgarian Ministers, but was not presented to the Prime Minister, M. Radoslavoff, as would have been usual, deeming it more discreet to fall in with the evident desire of Sir Henry, and not have anything to do with his sphere of action in that direction. At the War Office, in the absence of the Minister of War, I was received by General Teneff, the Chief of the Staff. He assured me that Bulgaria did not want to fight, but wished to recoup. Bulgaria had lost 100,000 men in the last war, and had not now mobilized, although the countries round had done so, and it was dangerous not to follow suit.

At the Russian Legation I found that M. Nekliudoff who had just been appointed Minister when I left Sofia a few years ago, had now given place to M. Savinsky, whom I had known previously at the Foreign Office at St. Petersburg. He told me that the Three Powers had recently asked Turkey, in a kind of ultimation, what were her intentions. Turkey had promised to reply when her mission returned from Bukarest in a few days. Meanwhile the Bulgars had also been asked their intentions in case Turkey should go to war, whether they would maintain a strict neutrality, and especially whether they would oppose Turkey, should the latter Power march through their territory to attack the Greeks. The Bulgars apparently did not know what to say to that and had not replied.

In the street I met an old acquaintance General Radjko-Petroff, who was War Minister many years ago. He is an ardent Stamboulovist, so I was not altogether surprised when he shouted out his fiery opinions at me, so that people in the street turned round to look at us. He declared that Bulgaria was not going to be deceived a second time, and that he did not believe in the promises of Russia, Serbia or France. "Why did the Powers rob us of the fruits of victory in the last war?" I said I thought the Powers had accepted the " fait accompli " when Bulgaria was driven back. He then said that he held a document from the Russian Foreign Office to the effect that Bulgaria would be treated as an enemy if she took a port on the Sea of Marmora ; and he

KING FERDINAND.
Of Bulgaria.

added that he would use all his influence in favour of Germany and Austria who were bound to win. In spite of these sentiments we parted quite amicably. It is both useful and refreshing in diplomacy to come across a fine old fighter like this General who is of sufficient value to count, and who blurts out exactly what he thinks, but it does not often happen. Soon after I met Madame Petroff, his wife, who was also at that time an important figure in Bulgarian society. Her opinion was that the Russians were no good, and the French already beaten; also that had Bulgaria been properly treated in the last war, the Balkans would have remained united, and have plumped solid for the Entente, and the present war would have been avoided.

After this I made the acquaintance of my colleagues, French and Serbian, Colonels Count de Matharel and Kouchakovitch. I was glad to notice that the former did not appear much concerned at the news which had just arrived, that the French Government was preparing to move to Bordeaux that very night. He and I then both urged on Kouchakovitch the desirability of the Serbs pushing on against Austria, but he thought they might be beaten the next time, and then what about Bulgaria? We discussed the Bulgarian War Strength. Matharel put it at 350,000, the same as before the Balkan War, notwithstanding the casualities, as their territory had increased. Kouchanovitch thought 310,000 nearer the mark. The Serbs had recently received a large consignment of ammunition from France, so there was no longer any anxiety about that. The Bulgars were believed to have about 1,100 rounds per field gun.

On the 4th September I transferred my quarters to a hotel in the middle of the town and dined at the Union Club which was much patronised both by diplomats and the leading Bulgarians. I was warmly greeted by M. Zenoff, an old Bulgarian friend and habitué of the club. Opposite to him sat M. Tontcheff, the Minister of Finance. I began to suspect I had invaded a German camp, and this was confirmed soon after by the entry of the German and Austrian M.A.'s, Major von der Goltz, a son of the Fieldmarshal, and Colonel Lachsa.   Lastly came Kaufmann, a German Jew, nominally Krupp's agent, but in reality a special secret agent of the German Emperor, and consequently a dangerous and influential person, who had been here for years. A few nights later I was dining there again with our consul Blakeney, when in marched a fine soldierlike Bulgarian in uniform. He was greeted most effusively by our enemies, and sat down amongst them.   This was General Boyadjiew, Minister of War, who had just returned from a tour in the newly acquired territory in the South. He said in German that he was delighted with what he had seen, and that the Division quartered there really amounted to an Army Corps.   After this slight indiscretion he was given a wink and the German and Austrian Attachés began talking in a patois that I could not understand.

The following day I went to see General Elias Dimitrieff, late Chief Intendant of the Army, an old friend and the only Bulgarian Officer I had met who could talk fluent English.   Most of the younger officers of the General Staff spoke pretty good French, but with the senior officers it was my practice to speak in Russian, and they replied in Bulgarian, which I could understand, but not speak sufficiently well.   In this respect I had found a knowledge of Russian both an advantage and the reverse, the two languages being so much akin as to make it very difficult for a Non-Slav to speak both without muddling them up.   As Russia originated and trained the Bulgarian army, all their military literature was in Russian, so they could all understand it perfectly, but this was not the case with the uneducated Bulgar.

General Dimitrieff told me that prior to the Balkan war, the stores had been very much let down, and he had ordered 400,000 greatcoats and the same number of pairs of boots for that campaign, but the total ration strength amounted to 600,000 which probably included every kind of follower. He declared that Bulgaria could now bring out 500,000 men.

It is interesting here to note that the result of the two Balkans wars in terms of population was as follows:—

Country.	Before 1912.	After 1913.
Bulgaria	4,389,000	5,000,000
Greece	2,632,000	4,200,000
Roumania	7,250,000	7,500,000
Serbia	2,957,000	4,100,000
Turkey in Europe	6,139,000	2,083,000
Montenegro	285,000	500,000

So that, after all, Bulgaria, in spite of having been deprived of the fruits of victory, which doubtless would have been very great, had ended a disastrous defeat at the hands of her former allies nearly three-quarters of a million stronger than before.

On the 8th September I paid my official visit to General Boyadjiew at the War Office. After a few words he took out a map of Central Europe and began to criticise the conduct of our allies. He didn't think much of the French, they were not a reliable people. They should not have pushed into Lorraine. They had a very good line of defence with forts every 50 kilometres, and that space was only sufficient for a moderate German force to get through. They could have waited behind that line and have mopped up the German forces as they emerged. They should have spared more men for the North, and have remained on the defensive all along the line. The Russians also had done wrong. They had sent the mass of their troops against Austria, and were pushing on to cross the Carpathians and crush her when they should have been concentrating their strength against Germany. They ought not to have got mixed up in the marches of Gumbinnen, but should have cut in from Warsaw. They were being pushed back again. Evidently their concentration of troops was not complete. They were wrong to attack the Germans piece-meal. He thought that France was already beaten and that

Paris was France. I did not agree with him in that respect, and declared that even if France were beaten, that would make no difference to us in the end. We could crush Germany with the help of Russia alone, and we were preparing for a three years' war. He was impressed with my account of our ultimate resources, and with the tenacity of the British character.

I said that I had come here in the hope that Bulgaria might form a "bloc" with the other Balkan States and march against Austria. He replied that naturally Bulgaria would want something in return, that so far she had been very badly treated. I presumed that it was not of much use to discuss what Bulgaria wanted, because she had not yet decided who was going to win the war, and consequently which side would best be able to carry out its promises. He replied that it was not that so much which weighed with him, as that they could not trust Russia's word. Her promises were of no value. "But," I asked, "supposing they were also guaranteed by Great Britain and France, would not that make a difference?" He thought it would. I then asked him what Bulgaria wanted. Was it the line of the Vardar? Was it Salonika? He replied: "No, what we want is Bulgaria as defined by the Treaty of San Stefano."

General Boyadjiew is himself a Macedonian, like many of the principal statesmen and soldiers of Bulgaria, but all Bulgars are united on this question. I have always found a Bulgar more level-headed than either a Greek or Serbian in regard to his aspirations. He is very persistent, but does not ask for more than he can digest, whereas the other two are unbounded in their territorial ambitions. A Bulgar, as he will himself boast, is first and foremost a Bulgar, and after that a Pro-Russian, Turk, German, or what you will, according to circumstances.

The next day I met General Papodopoff, a former colleague of mine in Petrograd. He confirmed what others had said about not trusting Russia but thought a promise of territory in Macedonia from

Sir E. Grey might induce Bulgaria to join the Entente. The General is a man of sound judgment and wide experience. He was Chief of the Staff to the Commander-in-Chief during the last Balkan war, and now commands a Division. He declared that in no case would they help Serbia, and this made it difficult to attack Austria. Besides, they would themselves in that case be attacked by Turkey. I suggested they might let the Greeks through their territory to stop Turkey. But he thought the Greeks would not be strong enough, as the Turks had 150,000 men in Europe. The only thing the Bulgars could do would be to attack Turkey themselves. One should ask Radoslavoff. Had I seen the War Minister? What did he think of it? I replied "Yes," and that I thought him favourably inclined.

Then I decided to write an official letter to Sir H. Bax-Ironside asking him to wire that I had reason to believe from conversations with the Minister of War and other Bulgarian officers, that a definite and satisfactory offer of Macedonian territory would induce the Bulgarian army to go either against Turkey, or in any other direction except in direct aid of Serbia. I added that I had no means of ascertaining what the Bulgarian Government might do. That meant that I relied on what the officers told me. Bax-Ironside had been careful not to present me to the Prime Minister, and expected me to confine myself strictly to military questions and not meddle with politics. Even in times of peace the position of a M.A. is most difficult. He must be careful not to encroach on political matters which are the special concern of his Ambassador or Minister. At the same time it is almost impossible to keep military and political matters entirely separate. Besides the opinion of military Chiefs in most foreign countries is a factor that cannot be neglected. And on the occasion of a great war when everything is of such vital importance, one cannot afford to let etiquette stand in the way. My situation was that I had been sent out by the War Office in a great hurry with no definite instructions or even outline of the general policy of the Government. I took it for granted that we should want to have the Bulgars on our side. But when I arrived at Sofia, I soon discovered that there was a general agreement among the neighbours, Greece, Serbia, and Roumania, to squeeze Bulgaria, keep her neutral and prevent her from getting anything out of the war. This was the result of the last Balkan War and the Treaty of Bukarest in 1913. Bulgaria's attitude, though she was much broken in spirit, was still sullen and defiant, like a hedgehog rolled up with his bristles against all the world. Consequently, by appealing to their instincts of revenge, especially against Serbia who was in possession of their promised land, the Germans had a far easier task than we, to win Bulgaria to their side.

Sir H. Bax-Ironside who had been in Bulgaria ever since I left it in 1911, was of opinion at this time that it was not only impossible but also undesirable to win her over to our side. He sympathised largely with Bulgaria's enemies, and especially with the Serbs, and did not think the latter ought to be asked to make concessions of territory. Turkey was at the time still neutral, and the stirring up of Bulgaria was calculated, he thought, to put the Turks against us.

Looking at the matter from a purely military point of view, I thought that it was an affair of the most urgent necessity to get Bulgaria in on our side at any price. I had great belief in the fighting powers and obstinacy of the Bulgars, once engaged, on whichever side. I also saw that Bulgaria alone of all the Balkan Powers was capable, from her geographical position, of smashing up the Turks single-handed, and that, from our point of view, being the communicating link with Germany, and the Turkish Empire, she was worth more to us than all the other Balkan States put together. I therefore made up my mind to do everything in my power to procure her entry into the war on our side.

Knowing the warlike character of the people, I did not much believe in Bulgaria remaining neutral.

But in order to bring her in, it soon became evident that it was necessary to have some arrangement with Roumania, and that if possible the two countries should enter side by side. I accordingly obtained Sir Henry's permission to visit Bukarest where we had at that time no military attaché.

Just before my departure, the brothers Buxton suddenly arrived on the 11th September from England. Noel Buxton, according to his own account—the Legation had heard nothing—seemed to have been given a kind of unofficial "carte blanche" by Government to re-establish an active Balkan League. I told him exactly what I thought and had done, that it was a waste of time to try and bring Bulgaria, Serbia and Greece together, but that it remained to be seen whether Roumania could not be induced to combine, and that I was going there the next day to see the lie of the land. Noel told me that Lloyd-George and Grey were very keen on forming a league, and were willing to pay liberally in the shape of easy loans to Bulgaria, but not to promise territory. He was surprised that Bax-Ironside had received no instructions from Government in that sense. The next day I went to Bukarest as arranged.

Chapter Two.

AT BUKAREST—OVATION TO FILIPESCU—TAKÉ YONESCU—
REVOLUTIONARY CONDITION OF ROUMANIA—LIKELIHOOD OF WAR
WITH AUSTRIA—GENERAL FITCHEFF REPLACES BOYADJIEW AS
MINISTER OF WAR—SUGGESTION OF CO-OPERATION WITH
ROUMANIA.

THE situation at Bukarest was very interesting. Our Minister, Sir George Barclay, kindly gave me letters of introduction to M. Bratiano the Prime Minister, and to M. Také-Yonescu the leader of the Conservative Democratic party now in opposition. Both these gentlemen being away at or near Sinaia in the mountains, at the summer resort of Bukarest, I was not able to make their acquaintance at once. Meanwhile the daily papers announced in huge headlines that M. Filipescu, late Minister of War, was arriving that evening from Sinaia, and had declared himself in favour of fighting on the side of the Entente. He belonged to the Conservative party, also in opposition. Sir George had told me that Russia had offered Bukovina to Roumania, and Sir E. Grey had practically offered to bear the whole expense of a war, if she came in on our side. These offers had been made about a fortnight previously, and Roumania had asked if they could remain open. The people were all in favour of war, but last year the King had signed a convention with Austria before the present Ministry came into office. He could therefore never fight against Austria, and would have to abdicate before such an event took place. So I went to the station to see what kind of reception Filipescu would receive at the hands of the people. A dense crowd, both of carriages and foot-passengers, rendered approach to the station difficult, and when at last the train did arrive, Filipescu himself was not there, only some members of his family. I went away, but the crowd showed no signs of dispersing, and I was told that when at last he did arrive, he was greeted with great enthusiasm by large crowds, and a small demonstration past the palace took place, French and Serbian flags being displayed. I noticed a company of infantry drawn up in a side street close to the station, so the Government was evidently prepared to maintain order.

Next day Bourchier was lunching with me at the Hotel, and by good luck was able to introduce me to Také-Yonescu, who happened to be passing through, and invited me to lunch at Sinaia. I then went on to see the French M.A., Captain Pichon, who was very kind and gave me several details about the Roumanian army, which he considered was now bound to be used against Austria. He said that 10 classes of reservists had been mobilized a month ago. Then in the last ten day they had sent four of these to their homes, with all their uniform and equipment except rifles, and had called out another four classes, who were now with the colours. A complete mobilization could therefore be carried out in four days, horses having been already requisitioned. These 14 classes comprised all the reservists required for the active army. The total number of combatants of the 1st Line amounted to 400,000 and 625 guns, with another 200,000 in depôts and auxiliary services. They were to be divided into three armies, two of 6 and one of 5 Infantry Divisions.

On the following morning I started for Sinaia, and, meeting Také-Yonescu on the platform, accepted his kind invitation to travel in his reserved compartment. I thus had the great good fortune of a three hours' tête-à-tête with this famous man. I found him shaking his head over Filipescu's rashness in having declared for war against the Central Powers. I did my best to persuade him that there was nothing else for Roumania to do, and the sooner done the better. He thought it would be a long war, and was anxiously searching the papers for telegrams from Berlin announcing German victories. I on the other hand inclined to the opinion that it might all be over in three months, if Italy and the Balkan States came in on our side. I found him a most interesting companion. There was hardly anyone of note in Europe whom he had not met. He was in London just before the war, and used to see Lichnowsky every day. Lichnowsky was not deceived about England's attitude. The German Emperor was in favour of peace. But the Germans were mistaken about Italy and also about Roumania. I could not repeat a quarter of the interesting things he told me, but the essential facts of the present situation as regards Roumania were that $99\frac{1}{2}$ per cent. of the people wanted war against Austria, but they were accustomed to look to their recognised leaders, and therefore public opinion could be kept under control. The King was the great restraining influence, and at 75 years of age, could not go against all his past. For 31 years there had been agreements with Austria, the last one having been signed only in January of that year. It would take some days to arrange a crisis. The King could not conceive any possible result of the war other than the ultimate victory of Germany. Still, he would have to give way, and if he abdicated, it was not improbable that his nephew, the Crown Prince, would also refuse to govern, and the crown of Roumania would then go to the latter's eldest son, who was now 21 years of age and a thorough Roumanian. As regarded Bulgaria, he, Také-Yonescu, would be prepared to give her a part, but not the whole of the territory recently taken from her in the Dobrudja in return for an understanding, and thought they must also get the Enos-Midia line in Thrace. Také Yonescu left me at Sinaia, as I wished to continue a few stations further in order to see the Bulgarian Minister, M. Radeff, at Bushteni. Here I was met by a Secretary, and taken to see Radeff, who was in bed with a chill. Radeff, an old acquaintance, declared that he was quite in favour of an alliance with Roumania. He said it

M. TAKÉ YONESCU.

was a mistake to suppose that the Stamboulovists*
were Austro-phil. But the stupid policy of Russia,
and Savinsky's "street politics," had spoiled the
situation. He was very glad to hear that the
Buxtons had come out to the Balkans, and assured
me that the Bulgarian Government had no engagements towards Austria, and that the King of Bulgaria was still less inclined to any binding treaties
with Austria than was the Government. The next
day I asked Sir G. Barclay to telegraph my report
on the situation, namely: that it was probable that
Roumania would declare war on Austria, and that
Bulgaria might join her if supported by Great
Britain. I suggested that Greece might be asked to
safeguard Bulgaria from Turkey, and proposed
myself as M.A. to Bukarest as well as Sofia. This
latter suggestion was adopted by the Government,
and I was in due course accredited to Roumania.
I then returned to Sofia, believing that things were
trending towards a revolution in Roumania, and a
speedy declaration of war against Austria.

On the 19th September, Bax-Ironside suggested
my asking the War Office to be sent to Serbia, to
replace Colonel Plunkett, who had been wounded.
I declined, because I thought the situation where I
was much more important with the great probability
of Roumania coming in, and the possibility of Bulgaria following suit. Bax-Ironside said that
Bulgaria would certainly remain neutral, that Radoslavoff had told him so. Nevertheless, I postponed
asking to be sent to Serbia until the situation
developed further.

About this time, hearing that an old acquaintance,
General Fitcheff, had just been appointed Minister
of War in place of General Boyadjiew, I went to the
War Office to pay him my respects. I told him
there was a good chance of Roumania coming in on
our side and asked him what he thought about Bulgaria joining with us. He replied that they did not
wish to do anything to help the Serbs. It was

---

* A Bulgarian political party, to which Mr. Radeff belonged, and at that time in power.

Military Attaché C.

impossible to put Bulgarian troops side by side with Serbian, and if his men met Serbs in the field they would cross bayonets. I suggested that Bulgaria might move against Austria on an independent line, between them and the Roumanians, and urged upon him the advisability of Bulgaria joining the Entente, even without guarantees of territory, in order to secure a place as our ally in the great conference that would take place at the end of the war. He promised to speak to Radoslavoff on the matter, and added that negotiations had already begun with Roumania. This latter remark was not quite correct, as I afterwards found out. Guranesco, the Roumanian Chargé d'Affaires, had held a conversation with him on the subject, but it was quite informal. General Fitcheff had been Chief of the Staff during the first Balkan war against the Turks, and he it was who planned and practically carried out the strategy which was so successful in that campaign. When the Bulgars quarrelled with their allies, he resigned his post, as he did not approve of either the strategy or the policy which dictated the second war. I thought possibly his appointment might be a sign of activity on the part of the Bulgars, but Bax-Ironside's opinion was that Radoslavoff wished to reduce Ghenadieff's influence in the Cabinet, Boyadjiew being, like Ghenadieff, a Macedonian. This was probably the real reason, although venality on the part of Boyadjiew was hinted at by the Premier.

On the 20th September I saw Bourchier and Buxton. They both thought that our Government ought to grant territorial compensation to Bulgaria in Macedonia, and that the situation might become dangerous if this were not done. On the other hand our Minister was at that time entirely opposed to any such thing. Buxton said he was going to ask him to cipher a telegram from Buxton to Sir E. Grey, to be passed to Lloyd-George and Churchill, and Bourchier was going to wire in the same sense to the "Times." Buxton asked me also to wire in that same sense to the War Office. I said I had

GENERAL FITCHEFF.

already done so about ten days ago, and could not send another without some definite reason.

On going to the Chancery next morning, I found that Buxton had sent a wire through the Minister, urging that territorial compensation should be given. I accordingly asked the Minister to send a wire for me to the effect that in my opinion, if compensation were considered, it should be made conditional on Bulgaria actively supporting the Entente. This point had not been mentioned by Buxton. I added that if Roumania were to attack Austria, it was most important that Bulgaria should do the same. Otherwise Roumania might not march; or if she did march, and no arrangement had been made, Bulgaria might attack Serbia or occupy Macedonia. I could see that the Minister did not approve of this at all. Just then a public telegram was handed in to the Chancery to say that Turkey, made uneasy by the attitude of Roumania, was on the point of going to war. The Minister said: "Do you still want to send your telegram after reading that?" I replied: "Well, if Turkey attacks Bulgaria first it will be difficult to get Bulgaria to send troops against Austria at the same time, so I will omit about her doing the same." This I did and the telegram was sent.

On the 22nd September I lunched with Sir H. Bax-Ironside at the Legation, and there met M. Antitch, the Serbian Minister. He was evidently very jealous of the idea of Roumania and Bulgaria treating separately, and feared it might be at Serbia's expense, and that the Serbians would be offered hypothetical gains in the future in Bosnia and Herzegovinia. Meanwhile, Bulgaria would be given actual compensation in Macedonia. This would, however, as far as was foreseen at this time, only be contingent on Serbia's gains elsewhere. I met the Roumanian Charge d'Affaires, M. Guranesco, who expressed great sympathy with the idea of an understanding between his country and Bulgaria. He thought it most important that the Bulgars should send some troops against Austria. 50,000 would be enough, and that would compromise her for years with the Germans. He asked me what General Fitcheff had said and I replied that I thought he was favourable to the idea.

Bax-Ironside's opinion, expressed at this time, was that there was no chance of Bulgaria going to war, and not much chance of Roumania doing so. Somehow or other Roumania had evidently cooled off, and there was no word of King Charles abdicating. It was not until two months later that I heard in Bukarest the reason for this change. It was that Poklewsky, the Russian Minister in Bukarest, got alarmed at the prospect of a revolution and the upset of the Hohenzollern dynasty, and induced his Government to offer Roumania all the compensations which she was to have obtained for going to war, in exchange for her neutrality. This unfortunate proposal was accepted by the Roumanian Government, and the army was at once demobilized. Doubtless Bulgaria was also affected by this change of front, and remained sitting on the fence.

During my subsequent visits to Roumania, I never saw such enthusiasm for war as there was in September. Had it been possible to secure the entry of Roumania and Bulgaria together with Greece, what might not have been the result when Russia was still strong?

It may be considered that I was much too optimistic in my view of the possibilities of achieving a Balkan "bloc," but in order to achieve anything, it is necessary to be optimistic. Besides, my former experience as M.A. in St. Petersburg had taught me that nothing was impossible in diplomacy. At the close of the Russo-Japanese war, within six months of the Dogger Bank incident, which so nearly led to war with Russia, and when the long-existing bad feeling between Russia and Britain had reached its zenith, an agreement was brought about between the two countries in an incredibly short time, engineered by a few leading statesmen on either side. It is true that in the present case one had to deal on the one side with three foreign Ministers, namely those of

Great Britain, Russia and France, all of them co-equal, and on the other side with four little States, all profoundly suspicious of one another, and one of them at daggers drawn with the other three. No wonder that Sir E. Grey found it a harder task than reconciling Russia and Great Britain in the past! The result really depended more than anything else upon the course of military events

Chapter Three.

SERBIAN VIEWS ON BULGARIAN CO-OPERATION — DANEFF EXPLAINS OUTBREAK OF SECOND BALKAN WAR—DIAMANDIS'S VISIT TO ROME — CRITICAL STATE OF AFFAIRS IN TURKEY— DEATH OF KING OF ROUMANIA—ATTEMPTED ASSASSINATION OF BUXTONS — GENERAL SAVOFF, LATE COMMANDER-IN-CHIEF — FALL OF ANTWERP—THE BULGARIAN PEASANT.

ON the 24th September I called on the M.A. at the Serbian Legation and discussed the possibility of an arrangement with Bulgaria. Colonel Kouchakovitch said he thought that Serbia would be ready to cede the Vardar Valley and Monastir, in the event of her getting Bosnia and the coastline. During our conversation the Serbian Minister, M. Antitch, entered the room and took part in the discussion, but did not share the Colonel's view. He declared that Bulgaria's present frontier on the mountain chain, just beyond Kustendil, was the natural one, and that the valley of the Vardar made one line with that of the Morava. That to cede up to the Vardar was to cede Ovche Pole, and whoever dominated the Ovche Pole dominated the whole peninsula, as this was a strategic point from which Nisch could be attacked. That even if the Bulgars were given a conditional promise of the Vardar and Monastir, the condition being that Bosnia, etc., fell to Serbia, they would want their bargain carried out unconditionally, and they would say, supposing the Serbs did not get Bosnia after all, that the conditional offer of Monastir was a proof that the Bulgars had an ethnological right to Monastir, and that therefore the claim was just and should be carried out. He considered it an ideal arrangement, and all that was needed, if Serbia, Greece, and Roumania had an agreement among themselves to keep Bulgaria within her present limits. I said they would want to crush Bulgaria, which was not in our interest. Like most Serbians, he was impervious to argument. It was almost hopeless to expect them to come to any arrangement. They could not be persuaded to take in a wider horizon than the Balkans, or to work for the common good, even if it were to help their own side to win.

The Serbian M.A. then gave me a sketch of the condition of the Serbian army as it was at that time, as follows.—There were 5 Infantry Divisions of the First Ban, each Division being about 20,000 strong in combatants, and consisting of 4 regiments (each of 4 battalions), one artillery regiment of 3 groups (each of 3 batteries), and two or three squadrons of cavalry, engineers, etc. Since the outbreak of war there had been formed 5 more Infantry Divisions of the Second Ban, each being about 15,000 strong in combatants and consisting of 3 regiments (each of 4 battalions) one artillery group of 3 batteries, and 2 squadrons of cavalry together with the usual auxiliaries. Besides the above 10 Divisions, there were also one Division of Infantry of 20,000 men, one Division of independent cavalry of 2 brigades of 4 regiments of 4 squadrons, and 2 batteries of Horse Artillery. There was also a regiment of 9 batteries of 12 c.m. Q.F. Howitzers, and a regiment of 9 mountain batteries.

The actual situation of the Serbian army at that time was that the Serbs were holding their own against various points on the Danube, the Austrians had crossed the Drina in the North-west corner of Serbia, and had established themselves on the Serbian bank, but had not gained the heights overlooking the river. Further south a column of 30,000 Serbs were marching on Serajevo. They were based on Ujitze at the end of a railway some 60 kilometres from the Western frontier and had reached about half-way to Serajevo. The Austrian force opposed to them was quite independent of the one operating against the North-west corner near Shabatz. The strength of the Austrians was more than $4\frac{1}{2}$ Army Corps.

CHAPTER THREE.

The Colonel had served in the first Balkan War alongside both Serbian and Bulgarian troops. To my question as to his opinion regarding their respective merits, he replied that the Serbian artillery was better served, because the Serbian officer was more intelligent and better educated. Since the annexation of Bosnia in 1907-08, the Serbs had made great progress. The Serbian cavalry was better than the Bulgarian. But as regards the infantry there was very little to choose between them, the Bulgarian being slightly superior. The Bulgars had more machine guns and more mountain guns than the Serbs. In the recent fighting against Austria, they had found the Slav troops much better than the German-Austrian. They returned to the assault ten or twelve times, whereas the latter had always had enough after one or two unsuccessful attacks. The Serbs were fairly well off for men, but there was a great shortage of officers.

On the 20th September a telegram arrived from the Foreign Office authorizing the British Minister to tell the Bulgarian Government that they would get compensation in Macedonia from Serbia in proportion to the amount of territory acquired by them elsewhere, and that the more heavily the Central Powers were beaten the larger would be the gains. That was the nearest approach that Grey had allowed himself, up to that time, towards suggesting that the Bulgars should take an active part in the war. I hoped that my last telegram had contributed in some slight degree to this concession, but doubted much if it would be sufficiently explicit for the Bulgars.

The following day I heard from the Serbian M.A. as to the course of events, and the position of the Austrian troops between Shabatz and Zvornik and those defending Sarajevo against the combined forces of Serbia and Montenegro. There were about 150,000 troops on either side, and the fighting had been more severe than hitherto. In telegraphing details to the War Office, I took the opportunity to ask permission to visit these operations pending possible action by Roumania.

About this time I went to see M. Daneff, late Prime Minister and Minister for Foreign Affairs, and an old friend. He gave me an interesting account of the way in which the 2nd. Balkan war broke out, as follows:—

"We had long before agreed to hold a conference at Petrograd to settle the line of demarcation between Serbia and Bulgaria in Macedonia. The point of difference between Pashitch the Serbian Premier and myself was that the original agreement between the two countries provided that a certain boundary line should be followed, and in the event of a disagreement, the Emperor of Russia was to be the arbitrator. The Serbs wanted to disregard this document altogether, because they had failed to secure the outlet on the Adriatic which they had expected. I was prepared to give them some concession in Macedonia, but naturally insisted on regard being had to the agreement. Pashitch and the Serbian Parliament eventually gave way, and I had told General Savoff, the commander of the Bulgarian troops, that he was to commence quietly to demobilize the army, that the matter was now in the hands of the diplomats, and no fighting was to take place. Savoff told me that he was going to Paris on leave, and the whole affair was settled as far as I was concerned. I had not seen the King for several days, but in my capacity as Premier and Foreign Minister had informed him of the Government's policy. There had been several little skirmishes between the opposing outposts, but one afternoon, a few days after Savoff had announced his intention of taking leave, there was a rumour of something more serious. I asked Savoff what had happened, and received an evasive reply. The next day it became clear that fighting had taken place on a wide front, and I ordered him to break off and withdraw his troops. This order was duly communicated to the troops, and a Bulgar regiment in consequence suffered very heavy losses by refusing to reply to the Serbian or Greek fire. It was then too late to stop these Powers who had quickly perceived Bulgaria's weak extended front, and the fighting continued. I telegraphed to the Emperor of Russia, begging him to order Serbia and Greece to desist, but they could not then be held back, and the Emperor replied that Bulgaria was not the only Power who was privileged to disobey. Then the Roumanians came in on our rear and all was over. Savoff declared that he had acted on superior authority, meaning that of the King."

Evidently Daneff had relied on the Emperor to restrain the Roumanians, and probably the King had expected Austria to do the same by the Serbs. No doubt Daneff was to blame for having allowed a dangerous situation to be unduly prolonged. One very interesting item of news was also told me by Daneff, namely that Guranesco then, as now, Chargé d'Affaires, had intentionally and falsely given the Bulgars to understand that Roumania would not move. Austria's motive was of course to break up the Balkan "bloc," and Roumania wanted the opportunity of rectifying and extending her Southern frontier. It was not surprising, therefore, that Guranesco was now looked upon with some suspicion when advocating an understanding between Roumania and Bulgaria.

On the 29th September, I went to the Bulgarian War Office to see Colonel Stancioff, Assistant to the Chief of the Staff, and for many years M.A. at Bukarest. He gave me his opinion that there was no chance of Roumania coming into the war. The King, he said, was very clever and master of the situation. When he was pressed by the Germans, he got up popular demonstrations, and then told his German and Austrian friends how impossible it was to go against the people's will. When assailed by the Triple Entente, he fell sick and nothing was done. He was also very afraid of Bulgaria.

Stancioff had some reason for his cynical remarks which rather impressed me, and I thought that, after all, it might be worth while to go and watch the fighting in Serbia. But the reply of the War Office to my telegram was, that I might visit Nisch, but was not to go to the front. That meant that the War Office considered my work here as the more important. As I could see no immediate object in going to Nisch, I remained in Bulgaria. I was afterwards to learn how the revolution in Roumania had fizzled out owing to the action of Russia, that the King had been really ill, and in fact died not long after.

About this time I met Tchapraschikoff, Bulgarian Minister in Serbia, back on short leave from Nisch. He was evidently on very good terms with the Germans as I could tell from his behaviour at the Union Club. Although a cautious man, he burst out about the necessity of getting back Macedonia, and was very strongly anti-Serbian, which is however, the case with all Bulgars. He saw no reason why the Radoslavoff Government should not go on for a long time, and no reason to change it. As he, himself, was on terms of intimacy at the Palace, his opinion was worth noting. I noted also that Guranesco who was dining with me, together with Tchapraschikoff, was despondent about the relations between Bulgaria and Roumania.

A day or two later I invited the brothers Buxton to dine and meet Guranesco, with whom they were much impressed, and I rather encouraged Noel Buxton in his suggestion of communicating to the Press the idea of a Bulgaro-Roumanian alliance, and a combined march on Austria. What a row there would be! It might cause the Turks to attack the Bulgars, but that would be a step in the right direction!

On the 30th September I again saw the War Minister and asked him what progress was being made with Roumania. He replied "None. The Roumanians are very vague, and have not made any definite offer. If the Entente and Roumania want Bulgaria's help, there must be more serious and definite proposals. Even if the Government ordered them to fight, the Reserve men would want to know what they were going to get out of it before they would respond in a satisfactory manner."

I was delighted at this time to note a change in our Minister's attitude towards the idea of offering Bulgaria a part of Macedonia. A few days previously I had written a despatch to the Foreign Office strongly condemning from a military point of view the policy of squeezing Bulgaria between Serbia, Greece and Roumania, on the ground that this tended to drive her into the arms of Turkey, rendered her useless for service against Austria, and prevented Roumania from coming in on our side. Bax-Ironside, to my astonishment, expressed himself as pleased and as having read it with great interest.

On the 6th October Guranesco told me that M. Diamandi, a prominent Roumanian, and brother to the former Roumanian Minister here, had just returned from an unofficial visit to Rome, where he, together with some of his fellow-countrymen, had approached the ambassadors of the Triple Entente with the suggestion of joining them if Russia would, besides promising them Transylvania and Bukovina from Austria, give them also the province of Bessarabia, taken from them by Russia in 1878. This suggestion also included the placing of two Divisions of the Russian army on the Bulgaro-Roumanian frontier, the idea being that the Bulgars would not attack Russians. I gathered that they had not succeeded in inducing Italy to join the Entente, although they had offered her the Kutzo-Vlachs of Albania should she decide to do so. Guranesco also said that some ten days previously Radoslavoff had offered Roumania the neutrality of Bulgaria free of charge, in case the Roumanians wished to invade Transylvania. That looked as if Radoslavoff wanted Roumania to become involved in Transylvania, in order to be free herself to attack Serbia in Macedonia, unhindered by fears for her rear ; or it might indicate merely a general desire to see her neighbours exhaust themselves in fighting while she kept her forces intact, and so would be capable of settling the Balkan problems after her own heart at the end of the war. Some such feeling was no doubt at the back of the mind of more than one Balkan Power, and added to the difficulty of inducing them to move. Fitcheff, too, at this time changed his attitude, and declared that Bulgaria stood to win all that she required by remaining neutral. Meanwhile the situation in Turkey had been getting lively. The King's Messenger arrived from Constantinople with the news that all the English ladies had been advised to leave, and were probably already on their way to Dedeagach, and in fact they arrived at Sofia a few days later.

On the 7th October I saw Savinsky at the Russian Legation, and sounded him as to the alleged negotiations with Rome. He said it was true in the main that the Roumanians had put forward some suggestions, but there had never been any question of giving them more than half of Bukovina, the whole of Transylvania, and only a small portion of Bessarabia. I also asked him about the Russian troops on the Bulgaro-Roumanian frontier which I thought an unfortunate proposal, and one which would be regarded with suspicion here. He said it was Colonel Romanovsky's the Russian Military Attaché's proposal, but it had been vetoed by the Russian War Office, as they did not wish to spare the troops.

On the 8th October I wrote to Lord Kitchener, at the suggestion of Noel Buxton, who asked me to let Lord Kitchener know my views. In my letter I advocated that the Triple Entente should promise the Bulgars a definite line in Macedonia, from the junction of the three frontiers to Lake Okhrida, dependent on Serbia getting compensation in Bosnia, Herzegovina, and on the Adriatic coast, the Entente to be arbitrators. That the arrangement should be made in conjunction with a treaty with Roumania, in order to bring Bulgaria into line against Austria, or against Turkey, if the latter direction were preferred. This suggestion did not quite coincide with Noel's, his being somewhat more complicated.

CHAPTER THREE.

About this time the brothers Buxton went to Bukarest, followed shortly by Bourchier.

On the 10th October news arrived of the death of the King of Roumania, and on the 11th came the announcement of the fall of Antwerp and the capture of 60,000 Belgian and British prisoners. Unfortunately the censorship of the Bulgarian Press had fallen into German hands before the war, and some of the papers, such as the "Utro," in which the fall of Antwerp was first announced, were undoubtedly subsidised by Germany.

On the 12th October I paid a visit to Tirnovo, the ancient capital of Bulgaria. The train left at 11.0 p.m. and reached Tirnovo at 8.30 the following morning. The sight is magnificent. Approaching by rail, one tunnels right under the town, which rises in terraces from the river. At the end of the town are two hills, round which the river serpentines far below. One of them is connected with the town by a natural causeway of rock. Facing the causeway and the town is the site whereon Ferdinand a few years ago declared himself Tzar, and where once stood the palace of Asen II., King of Bulgaria, before the Turkish conquest. The remains of houses and a city wall are still to be seen. The other hill, which was sacred, contains the ruins of numerous stone-built temples, facing East, and each provided with a round pillar about 8 feet high. None but priests were permitted to live on this hill which is altogether a most romantic spot. The town is a primitive place now, with a few insignificant shops, the usual dirty inns, a fine school and good barracks.

I inspected two infantry regiments which were composed of an excellent type of soldier. There was no sign of mobilization, the 36th class having just been dismissed, and companies being from 60 to 85 men strong. There were three battalions per regiment, but the new 3rd battalions were not completely formed, and only numbered 200 men. The machine guns were of excellent type, from the "Deutsche Waffenfabric" at Berlin.

From Tirnovo I went by train across the Balkan range to Stara Zagora, and thence to Philipopolis. This is the second largest town in Bulgaria and a place of historic interest in connection with the Russo-Turkish war of 1877-78. It is picturesquely situated amongst some half dozen rocky hills on the banks of the Maritza, the great river of Bulgaria which forms the theme of the Bulgarian national anthem, "Shuma Maritza." Here I was received with great cordiality by an old acquaintance, General Gueschoff, commanding the 10th Division, and was shewn a battery of French Q.F. field guns at fire practice, and a number of good Krupp guns recently captured from the Turks. Thanks to the latter they were able to fit the Division out complete with Q.F. guns.

No sooner was the morning drill over than I was shown a copy of the "Utro" containing the news that both the brothers Buxton had been shot dead by a Turkish assassin. This gave me a shock, especially as I believed it was partly on my advice that they had gone to Bukarest. It was also very strange that they were apparently the last people to see King Charles, as they had an audience at 9.0 p.m., and the King died at 6.0 the following morning. I wired to Bukarest for information, and was much relieved at receiving a reply from Sir George Barclay the next morning that they had been wounded only and were doing very well.

On the 17th October I travelled back to Sofia, and found myself in the same train with General Savoff, the late Commander-in-Chief of the Bulgarian army in the last war. He kindly invited me into his compartment, and we had a very interesting conversation.

He said the King was much depressed, was afraid of the Czar, and would do nothing against Russia. He himself was in favour of mobilizing all the available troops at once as first line troops. Germany did this and now had at its disposal 75 army corps. The French and Russians waited till they had formed their first line troops before mobilizing their second line. That was an error. If strategy now demands that you should put your whole weight into the field at once, then you should draw up your plan of mobilization to correspond. Bulgaria could never have beaten the Turk had she not done this, or had Turkey been able to do the same.

The Bulgarian army took 5 days to mobilize and 15 more to concentrate ready for action. The combatant strength was 460,000, but counting every enlisted man, the total swelled to 700,000. I had heard this figure put by the Chief Intendant of the army at 600,000 and thought he had exaggerated, but he was probably correct, or not very from from the truth.

General Savoff gave me the impression of being a good leader, quick, bold and decided. Whatever his judgment might be, he would not hesitate in the execution. I asked him how the fighting occurred with Serbia, and he replied that the Serbs kept on advancing the whole time so he had orders to attack them, which he did. Even then it might have succeeded, had it been carried out whole-heartedly, but he got orders and counter-orders. When finally Daneff gave him the order to break off fighting, it was no longer possible to do so because the Serbians then would not stop. At one time he got the order from the King to retire on to Sofia, when he was facing the Greeks and Serbs somewhere in the direction of Kustendil. Papodopoff was his Chief of the Staff, and brought the telegram at night. Savoff said: "I cannot possibly retire. That would be fatal. I couldn't hold back the enemy from the capital, and the dynasty would go!" Papodopoff agreed with him. He gave the order to advance with every available man against the Greeks, and telegraphed to the King for other orders, that the enemy must be held or the men must die at their post. The attack succeeded, and they were able to make terms with the enemy. Savoff was educated at St. Petersburg, and as a young Bulgarian Lieutenant, attracted the attention of the Czar, Alexander III., when out sketching in the neighbourhood of Gatchina. Savoff replied to the Czar's questions so intelligently that he was pleased, and when Savoff got back to the village where he was staying he found awaiting him a present of cigarettes and eatables from the Emperor. Months afterwards, when he was presented to the Czar on passing out of the military college, Alexander recognized him, and sent him a present of 1,500 Roubles, and a message to enjoy himself at St. Petersburg before returning to Bulgaria.

But, like other Bulgarian officers who had been educated in Russia, Savoff knew too much about the Russians to have any special regard for, or confidence in them, and still less of gratitude. Before leaving him, I took the opportunity of sounding him as to a possible alliance with Roumania. He seemed to think it feasible, and that the men would march well enough, if they knew what they were going to fight for and they were quite intelligent enough to understand attacking Austria in order to get Macedonia.

On October 8th further bad news appeared in the public telegrams regarding the amount of material captured at Antwerp, together with reproaches by the "Morning Post" to Churchill for having undertaken to defend Antwerp with a weak force of Marines, against the advice of responsible military chiefs. The military correspondent of the "Times" remarked that it was possible the Germans might undertake an invasion of England, though the chances of success were small. Fancy owning that there were any! Worst of all, another of our cruisers had been sunk by a German submarine. This meant that Germany might gradually whittle away our naval strength while keeping her own intact, and so prevent us from continuing the war indefinitely.

On the 24th October I started for Bukarest, but had arranged a little shooting party with Royaards, the Dutch Minister, an old friend of St. Petersburg days, and Motte, a Belgian, formerly in the diplomatic service, and now in business at Sofia.

Military Attaché D.

CHAPTER THREE.

We stopped at the station beyond Plevna and shot that afternoon and the following day, bagging a few woodcock, hares and partridges. At night we stayed in a country inn, and conversed with the peasants in a large square low-roofed room containing a big stove, a bar for drinks and a wide oak bench all round the walls. They were very intelligent and well-informed. Most of them had taken part in the Balkan wars. One man was able to illustrate a tactical point by drawing a plan on the ground. They all seemed favourably inclined toward England, and said that she was their only friend. They believed in her honesty and disinterestedness, but doubted her power of doing anything at the end of the war to prevent Russia from taking the Dardanelles, and therefore from gradually swallowing up the Balkan States. That was really one great reason why many of the "Intelligenzia" of the towns had mixed feelings. They also knew that Germany was more efficient than Russia and therefore thought that she would win. The best informed knew that if Germany and Austria were to win, there would be small chance of the Bulgars getting Macedonia, as eventually the Austrians would take it as well as Salonika. Consequently these latter hoped that neither side would win, and wished to keep strong themselves in order to be able to settle the Balkans after the war as they pleased. For the moment they had had their bellyful of fighting, and did not want any more unless they saw a clear profit. About this time I noticed that Royaards, who was at first very Germanophil, began coming round to think that we might perhaps win. He reflected that the Britisher had something in his composition that neither the Dutchman nor any other continental possessed. He did not quite know how to define it, but thought it might make all the difference.

On returning to the railway I went for a stroll into the village of Pordim, about three-quarters of a mile from the station, and there, to my surprise, I found two museums, one Russian, the other

Roumanian. Although I had once or twice visited the field of Plevna I had not been told of these. It was here that the Emperor Alexander II. and King Charles of Roumania spent some six weeks before the fall of Plevna. The Emperor lived in quite a nice little house with four decent sized rooms, while King Charles had to put up in a hovel. Both are now preserved as museums, the latter having been enlarged. There are life-size wax figures showing the different uniforms of the two armies. The Emperor slept in a four-poster which is gone but the camp bed of the Commander-in-Chief, the Grand-Duke Nicolai Nicolaievitch, father of the present C.-in-C., is still to be seen. There are numerous weapons, photographs, etc., and in the little garden surrounding the museums are Russian and Turkish weapons and guns. The village looked particularly smart and prosperous, and the young women in their national embroidered dresses appeared to be handsomer than the usual type, which might well be the case.

The next day, 27th October, after a somewhat troublesome journey, I reached Bukarest, and put up at Athenée Palace Hotel. I visited the Buxtons in hospital. Noel had been hit in the jaw, and had had a narrow escape besides, as the first shot was turned by the corner of his pocket-book. Charles, likewise wounded, was still in bed, but was looking well.

Chapter Four.

SECOND VISIT TO ROUMANIA — BUXTONS IN HOSPITAL — EXPLANATION OF ROUMANIAL'S INACTION—INTERVIEWS WITH FILIPESCU, TAKE YONESCU AND BRATIANO — SUGGESTION OF PROPOSALS TO EMANATE FROM LONDON—STATE OF GERMANY AND AUSTRIA—LETTER TO CROWN PRINCE OF SERBIA—BUXTON'S INTERVIEW WITH TURKISH ASSASSIN — GENERAL ILIESCO—BUXTON'S AUDIENCE WITH QUEEN—INSPECTION OF ROUMANIAN TROOPS, ETC.—LUNCH WITH GENERAL ILIESCO—INTERVIEWS WITH FRENCH AND RUSSIAN MINISTERS—BULGARIA DECLINES OFFER OF LINE OF THE VARDAR AND ENOS MIDIA—TAKE YONESCU IN CORRESPONDENCE WITH VENIZELOS.

A FEW days later Sir George Barclay took me to pay a ceremonious visit on M. Porumbaru, the Minister for Foreign Affairs. The American and German Ministers were waiting in the ante-room, and though we took no apparent notice of the latter, he struck me as being a very smart and capable man. I afterwards ascertained it was Von dem Busche.

The conversation with M. Porumbaru turned on the visit of the Buxtons who, during their audience with the late King Charles, had told the King that England would continue the war to the end. "But what will be the end?" asked the King. The Buxtons, according to M. Porumbaru, were quite nonplussed, and confessed they didn't know. The Buxtons were the last people to see the King officially, as their audience was at 9.0 p.m., and he died the following morning. The King evidently thought he had scored, and presumably told the Queen or some member of his suite, and so it got to the German Minister who had just related it to the Minister for Foreign Affairs. From here I happened to go on to see how the Buxtons were progressing, and ascertained from them that this little incident was correctly stated. So I fear they lost an opportunity of boosting up the British Empire.

They also told the King that England took a great interest in Roumania now, to which the King replied that it was a pity she had not done so before. It was therefore clear on whose side the King's sentiments lay, and that he was not in a very amiable frame of mind, which is not to be wondered at under the circumstances.

I then called on Captain Pichon, the French Military Attaché, and he told me that after I had left Bukarest the situation was coming to a climax, and the King would have been obliged to give way, when Poklewsky came in with the ridiculous promise of giving Roumania permission to occupy Transylvania and half of Bukovina in exchange for her mere neutrality, instead of a reward for her active participation, at the same time guaranteeing her present frontiers. He added that the Roumanians had extorted this promise from Poklewsky, and the Russian Government was obliged to acquiesce and see him through. The Russian Military Attaché was furious, and the thing was done without consulting the Triple Entente. The result was the immediate demobilization of the Roumanian army. On the other hand, Barclay, who was a friend of Poklewsky, declared that the latter got his instructions quite definitely from Sazonoff, the Russian Foreign Minister, and had no choice in the matter.

Next day, the 30th October, I called upon M. Nicolas Filipescu, late Minister of War and member of the Conservative Opposition party. He told me about the agreement with Russia which had been signed about 8 days previously, and committed Roumania entirely to the side of Russia. He was, however, not quite as easy in his mind, as the engagement said that Roumania might occupy, but did not say "annex" the territories in question. Still, he said, they were certain now to come in against Austria unless some frightful catastrophe occurred to the Allies, which would entail their ultimate defeat. Just then he was called to the telephone and returned with the news that Russia had declared war on Turkey, and that to-morrow

Bulgaria would openly declare herself on the side of Turkey, and march in Macedonia. I said that if Bulgaria did so, it would be the fault of Roumania for not having squared her before, and also of the Triple Entente, who might have ranged her on our side. He seemed surprised at that, and said the Germans had told the Roumanians that Bulgaria had made engagements with Germany and Turkey. I replied that we had the most positive information that such was not the case. He then discussed the value of the Bulgarian army, which I put as strong as before the Balkan war, he thought they were in a bad way and that one army corps left behind on their frontier would be sufficient to keep them south of the Danube, a totally inadequate figure if they meant coming.

The same evening I dined with Take Yonescu tête-à-tête (his wife being still at Sinaia) in his large and luxurious house. I found that his attitude although quite as friendly as before, was different from what it was a month previously. He was no longer keen on a Bulgarian alliance, or on making any arrangement with her which would, he said, only be leaving her free to occupy Macedonia. I said " of course you would only offer her something in the Dobrudja, on condition that she entered the war on the side of the Triple Entente, not merely for remaining neutral." Altogether I was discouraged by Take Yonescu's attitude, and did not think Roumania seriously meant coming into the war.

Next day I had an interview with M. Bratiano, Premier and Minister of War. He was an intelligent looking man of about 40, with a small brown beard. I asked him what was the state of affairs in Roumania. He replied " I did not send for you to tell you that, but to find out from you what was the state of affairs in Bulgaria." " Bulgaria's attitude depends on that of Roumania, and that is why I took the liberty of asking what was the position here, otherwise the position in Bulgaria is that of a general friendliness to the Triple Entente, and especially towards England," said I. " Really, what—more friendly towards England than to Russia?" I replied yes, they had more confidence in England. Whatever the result of the war, the Bulgars thought England would emerge strong when all the other Powers were more or less exhausted, and Bulgaria knew that England wished to see a strong Bulgaria.

"Well, you have told me something I did not know before," was his somewhat incredulous reply. I then asked him point blank whether Roumania was really better disposed to the Triple Entente than to Germany and Austria. "Yes," he hesitated rather, " it is no secret. Everybody knows we are on the side of the Entente." I suggested what a great effect it would have if they and the Bulgars both joined actively in the war, and whether it would not be possible to make an arrangement with Serbia, by which Bulgaria would get the Lake Okhrida line in Macedonia, and recover from Roumania that part of the Dobrudja which they had lost in the late war. He declared that the Serbians would on no account give up Monastir. They considered that they had sacrificed themselves to Russian interests, and demanded special treatment, in the same case as Belgium. They would not realise that in point of fact the Great Powers had made immense sacrifices to save Serbia from annihilation. The utmost that she might be persuaded to give up would be the line of the Vardar. As for the Dobrudja, he professed to be quite firm in refusing to give up a single inch of it. Roumania might have taken a great deal more, but had been content to seize the minimum requisite for strategic reasons. He was quite prepared to enter into amicable relations with Bulgaria, and was in no way hostile to her pretensions in other directions. He had twice last year given proof of this, in refusing to join a coalition with Serbia and Greece against Bulgaria. Now, as the British influence was so great, we might ascertain the maximum that Serbia was content to give, and let Bulgaria have also the Enos-Media line, and use her against Turkey. Roumania intended to enter into action against Austria, but the time had not yet come. They would wait to see what Bulgaria did. If she joined the Turks, and attacked Macedonia, she would gain nothing by it, as we should certainly attack her if she made war on Serbia. No, it would be much better for her to take what she could get from Serbia without fighting. Such was the gist of Bratiano's remarks. Although there was much sense in what he said, it was clear that he had no intention of taking the initiative towards forming a Balkan "bloc," and the same might be said of the leaders of the other Balkan States.

I accordingly took the opportunity of another visit to the hospital to prime Noel Buxton with suggestions for a wire to Grey, Churchill & Co., with the object of initiating a deal in London about Macedonia.

The following day, the 2nd November, on arriving at the Legation, I found things humming. It seemed that our people had at last realised the supreme importance of roping in Bulgaria. At Barclay's invitation I drafted a telegram urging the Foreign Office to tackle the Macedonian question. it was signed by Sir George and ran much as follows —"Col. Napier believes that proposals emanating from London will be more efficacious in Bulgaria than any coming from St. Petersburg. Essential to offer Bulgaria some definite Macedonian territory in addition to Enos-Media line. Action by Bulgaria will not only entail co-operation of Greece, but may inspire Roumania to move at once." What I wanted the Buxtons to wire to Grey, Churchill & Co., was "Present critical situation may now be saved if Grey immediately sends for Roumanian, Bulgarian and Serbian Ministers in London and arranges on his own initiative, subject to consent of France and Russia, that Serbia surrenders to Bulgaria unconditionally line of Vardar at close of war, and Bulgaria has permission if undertaken immediately, to reconquer Enos-Media line from Turkey, Roumania observing benevolent neutrality towards Bulgaria." But they spent all Sunday talking about it, and didn't send anything until

Monday afternoon, and then very much what I had said in the morning. I couldn't personally invite Grey how to act, nor could the Minister, but I hoped to have got the Buxtons to do so.

Then I happened to meet Yacovaki, First Secretary of the Roumanian Legation at Berlin, whom I had known formerly at Sofia. He was here for a few days leave, and told me that the whole of Germany was absolutely united, confident, and determined to fight to a finish. Not so, however, Austria. This was the weak spot in her armour, and Germany knew it. She had sent lots of troops there, and had taken over all the high commands. His idea was that if we could destroy the Austrian army, and take their country, that would finish the war. He thought that England had been too backward, and Russia too forward in declaring their policy. He also thought a lead from us would do very much towards establishing a firm alliance between Roumania and Bulgaria. They didn't trust each other. The trouble began fourteen years ago, when the Bulgars took to sending assassins here to kill certain eminent Roumanians. I was glad to hear such a speedy confirmation of the views I had just telegraphed about the advisability of England taking the initiative, and that from a totally different source.

The same day I saw Radeff, the Bulgarian Minister, who was rather low about the whole affair, and said that someone ought to approach Prince Alexander of Serbia, who had everything over there in his own hands. I said nothing, but thought perhaps I might usefully put in a word there. I then proceeded to encourage Radeff and said things were going all right, and that the Germans had done us an immense service by forcing us to declare war. It was a great pity we had not done so many years ago. Radeff's M.A. Captain Samardjieff, an old friend, was there also, and asked me to lunch with him some time. He is married to an Italian lady.

When I got back to my hotel that night, I thought of telegraphing to Prince Alexander of

Serbia, but could not have done so through the Legation, or "en clair" without attracting too much attention. So I wrote him a long letter describing the whole situation, and what a great service he would do both to the Triple Entente and to Serbia, if he gave up something in Macedonia. I didn't know what their price was—Vardar line or Okhrida Line, but if we got the Bulgars in, we should get the Greeks and Roumanians in also, and finish the war. I did not add the Italians, because I thought Serbia might not be so keen about that. I reminded Prince Alexander of our time together at the Coronation in London, (I had been attached to his suite) and said how much I had wished to accompany his army in the field, and to have had the opportunity of expressing my great admiration for his many magnificent achievements. It was a fact that he had saved his country over and over again. Now he would have an opportunity of doing so once more. I said I would not tell my Government that I had written to him; that it was private and confidential for his personal information.

I couldn't register the letter without attracting attention, so I just stamped it and stuck it in the post to take its chance. It could do no harm if the Roumanians read it, but I thought my Chiefs would have a fit if they heard of it.

On the 5th November I lunched with Radeff and found him very disgusted with Bratiano, who had told him, as he had told me, that he would not give up an inch of the Dobrudja to Bulgaria. He also told me that when we were being pushed back on Paris the Roumanian Government encouraged Bulgaria to march into Macedonia and promised not to interfere with them, but the Bulgars refused out of regard for England. Of course one must take that latter remark with a grain of salt. Then I asked Radeff what would be the result if the Entente were to force Roumania to decide definitely for or against the Entente? He said Bratiano would probably try and get out of it, and if he couldn't, then he would resign. I then went back to the

Legation and wrote a despatch suggesting that perhaps the moment had arrived when the Entente could advantageously apply pressure. The following day, Barclay, after consultation with Poklewsky, who strongly condemned my suggestion, sent a wire informing the Foreign Office of Bratiano's remark to Radeff, and of my suggestion that a strong lead from the Entente headed by England might remove the deadlock here, in the event of negotiations regarding Macedonia and Thrace being otherwise successful. Poklewsky, however, thought anything of the sort would do more harm than good at present. Evidently he, and possibly the Russian Government, were not keen on Roumania's help, or Bulgaria's either.

That afternoon I spent at the Palais de Justice where the Buxtons were interviewing their would-be assassin. He was rather a good-looking young man of about 20 years of age, with an intelligent and determined face. The Buxtons had spent nearly an hour with him discussing Young Turk questions and politics before I arrived. I asked him whether he was sorry that he had not killed them. He replied that he was sorry he had wounded Charles, but had rather regretted Noel's escape. Now, however, that the latter had persuaded him that he was a Turko-phil, he was not quite sure. The conversation then turned on India. Being a Turk, a Mahomedan, and a cheeky youth, he reproached the British for having neglected to educate the Indians, and said that that was why we had so much discontent and rebellion. I said I thought it was because we had given them the wrong sort of education, and allowed them to imbibe all kinds of socialistic doctrines, and that we were perhaps too liberal in that respect. "Why did we send missionaries to convert the Indians?" he asked. I said everyone was free to preach whatever religion he liked, and if he were free he should go to see for himself, but not judge from hearsay. Anyhow, whether we had failed or not, had Turkey done any better, or as much for her people? to which he gave no reply. We then asked him where he had studied. The answer was —chiefly in France; he had been to London and visited Munich, but had made no long stay in Germany. I could not find anything to implicate Germans in his attack on the Buxtons. He was in Sofia with them but it was not until he got to Bukarest that he seemed to have received his instructions, and he refused to give away any of his accomplices. The Buxtons shook him warmly by the hand, and they parted on the most friendly terms as he was conducted back to prison by the Roumanian police.

I had really visited the prison in order to catch the Buxtons, because I had heard they were going to see the Queen of Roumania on the following day, and I wanted to ask them to try and put in a little political work. The Queen had apparently not allowed any political conversation on the part of our Minister. Perhaps it would be easier for the Buxtons.

On the 7th November the papers had news from Vienna that the Amir of Afghanistan was advancing against India with an army of 170,000 men. I was rather uneasy about this, as it was a vulnerable point, and I remembered that Lady Bax-Ironside had received an anonymous letter about a month previously to say that German officers were going to Afghanistan. The Afghans were said to have destroyed the Herat-Kushk railway to prevent the British troops from concentrating. So far as I was aware, no such railway existed, and if it did exist, it would have been of use to the Russians, not to ourselves. So the whole news was rather confused. As a compensation, however, there were rumours of a big Russian victory in Galicia.

That morning I had an interview with General Iliescu, Secretary General of the Ministry of War. He was directly under Bratiano, and appeared practically to run the whole army. He received me very warmly and informally, and asked me about the Bulgars. I said they were all right and friends of ours, and it was a pity Roumania could not

GENERAL ILIESCU.

(Presented to the Author).

arrange something with them. Iliescu declared they were ready to march into Transylvania now, and it was only the Bulgars that stopped them. I replied that the Bulgars were disappointed that Roumania had not approached them, and that Bratiano had now said that he would not give them an inch of territory so that things would be worse. Iliesco said "Once get the Bulgars to come in with the Entente, and we will arrange with them in 24 hours. But you must settle about Macedonia and Turkey first, and it will be all right about the Dobrudja." Just then the Minister of Public Works and another civilian whom I did not know came into the room and took part in the conversation, and repeated that it would be all right about the Dobrudja. I said they would certainly have to give the Bulgars a small piece, even if it were only Dobritch and Baltchik, as a proof that they were in earnest. He and the General both seemed to think that feasible. Just then General Iliescu rushed off to the Palace as he had to see the King, and I was left with the Minister. I asked if I might quote him about the Dobrudja. He replied "No, it is not my job, but it will be all right. Go on and square the matter up yourself, working unofficially." This was rather funny language from a Minister to a Military Attaché, and made me wonder whether the Roumanian Government had intercepted my letter to Prince Alexander. The very marked attention that I was shortly to receive at the hands of the King of Roumania through General Iliescu, made me wonder still more.

After lunch I saw the Buxtons again. Barclay had not telegraphed my suggestion, embodied in a despatch, that perhaps the time had come to put a little pressure on to Roumania to induce her to get off the fence, even if it were to involve Bratiano's retirement, but the Buxtons had had a good yarn with the Queen. Noel didn't, but Charles did carry out my suggestion of kissing the royal hand, and he reeled off a sentence or two of my prompting that we were now closing in on Germany like a boa-

CHAPTER FOUR.

constrictor, etc. I didn't suppose she often heard a favourable opinion of the war. Charles told me that the Queen was very jolly, and told them some most amusing yarns about King Ferdinand of Bulgaria, and he was able to put in a word or two, I believe, about Bratiano being a trifle sticky.

On November the 8th, the papers contained a message from the Grand Duke Nicolas to Lord Kitchener to say they had gained the greatest success of the war against Austria in Galicia, and a private telegram in the Press said that Yaroslav had fallen and the Austrians had lost 18,000 men, but this sounded too small a number to explain the Commander in Chief's telegram.

During the next few days, General Iliescu having, true to his word, attached an officer of the General Staff to show me round, I spent my time in looking at Roumanian troops, factories and stores. Lt.-Colonel Rascano, Chief of the Operations' Sections, fetched me one morning to see a battalion of infantry, a group of three batteries of artillery, and a regiment of cavalry on parade. The turn-out was smart and the parade movements were well carried out. The infantry soldier is small, but looks fairly tough. Either as a fighter or in point of intelligence he is not to be compared with the Bulgarian soldier. But on a horse he shapes much better than the Bulgar, and his cavalry is consequently better than theirs. The artillery looks smarter and moves quicker but I had no opportunity of judging its shooting capacity. In the afternoon I went over the barracks, where the men were very closely packed. The discipline was very severe, and in the guard room prison, a dark room with hardly any light, there were ranged round the wall a number of very slender looking sentry boxes, each with a square aperture and a man's face looking out of it. The men appeared to have two kinds of confinement, one in these sentry boxes, where they cannot sit down or even turn round, and the other in a room with one or two beds and large enough to walk about in. The sentry box confinement must not

October 29th—December 7th, 1914.

extend for more than 8 days and nights, during which a man must have one rest in the other room. One man I saw and interrogated; he had been in his box for 24 hours for having absented himself at night without leave. That is the usual crime, the men do not get drunk much, but yet the Commanding Officer said they were a very refractory lot to deal with. I could not say they looked it. In the barrack yard of this regiment there were squads of non-commissioned officers qualifying to be instructors, and a detachment of machine guns drilling. The latter were particularly smart in bringing the machine guns into action, firing in a recumbent position to avoid exposure. The regimental transport was complete and in the company mobilization stores were bundles of clothing all ready with the reservist's name and number, and to his measure. A bundle contained 2 pairs of ankle boots, one pair of sandals, two pairs of socks, an astrachan fur cap to pull over the ears, shirt, drawers, great coat, uniform, and an entrenching tool. An inspection of the artillerymen's kit disclosed the same articles with the addition of a fur waistcoat. This was being supplied for all troops, 800,000 having been ordered. The foot gear did not seem to be sufficient protection against the snows of Transylvania, but I was told that every soldier brought his ordinary peasants felt foot gear that is worn with the sandal, and the Government takes it over at a valuation. The ammunition and ambulance columns appeared to be all complete, carts of every description having been manufactured here and standing all ready in good masonry store houses. In the store houses were piles of boxes, rooms full of sugar, biscuit, maraconi, rice, of which the men are large consumers, tea, tobacco, chocolate and tinned fish, the last two articles being exclusively for the use of officers. The recent campaign in Bulgaria, though inglorious and bloodless, had been of the utmost use as a mobilization manoeuvre test, and they had been able to rectify all their weak points.

I noted a few details about the larger units. Each Army Corps had two Divisions. Each Division had two regiments of field artillery of two groups of three batteries (12 batteries). An Army Corps thus had 24 batteries plus 6 batteries of howitzers, plus some heavy artillery. Howitzers were of 10.5 c.m. and 15 c.m. Thus there were 30 batteries—120 guns to an Army Corps which was over 60,000 strong and nearly 55,000 combatants. This is a higher proportion of artillery than Bulgaria can boast of. Infantry regiments are of 3 battalions, including the reserve regiments of which there are 40.

The cavalry consists of 2 Divisions of 6 regiments each, plus 5 brigades of 2 regiments each. The black regiments, so called from the colour of their uniforms, not of their skins, amounted to nearly half of the total, and were "silladar" cavalry, to use an Indian word to describe irregulars who bring their own horses with them to the colours, a long existing system. Each regiment had 2 machine guns mounted like artillery, with gun and limber, 6 horses and 2 ammunition wagons. Thus a cavalry Division had 12 machine guns divided into 2 groups of 6 guns each. It also had in addition a force of 250 bayonet bicyclists. Of aeroplanes there were 24 (12 monoplanes and 12 biplanes) in all. The corps of officers amounted to some 10,500, of which about 5,500 were on the active list and 5,000 in reserve. These figures included the whole army.

I visited the arsenal, which employed 1,000 men and manufactured 600 rounds of field artillery ammunition per day, and 50 ammunition wagons per week, likewise the cartridge factory, employing 3,000 men and turning out 200,000 small-arms cartridges daily, as well as brass cartridge cases for heavy and light artillery. The plant is said to be capable of turning out 1,000,000 rounds per day of 24 hours. The workmanship was excellent.

I then inspected the medical stores at the general depôt, and also at the depôt of the 2nd Army Corps.

There were enough stores in reserve to last for 6 months, and, compared with the Bulgarian army, the Roumanian was extraordinarily well supplied. Each Army Corps had about 36 ambulance wagons all fitted with the usual appliances, operating tables, laboratory, etc. Besides these I was told there were 5 trains in the General reserve, and 700 to 800 third-class carriages fitted with stretchers. Every man, including the reserve of the army, had already been inoculated for cholera, and I was told that for amputations they would use a liquid injection called " Stovain," the effect of which lasted half an hour, and was quicker applied than chloroform.

In the afternoon, thanks to a rapid car, I was also able to see the munitions factory. This is evidently very well run ; in fact I was told it was one of the best managed in the world, German chemists being employed in the laboratories. The propellant was a kind of guncotton used for all kinds of projectiles, quite different from our nitro-glycerine propellant such as cordite. First I saw the bales of cotton pulled out, then put into cylinders in order to extract all moisture by impregnating it with alcohol under pressure. The excess alcohol was extracted and it was then dipped into an acid at a high temperature in small covered vats. This was the only dangerous process. It was afterwards put into water, and then cut up into the required lengths. A blend was then made of the various brews, and they were packed damp in sacks for storage. About 300 men were being employed in the powder factory, and 1,000 kilograms of powder and 2,000 of ether were being manufactured daily. An electric engine of 500 horse power was driving the machinery.

The following day I looked at the Supply depot. Here were sufficient supplies of all sorts for an army of 700,000 men for two months. The store rooms were solidly built, with two or three stories, well ventilated and provided with a lift. Among the stores were included sugar, biscuits, beans, macaroni, sago, rice, tea, tobacco and tinned fish.

CHAPTER FOUR.

We then drove off in the car to a large mill hired by the Government. The capacity was 10 wagon-loads of flour per day and there were altogether 8 such mills in Roumania. Taking a wagon at 10 tons, this would mean that they could easily supply the whole army with a ration of 2lbs. of bread daily. I concluded my survey of foodstuffs by looking at three sheds, each about 400 metres long, full of nothing but sacks of oats, said to suffice an Army Corps for two months. From there, one or two stations along the line to Constanza, I was conducted by Colonel Rascano to an old and shabby-looking restaurant in the old part of the town, where I was invited to lunch by General Iliescu. No one else was there besides ourselves and one aide-de-camp.

We discussed a good many things, and the difficulty of settling with Bulgaria, etc., when the aide-de-camp said "What the triple entente ought to do is to present an ultimatum to each of the Balkan States—Greece, Bulgaria, and Roumania—to declare in 24 hours whether they were for or against the Entente." I thought that was a very good idea, and asked the General his opinion. He agreed that it would be an excellent thing. I said I was sure that Bulgaria would come in on our side. They were not so certain of that. In fact what was in their minds was that they would be able to keep in with both sides, Germany and ourselves, by attacking Bulgaria. But, they said, before making war on two fronts (an impossibility for Roumania) they would like to be assured of being able to procure more raw material for making cartridges. They could not get it from Russia as she could not spare it, and England would not give it as the Roumanian attitude was uncertain. Would they do so if Roumania joined the Entente? General Iliescu added that a Commission of Roumanian Officers was still in England, and Roumania had now quite gone over to the Entente. In that case, I asked, how was it that a few days ago, Roumania had let some wagons through Turkey with munitions of war?

He denied that any such had passed since Turkey went to war, and asserted that they had even stopped the Turks from using the International waterway of the Danube for the passage of torpedo boats to attack the Russian town of Reni, and were permitting stores to be imported from Russia into Serbia. I expressed great satisfaction at these proofs of friendship, and then hinted that it would be very advantageous if I might have the opportunity of being presented to the King. There was a difficulty about doing this diplomatically, because our Minister had not yet got his letter of credit since the death of the late King, but if I could thank His Majesty for having let me see so much of the army, I would be very glad. They asked if it should be done through the Premier. I said "No, but unofficially, through the King's own Household." In Petrograd that was how it had been done. The A.D.C. then asked if I would like to see the Queen also, to which, of course, I replied that such was my ardent desire, she being an English Princess. I did not add a very pretty and amusing one!

I then went back to the Legation and drafted a telegram describing the incident briefly, that a Roumanian officer had suggested the Triple Entente sending an ultimatum to Greece, Bulgaria, and Roumania, and that failing an agreement regarding Macedonia, I thought it was a good idea and might break the vicious circle. I added that the supposition here was that Bulgaria was waiting to enter Macedonia until Roumania was involved in war and Serbia was exhausted. I also asked whether England could supply the brass for cartridges if Roumania joined the Entente. I signed it and Sir George sent it on, reserving his comments until after he had seen the French and Russian Ministers. I thought the time had come to try and get our Foreign Office accustomed to the idea of ultimatums, but I did not expect to be supported by the diplomats. Next day I went to see Radeff as the papers had mentioned some incidents on the Greco-Bulgar frontier. I told him I had heard people saying that Bratiano was making too much money out of the present state of affairs to wish to go to war. Radeff agreed that that was a calumny as far as Bratiano was concerned, but these rumours of frontier incidents might be due to him. I said the Roumanians were suspicious of Bulgaria's attitude and thought she wanted to go into Macedonia. "Why then did not we go some weeks ago, when the Germans were near Paris and the Roumanians were pressing us to go in?" That was rather difficult to answer if true. Roumania had a bad conscience after what she had done the year before in stabbing Bulgaria in the back, and that might be the reason for her suspicions of Bulgaria now. Radeff went on to say that Take Yonescu took advantage of M. de Giers passing through here from Constantinople to get him to propose that Serbia and Roumania should make an offer to Bulgaria of such and such territory, and that the Triple Entente should then put it before Bulgaria to accept or refuse, but Bratiano would not agree. Bratiano was still the obstacle, and Take could not turn him out. If Bulgaria were to join the Triple Entente, Radoslavoff, he said, would have to make a combination Government with Toderoff and Malinoff as representatives of the other parties in the State.

The following day, November 15th, I went to see M. Blondel, the French Minister. He had been here a great number of years and said that the people were very proud and sensitive, and he himself was dead against any summary measures. He was frightfully disgusted with Poklewsky for having given away the whole show nearly two months ago when there was a great agitation for war and had only just begun to work again for Roumania's entry into the war. He said that the Triple Entente from the beginning had offered Roumania Transylvania and half of Bukovina in return for co-operation, and could not go back on that offer which Roumania was apparently able to keep open until the last moment before peace was declared. Roumania had begun to realise that it was the Triple Entente and not

Russia only that would arrange the map of Europe if successful. I suggested that we might say we wanted her co-operation now or the offer would be withdrawn. Blondel was against that and said how could we tell it would not be of use to us also later on? The only way was to begin again and gradually work up Roumania to the sticking point.

I then went on to see Poklewsky and told him that although the peasants in Bulgaria were in favour of Russia there was a strong feeling amongst all the "Intelligentzia" that Germany was much more efficient militarily than either Russia, France or England, and there was also a great bitterness, more especially against Russia, as the result of the war last year. I asked if anything further had happened about negotiations with Serbia. He said he had heard nothing and that there was nothing to be done. The Serbians might give the Vardar Line but never Monastir, and so there was a deadlock. I suggested that it would be a good thing to make Bulgaria a definite offer, even if it were only the Vardar Line, and the promise of the Enos-Midia Line in return for action against Turkey, and then we should know where we were. All these people began by asking more than they would eventually take, but at present Bulgaria said "If you want our help you must make a serious proposal; up to the present we have had none." I was speaking of two or three weeks previously, perhaps it had been already done, and Poklewsky promised to bear this in mind if no definite offer had yet been made.

I then went back to our Legation and found them lamenting over a most unfortunate (?) mistake. Two telegrams had just arrived, one from Sazonoff, Russia's Foreign Minister, telling Poklewsky to thank Bratiano for what the latter had told him, viz., that Roumania was ready to attack Austria if she were assured of getting raw material for cartridges, and of non-interference by Bulgaria. (Just what Iliescu had said to me!). And another telegram instructing the Triple Entente representatives at

Sofia to demand the necessary assurance from Bulgaria.

Apparently Poklewsky had received Sazonoff's telegram the day before, and was much upset by it as Bratiano had mentioned this in the course of an informal conversation and not officially, and Poklewsky had wired back to his Government that there was a misunderstanding.

I said "What a pity! Why did not Poklewsky go to Bratiano and say ' My Government have made this mistake, are you now prepared to make it good?' I thought Sazonoff had intended to rush Bratiano and why should he not be rushed? But all that the Diplomats think of is "Roumania must not be given away. Hope it is not too late to stop the instruction to Sofia," etc., etc.

In the evening I went to see Captain Samardjiew, the Bulgarian Military Attaché, and put to him in the course of conversation a casual question as to whether Bulgaria would give Roumania assurances of non-interference if she wished to march against Austria. He replied " Of course, we have done so already. But that is only a pretext. Roumania would never march!" I said "But she is so suspicious of you. How would it be if the assurances were given to the Triple Entente?" "Why not," he said. We then went into a long discussion about Radoslavoff's speech to the Sobranie (Parliament) and the letter in the Press from a Serbian ex-Minister, who, when staying at the Legation at Sofia, wrote to the papers to say that it would be treachery for Bulgaria to attack Serbia. And the Bulgarian reply to it, that no one but a Serbian would have the impertinence to say such a thing, and that the Bulgarians were going into Macedonia as soon as the Serbians were exhausted.

Samardjiew was not at all convinced that the Germans would not win, and he was all for marching into Macedonia whether we liked it or not, and was dead against Bulgaria exhausting herself against Turks or in any other direction. The only argument against that attitude, namely "Who is going to turn us out?" that I could produce was that after the war England, with an expeditionary force of one million, would be in a different position from the England of 1912-13, and Bulgaria was now a Mediterranean Power and therefore assailable by sea. Still we parted friends.

On the 20th November a telegram arrived from Sir Edward Grey, dated 16th, suggesting that we should offer Bulgaria the 1912 line in Macedonia, and the Enos-Midia line in Turkey, in return for immediate action against Turkey. This proposal was to be put by the three Powers. That was following out my suggestion, but apparently Grey instructed Bax-Ironside to deliver it. The result was that Bulgaria declined, but Bax said that they considered the matter with the King very seriously before declining.* I thought that if Roumania had stepped in with an offer at that time to give up the portion of the Dobrudja and had promised to go in against Austria, Bulgaria might have accepted. Poklewsky was very disgusted at the "indiscretion" of Bax-Ironside, who had perhaps asked also for assurances that Bulgaria would not attack Roumania, the idea being prominent in Poklewsky's mind that he had given away Bratiano. He also declared that Bratiano only said he would attack Austria provided that Bulgaria attacked Turkey, not on the understanding merely that she would not molest Roumania. I saw him that afternoon in Sir George Barclay's study. He evidently thought I had been poking my oar in and doubtless all three Ministers here, English, French and Russian, were cursing me freely. But I did not mind. A day or two later I saw General Iliescu at the Ministry of War, and told him that we had arranged to remove the obstacles in Roumania's way, that prevented her from marching against Austria, and that the Triple Entente would probably give the assurances required about Bul-

---

* We heard afterwards from a Bulgarian source that Bax's proposal was: "Line of Vardar south of the 1912 line in Macedonia, and the Enos-Midia line"—but see Appendix A. Radoslavoff did not always inform his Ministers correctly of what was going on.

garia's attitude towards Roumania, and the ammunition would also doubtless be arranged. Iliescu replied that it was now all right about ammunition which they could get from or through Russia, but Bulgaria was still in the way. She had just now acquired the whole mercantile fleet of Austria, all of whose boats and barges were now flying the Bulgarian flag. This was a trick, he said, to enable the Austrians to go on supplying Turkey with ammunition. The Roumanian Government would not permit these boats to pass through Roumanian waters but would fire on them if necessary. This might cause war with Bulgaria. I said what would be the use of that? It would be much better before fighting her to try and negotiate an alliance. Now was the time to do it when we were in want of her help and were ready to arrange concessions in Macedonia. Bulgaria did not wish to fight against Turkey, but perhaps she would join with Roumania against Austria in return for part of the Dobrudja. No, he thought all their information from Bulgaria showed that the latter wished to attack them and had been getting pontoon equipment with which to cross the Danube. I said that if Roumania was persistently hostile, Bulgaria might be forced to take refuge in an alliance with Turkey. But I had heard that Roumania hesitated to negotiate with Bulgaria for fear of compromising herself with Austria. Iliesco denied that this was the case and assured me that they had finished with Austria. Then, I suggested, why did they not declare war on Austria at once, but without sending troops into Transylvania immediately, wait and see what the Bulgars would do; it might bring them in on our side? General Iliescu thought that was a good idea, and that Roumania was rich enough to remain mobilized all the winter, and promised to speak to the Prime Minister in that sense. The result of my interview with Iliescu was to give me the impression that the Roumanians would really do nothing against Austria but might attack Bulgaria. The Balkan States were unable to get away from the Balkan politics of last year. The moment Greece heard about concessions to Bulgaria she got alarmed and asked Roumania not to budge.

On the 22nd November I went to see Také Yonescu who kindly asked me to lunch, when I met his wife, an agreeable Englishwoman. Také was dead against moving until the Bulgars were committed, at the same time he would not commit Roumania. He showed me an interesting letter and telegram that he was sending to Venizelos to try and persuade him to make some concession to Bulgaria. He said he hated and despised the Bulgar more than he could express. The Bulgar was a pig, but one had to make use of them, so he was all for concessions which he hoped at some future period to deprive them of again. He wanted me to get the Legation to telegraph advising us to support Russia and France at Athens in favour of concessions to the Bulgars. Accordingly I wrote a despatch to Sir George Barclay in this sense.

I then went to see M. Filipescu (late Minister of War) who had just returned from a patriotic meeting advising action, and the crowd had afterwards broken the windows of the Liberal Union Club and of the "Minerva" newspaper office which favoured Germany. He told me that his Government had recently given the Serbians 100,000 great coats and as many pairs of boots, and the Russian Government had given them many Austrian uniforms which they had had to have dyed. The ammunition that came from Russia had to go through the Serbian arsenal at Kraguevatz for some slight alteration before being used. He added that the Roumanians did not know whether to put the bulk of their force on their right flank to join with the Russians or on the left with the Serbians.

On this day, 23rd November, the Russian Military Attaché told me of 10 submarines being put together at Bruges ready for Zeebrugge, and I telegraphed this home.

He also told me, and this was subsequently confirmed by the Bulgarian Military Attaché, that, owing to reports of Austrian troops being massed within 40 kilometres of the Roumanian frontier in the direction of Predeal, a partial mobilization of the 1st Roumanian Army Corps was ordered. Also the convoy to Serbia, consisting of 17 lighters with 20 batteries of a new Austrian field gun and 20,000 rounds of ammunition, had arrived safely from Russia with the help of the Roumanians, although the Austrians tried to intercept it at Kalafat. I also heard that the Roumanian Parliament was to be opened shortly, so I decided to stay on in Bukarest a little longer before returning to Sofia. I therefore pressed Sir George Barclay to ask for an audience for me with the King. This he was kind enough to do eventually, direct to the Maréchal de la Cour, in spite of the diplomatic difficulty about his letters of credit not having arrived. The reply was immediate, fixing the following Sunday, the 29th November, for the audience.

On the 28th, Akers-Douglas, the first Secretary of the Legation, returned from Salonika, and handed me two letters from the Legation at Sofia. One was from O'Reilly, the first Secretary there, telling me that the Ministers of the Entente Powers at Sofia had recommended their Governments to promise Bulgaria the whole of Macedonia with immediate occupation up to the Vardar. This had so completely put off their Governments that they had fallen back on attempting to secure Bulgarian neutrality only. A great pity! The other was a reprimand for me from the Foreign Office, dated 7th November, addressed to Bax-Ironside, warning me not to express political views to Bulgarian Ministers except with Bax's knowledge and authority, and adding that my statements as to the impracticability of an alliance between Serbia and Bulgaria were inconsistent with the efforts of the Allies and the opinions of His Majesty's Government. I thought that a bit stiff. First of all H.M.G. sends me out here without giving me an idea of what their views are. I make enquiries, talk to the Bulgars, ascertain from the Bulgarian Minister of War that help to

Serbia direct was out of the question, that if the armies met, the men would cross bayonets. I give the Government, our Government, information showing what policy they ought and what they ought not to pursue, and I get this sort of stupid wigging, which shows they have not even read my despatches correctly two months later! Every single Bulgarian I met said much the same thing as the Minister of War expressed so tersely. The only man I had heard advocating direct help to Serbia was Daneff, and his party at the time, I was told, was represented by one man, himself. But until I got back to Sofia and referred to the records I was unable to make any reply.

This day the Roumanian Parliament opened. Sir George was seedy, Akers-Douglas busy, and I was the sole representative of our Legation. The Parliament occupies a small house compared with those of Russia and Bulgaria. Diplomats are placed in a tiny box. I could not see the King, but he spoke in a clear voice. There was not much in his speech, but it was a very careful non-committal one. He praised the army and said it was the object of everyone's care and solicitude. The French, American, Serbian and Persian Ministers were to the right of me, and the goats, the Germans, Austrian and Spaniards were on the left, Russians in the middle. There were boxes all round like a theatre, full of men and ladies, relatives and friends of members. I noticed Také Yonescu in the centre among the members, and I think Marghiloman on the right. The King and Cabinet were facing the members and the audience.

Next day, Sunday, I was received by the King. I went down a long passage in the Palace and across a big room to his study. The King was standing a little on one side, the room was rather dark. He had on some sort of uniform. He seemed to be more nervous than I was. I had to wait for him to begin the conversation. After the usual preliminaries (I had told the Colonel in attendance that I had retired from the army a year or two ago, etc.,

CHAPTER FOUR.

and the Colonel had prompted the King just before my arrival) of where I had served before, I led the conversation into political channels by saying it was a very interesting and important time just now in the Balkans, and especially in Bulgaria. The King said "Yes, but those Bulgarians are very clever, they won't say on which side they are." I replied I had great confidence that they would not go against the Triple Entente, but Greece was in the way. "Yes," the King said, "Greece does not want to give up anything and does not want Bulgaria to get anything." I said I understood the situation to be that Roumania, Bulgaria and Serbia all wanted to expand. Greece had already got what she wanted and did not wish either Serbia, Bulgaria or Roumania to get any bigger, but I hoped she would not be allowed to stand in the way of the aspirations of the other Powers. The King said that Bulgaria concentrated her attention on Macedonia. I replied that if Bulgaria was determined to get Macedonia anyhow, it was better she should take it as our friend than as our enemy. I hoped that Roumania was not hostile to Bulgaria; there was a great lack of confidence between the two countries and I was doing what I could in my humble way as Military Attaché to improve the relations between the two countries. The King said that Roumania was not at all hostile to Bulgaria or her aspirations, and I said I hoped I might tell the Bulgarians that, to which he replied that King Ferdinand knew it already. I went on to say that there was a great opportunity for the Balkan States to realize their ambitions but they would have to work themselves, otherwise the war might end in a sort of stale mate as far as the Balkans were concerned, and if we got all we wanted out of Germany with the complete restoration of Belgium, etc., the Triple Entente would probably not prolong the war in order merely to obtain territory for the Balkan States if they had not helped us. The King was careful not to commit himself to any definite policy. I thanked him for having shown me so much of the

THE KING FERDINAND.
(Of Roumania).

By kind permission of "Julietta", Bucuresti.

troops, factories and stores, that I was struck with all I had seen, and the state of preparation of the army, and that I thought the late King must have worked hard for the army. The King replied that was so, and that the expedition of last year had been of great service as a kind of test manoeuvre, but that nothing was ever complete or perfect. I said I was glad to see that the army was so ready for war, to which His Majesty replied that an army must always be ready for war. The King then asked me what branch of the service I belonged to. I replied Indian Cavalry, and that my father had at one time been Commander in Chief of the Indian Army. "Was Lord Napier* your father?" he asked with surprise. "Is there not a statue of him somewhere in London? " Yes," I answered, "near the Duke of York's Column in Waterloo Place, but it is going to be removed elsewhere to make room for a statue of King Edward." And the interview terminated.

On the 30th November I dined at Capsha's, the smart restaurant of Bukarest, to meet Colonel Semenoff, the Russian Military Attaché, and Arsenieff, First Secretary of the Russian Legation. The latter had wished to make my acquaintance because of my knowledge of Bulgaria. Some weeks previously Arsenieff had written a report to Petrograd, strongly condemning the action of his Chief with regard to Roumania. Before sending it, he had shown it to his Chief, Poklewsky, who had refused to forward it, and said that if it went, Arsenieff would have to leave his staff. Arsenieff sent it; it made a sensation in Petrograd, and he was now preparing another report of a similar nature. The Serbian Military Attaché was asked to meet us. He was a fine-looking fellow, a Colonel Andonovitch. During dinner he got a telegram to say the Serbians had beaten back the Austrians at all points with heavy losses, which made us happy, but we knew the Serbians were being hard pressed. I told them what I thought the Bulgarians were doing, namely waiting for the Serbian army's total destruction, and for the

---

* Field-Marshal Lord Napier of Magdala.

ripe fruit of Macedonia to fall into their mouth without any trouble. That the Bulgars would not come to the assistance of the Serbs. The Serbian Colonel was astonished. "Have they forgotten, then, how we fought together with them before Adrianople, up to our necks in water?" "Yes, entirely," I said "All they think of is that you scored off them the last time you met, and they are waiting their turn to pay it back with interest." We then discussed what could be done to make Roumania move. I thought the best way would be for Russia to send an army corps at once up the Danube; not asking the Roumanian Government's permission, but warning them that Russia was sending some troops up the international waterway, in the same manner that the ammunition was sent a short time ago. Would Colonel Semenoff mention it to the Russian War Office? No, Semenoff didn't like to do this, because it would be equivalent to forcing Roumania to declare war, which would be a diplomatic move, and therefore not his immediate concern. But time pressed, as the Danube is liable to freeze up by the beginning of January, and although eventually superior in carrying power to many railways, its chief recommendation at the moment was, to my mind, as a means of getting Russian troops into this theatre of war without technically infringing the neutrality of Roumania. I assumed that such neutrality would not last long, and that the Roumanians would themselves place their railways at the disposal of Russian troops to transport them to Serbia or Austria as the case might be. Guranesco had in fact said to me at lunch that day, that the Russians might use the Roumanian railways to transport troops to Serbia. Semenoff was rather inclined to force the Roumanians to come in by pushing over the passes into Transylvania, but that also was a difficult operation needing many troops and would be a diversion in the wrong direction, so I reverted to my plan which was supported by Arsenieff. I said "Let me suggest the idea to Mr. N. Filipesco (late Minister of War) who is working up the people towards war with Austria, and see what he says." Semenoff agreed, and promised, if Filipesco agreed, to wire it to Petrograd, and add that the British Military Attaché approved of it.

The next day, December 1st, I went to see the Serbian M.A. and found him in a different mood. He had received another telegram from Serbia, dated 6.50 p.m. 30th November. He went over the position on the map with me, and was evidently of opinion that the position of the Serbs was desperate. He wouldn't let me tell anybody about it, which was absurd, but his Minister was out. I said it was so grave that I must wire the news to London at once, but it should be kept secret here if he wished, and so it was agreed. I accordingly went to the Legation and wrote out a telegram to the effect that the Austrians had turned the left wing of the Serbs at Ujitze, and that in consequence the Serbian army was obliged to withdraw from the line Ujitze—Belgrade to a line Kablar—Wenchatz—Surlainatz, thereby giving up the defence of Belgrade, Semendria and the whole of the Danube. The position was very critical, and I thought it necessary for Roumania to enter into immediate action. The estimate of the enemy's force was 6 or 7 Corps, of which one was German. This telegram was duly despatched by the Minister.

In the evening I went to see Filipesco by appointment. I put to him the question as to how it would be regarded by his party if Russia declared her intention of sending an Army Corps up the Danube. He tried to evade the question but eventually said he was in favour of Roumania going in herself, and therefore all the more in favour of letting Russian troops through, especially by the Danube. Just then a Mr. Sturdza came into the room with the news that the Serbs were badly beaten, and that there was a rumour that Russia was going to demand or had demanded permission to send two Army Corps up the river, and that Bratiano was as obstinate as ever and was doing his best not to let them through. Filipesco then said to me " The moment has come to say politely, not as to a vassal, gentlemen, take your choice, with us or against us." It was, perhaps, not right for him to be so frank as it might be misconstrued, he said, but it was quite clear to me that he thought his country needed this push in the right direction. He told me that Bratiano had seen him that day and was not in favour of moving before February. That was about noon, and Filipesco regretted that at that time he did not know of the Serbian débâcle, about which everyone was talking. But he gave me his word that Roumania had definitely gone over to the Triple Entente and there was no question of siding with Austria. There was a good deal to be said in favour of waiting another three months until the back of the winter was broken and they had got in their supplies of ammunition, etc. Against that, however, there was the loss of perhaps 300,000 men of the Serbian army, and the cutting off of Roumania's communications with Europe through Serbia. Filipesco thought the Bulgars would attack Roumania at once if they went to war now. I said "No, but if you wait three months we shall lose the Bulgars as well as the Serbs. By that time if the Austrians are allowed to score this success the Bulgars will have gone over to them." Filipesco then said that the Bulgars had a treaty with Austria or Germany, to which I replied that they denied it, and in any case it was not very important, as they were capable of breaking it. I thought that if the Roumanians were once openly declared on our side, that would turn the Bulgarian scale in our favour also. I did not doubt but that the two Ferdinands and their Ministers would do all they could to stop it, but I thought the people would have their way if we were firm and prompt.

After this interview I went back to Semenoff's house, and left a letter with his soldier servant, a Russian, and quite safe. Besides, I did not mention Filipesco's name. Semenoff was, of course, out, but I saw him again on the 3rd December and helped him to draft a telegram to the Russian War Office. This, however, was never sent. Prince Trubetzkoi passed through Bukarest at this time on his way to Serbia. Semenoff saw him the following day, and of course he was dead against doing anything. Diplomats nearly always are; it is their business to talk. Russia had no idea of sending troops. In fact they probably were not at all anxious for Roumania's help, or that of the other Balkan States either. Still it would have been a great strategic move, if the Russian Commander-in-Chief had in this way turned the Carpathians, and swept in with him Roumania, Bulgaria and Greece, on the flank and rear of the Austrian army. Meanwhile I informed our own War Office of my suggestion to the Russian Military Attaché.

On the 3rd December I went to see Také Yonescu. He had been very busy and had seen Bratiano. Things were not going well. The Powers were to offer Bulgaria next day, through their Ministers at Sofia, part of Macedonia and the Enos-Midia Line in return for neutrality, and complete realization of their ambitions in Macedonia in return for active co-operation. So far, good, but they were to inform Bulgaria that Greece was sending men to help Serbia, and that they guaranteed that at the end of the war, Greece would evacuate Macedonia. The Powers were going to ask Roumania to guarantee that she would attack Bulgaria in the event of Bulgaria attacking Greece. Také Yonescu had been unable to move Bratiano either to go to the assistance of Serbia, or to declare war before February, and he would not even agree to attack Bulgaria in the event of the latter attacking Greece. I then asked Také what he thought of Russia sending troops. "Yes, they could send them by the Danube," he said, "but we should have to mobilize, so they could not have our railways." "But after your mobilization was complete, could they not use your railways?" I suggested. He thought they might, but Bratiano might object and he did not know if Russia had any troops to spare. Poklewsky knew nothing of any Russian plan for sending troops.

Military Attaché F.

CHAPTER FOUR.

On December 4th the news was that the Powers were offering Greece the Southern half of Albania in return for her assistance to Serbia. That settled the difficulty about Macedonia for the Bulgars, and it seemed to be a good thing to shew these neutral States such as Bulgaria, that they might outstay their market if they waited too long, and that was apparently what the Triple Entente were now doing.

In the evening I went to the Cinema where I saw some films which must have been arranged by the German Minister, von dem Busche. An excellent German cavalry attack and German field guns being served by smart-looking German gunners. On other films, French wounded and a French cemetery.

On the 6th December I had an audience with the Queen of Roumania in the Cotroceni Palace, about 2 miles outside the town. The Queen received me with her back well to the light—a point of vantage sometimes neglected by the mere man granting an interview. She was charming and looked very pretty. Quite serious, and very interested in politics. I told her exactly what the position of affairs was ; that Greece had promised to send 80,000 men to help Serbia provided we could guarantee her against attack from Bulgaria, and the representatives of the Triple Entente were going to ask Roumania if she would guarantee to attack Bulgaria in case the latter attacked Greece. She appeared to be well informed and to know what I was telling her, but I could not be quite sure how much she knew. I told her that the Bulgarian War Minister, General Fitcheff, when Chief of the Staff in 1910, had prophecied to me that the big European war would break out in 4 years time, and that he had told me then that the task of the Triple Entente should be to induce Italy to secede from the Triple Alliance, which would suit Bulgaria very well. But I thought that now the Bulgarians were much impressed with Germany's immense military strength and prowess*, and having no sea-faring experience, were unable to realise the enormous

---
* Vide Appendix A.

strength of England's position, and that we were bound to crush Germany sooner or later. I told her that Roumania's chance was now, and that it was a glorious one. I thought a bold march on Austria, in co-operation perhaps with Italy and Bulgaria, might end the war. The Queen was most sympathetic to our cause and I thought she seemed a determined lady who had made up her mind to be a person of some importance in the kingdom. I had heard from old Mr. Green, a much respected English resident, the day before, that the Queen had told him it was lucky for Roumania that she was Queen of it; so I ventured to remark that it was lucky for England that we had an English Princess as Queen of Roumania, to which she seemed thoroughly to agree. She told me that in the old King's time he was absolutely convinced that Germany must win, and nothing could shake his confidence. With the present King, when he said the other day, "How shall I ever be able to set foot in Germany again or to offer my hand to a German Sovereign?" she replied, "Not at all, if you are strong, it is they who will offer their hand to you; that is the way of the world. Those who are powerful and strong are respected." I very warmly applauded these sentiments. I remarked that a great deal depended on King Ferdinand of Bulgaria. The Queen asked me if I knew him, to which I assented, and she then said he was a very clever and amusing person but one could not treat with him as he was absolutely unreliable. He had shifty eyes. I remarked that I thought it a wicked face, to which she quite agreed, but added that unfortunately she was supposed to be rather a friend of his. The Queen then asked how England was getting on. I said—full of confidence, and the recruiting had been wonderful. We had now introduced martial law and were beginning to make preparations against invasion. Perhaps this was to stimulate recruiting, I did not know. Anyhow, Germany's only chance of invading us would have been by a surprise war. We were now ready, and the war had been a splendid thing for us. The Queen then began to talk about what a dreadful thing it was for people who had relations on both sides, especially so for Royalties, and hoped that Roumania would realize what terrible sacrifices a King had to make to throw over all his kith and kin, his tastes and prejudices, everything, in favour of the country of his adoption. The eldest daughter then came in, and the audience was at an end, and I took my leave, the Queen showing me at the same time a magnificent Borzoi hound, a gift from Petrograd.

On the 7th December I found the Serbian Military Attaché smiling and confident again, after a Serbian victory. They were still holding Semendria and Eastwards to the Roumania frontier, but Belgrade had been occupied by the enemy. Meanwhile Bratiano had refused to guarantee Greece against a Bulgarian attack, and I was told that Prince Trubetskoi was going to Serbia to try and persuade the Serbians to give up Monastir. The news about Roumania was not very reassuring as they were shipping gold for Turkey, and the Russian Government had refused them the purchase of 3,000 horses from Russia, as there was not sufficient evidence of their devotion to the Entente. On the other hand the French Government had consented to sell them ammunition and a Roumanian Colonel was going to France to buy it.

THE QUEEN OF ROUMANIA.

By kind permission of "Julietta". Bucuresti.

Chapter Five.

RETURN TO SOFIA — OFFER OF RESIGNATION — REPLY — ASSERTION OF RIGHT TO TELEGRAPH MILITARY ATTACHE'S VIEWS TO LONDON — INTERVIEW WITH DIAMANDI — DUBIOUS ATTITUDE OF BULGARIA—WAR MINISTER NEUTRAL—TURKISH EXPEDITIONARY FORCE — RUMOURS OF AGREEMENT BETWEEN ITALY AND BALKAN STATES—BULGARIAN GENERAL'S VIEWS ON RUSSIAN STRATEGY—MINISTER OF WAR DEFINES BULGARIA'S WANTS IN MACEDONIA.

ON the 8th December I returned to Sofia, and there made enquiries regarding the Foreign Office wigging, and I sent a telegram through Sir Henry Bax-Ironside protesting that the opinion regarding Bulgarian and Serbian relations and the impossibility of bringing them together in the field was that of the Bulgarian Minister of War, and not my own.* I regretted if I had not made this point clear enough in my despatch in my ignorance of the views held by His Majesty's Government, and had thereby failed to convince H.M.G. of the impracticability of such policy at that time. But if this failure was due to want of confidence of Government in the Military Attaché, I felt that he should be at once replaced. Bax-Ironside added confidentially that my opinion, as derived from the Minister of War, was emphatically confirmed by telegrams from other sources on the 11th November, some two months later, and that the only thing that would change this attitude would be if the Serbians voluntarily gave up Macedonia. Bax-Ironside was kind enough to add that I might be of great use, especially if Bulgaria and Roumania came into action on our side. A reply to this telegram was received from the Foreign Office a few days afterwards in which Sir Edward Grey was pleased to say "he did not call in question my ability and

---
* Vide Chapter 2, page 33.

knowledge, and there was no question of want of confidence. But his desire was that I should confine my official activity when dealing with members of the Cabinet or local authorities to the military as distinct from the political aspect of the question. That the Minister alone was the channel between the two Governments although the Minister in communicating with him could always benefit by the views which the Military Attaché derived from his experience of Balkan affairs, which Sir E. Grey regarded in my case as interesting."

The question then arose in my mind whether I could let the matter rest there. Sir E. Grey assumed that I had been made a channel between the two Governments. If so, it was unofficial. If the War Minister gave me an opinion on the amount of territorial compensation demanded by Bulgaria it was unofficial, as he always took care to tell me. And my views on politics to Ministers I had always taken care to place in the same category. But this incident I regarded as a purely military one whether the army could or could not be used for a certain purpose. I was right to telegraph it, and would not have done my duty if I had satisfied myself by merely mentioning it to the Minister and had left it to his discretion to report or not. It was one of the duties of a Military Attaché to write despatches. In critical times, these, or extracts or summaries of them, must be telegraphed to be of any use. A Military Attaché holds a very responsible position, and you cannot hold him responsible and at the same time muzzle him.

Sir E. Grey's reply seemed to imply that I had not the right to indite a despatch containing political matter. The point on which the Foreign Office had challenged me showed how impossible it was to draw a hard and fast line between military and political affairs. At the same time it was not right to embarrass the Government further at such a time by telegraphic correspondence on the subject. So I decided to write a despatch in the above sense to my Minister. This I did. The following day, Sir H.

Bax-Ironside sent for me, said I was absolutely right and my case was most ably put forward, but asked me not to send it on. I agreed, but asked him to file it in the Chancery for future guidance, in case anything of the same nature were to crop up again, and the incident was thus closed.

On the 11th December I went to see M. de Russi, the Roumanian Minister at Sofia, and there found M. Diamandi, a prominent Roumanian, who had returned recently from a special mission to Rome. These gentlemen asked me what impression I had brought back from Roumania. I replied that I had returned in complete ignorance of what Roumania really thought and really intended. De Russi had been trying to convince me before Diamandi came into the room, with an elaborate explanation of h'er attitude, which resolved itself, in my opinion, into the simple expression of hunting with the hare and hounds. De Russi did not mean that exactly and began another explanation which was equivalent to saying that Roumania did not like to burn her boats. Then Diamandi came in and undertook to convert me. He said Roumania was entirely in sympathy with the Triple Entente. But small States as well as big ones had to look to their own interests first, and even more so than big ones. They could not afford to make mistakes. A big country might lose an army here or there and replace it and correct h'er mistakes. Or like Serbia, it might withdraw to the Hinterland. But Roumania had only 500,000 men and a limited supply of cartridges and no Hinterland to retire to. If Russia got a heavy defeat, the whole force of the Austrian and German forces might be brought against them. Would it benefit the Triple Entente if the enemy came into Predial and took all our petrol and food supplies? What good would Roumania do now by coming in, with the task of crossing the Carpathians in mid winter? I said I thought it might bring the Bulgars in too, and the risk was great; that if the Serbian army was destroyed, Austria and Turkey might bring pressure on Bulgaria to come in against us. Diamandi said that if the Austrians were such fools as to go into the heart of Serbia, nothing would suit the Roumanians better, as they would be able to cut them off their base. To this I agreed, but opined that before this happened, the moral effect on all the other neutral States would be very great. Then De Russi broke in, saying that Bulgaria's guarantee not to attack Roumania if the latter went to war with Austria was worth nothing, and asked me had I seen it. As I had not, he went to fetch it, and read it to me. It certainly sounded rather a non-committal document, and Radoslavoff had taken a long time about producing it. "But," I said, " Bulgaria would not dare to attack you, once you had adhered to the Triple Entente." The reply to this was: "You might punish her afterwards, but could do nothing to stop her at the time. That is not good enough. No, Bulgaria's interests and ours are identical, and one of the reasons we are on your side, and an important one, is that England supports the cause of nationalities, and we feel that she will see to it that we are not swallowed up after the war. (This was evidently a hint about Russia). Italy's interests are also very strongly bound up with Roumania. Italy was not ready two months ago, is perhaps ready now, but the Alps and winter prevent her from moving, but she will begin to move some time in February." By this time Guranesco had come into the room, and his attitude was " How has this child of mine become perverted after all the good counsels I have been pouring into his ear?" Diamandi tried to find out and said " If you tell me whom you have seen, I will tell you what ideas you have. If it is the French Minister, he talks in the same way to a journalist that he does to a Minister. He is half a Roumanian, and is so keen we should come in that he pushes too hard. It is impossible that Bratiano should 'déboutonner' himself to a person like that." I said "Would you mind my asking you really a frank question, quite between ourselves? People tell me that Bratiano is very Germanophil, or else that the King is very Germanophil. What is the truth?" Diamandi replied, "I will return you frankness for frankness. Neither one nor the other. How is it possible that Bratiano should be Germanophil—a man who was educated in France, and who last year or last winter, I forget which, denounced the Austrian treaty? But he does well to disguise his feelings when he is pressed on all sides. He cannot afford to give himself away." "But the supplies of ammunition, etc., which continue to pass for Turkey?" enquired I. To this Diamandi repeated the "quid pro quo" argument which I had heard before, and added that Roumania was trying to get 12 batteries of mountain guns out of Austria. Hitherto her policy had been directed towards fighting Russia in the Steppes. Now they were going to fight against Austria in the mountains and must have mountain guns. I suppose I still looked unconvinced, as Diamandi went on to say: "I see you still want more converting. You have evidently come back from Roumania in a bad state of mind, confess it." I said "Really, to tell you the truth, as I said at first, I was ignorant, but I assumed a very pessimistic attitude in order to extract the truth out of you. Thank you very much for having told me!" "Ah! we see you are a very dangerous fellow!" was the reply, and they gave me a lift back to my hotel.

They were going on to see the Italian Minister—Cucci, who is a very quiet unobtrusive man, but has a finger in every pie here, and I was afraid that they might be trying to form a Roumano-Bulgaro-Italian alliance which would consult its own interests independently of us or the Germans, and might be aiming at neutrality until we had cut each others throats, and they be able to settle the Balkans as they pleased. But in any case I thought Diamandi was the best Roumanian I had come across, and very like his brother who had been Roumanian Minister here in years gone by.

I then went to see the Russian Military Attaché, Colonel Tatarinoff. He thought the Bulgars were almost our enemies in spite of smooth words.

CHAPTER FIVE.

Tarnowski or Lakhsa, the Austrian Minister and Military Attaché respectively, were now almost always present at the council of Bulgarian Ministers. The Field-Marshal von der Goltz Pasha who was passing through Constantinople, was seen by the King that very day at the Vranya Palace some miles outside Sofia. This was bad news so I went on to see the Minister of War, General Fitcheff, and my interview with him bore out very much my previous suspicions that the Balkan States were now trying to make their own arrangements independently of either side. Fitcheff said he was unable to foresee the result of the war or when it would end. The chances for either side were at present even. Our opportunity for gaining the active support of Bulgaria had now gone by, but we could be sure of neutrality. The Serbs had opposed to them two active and four reserve Austrian Army Corps, but no Germans. They could hold out all the winter against a force of this size, but even if Serbia were crushed by superior forces and occupied by Austrian troops, Bulgaria could not be forced into an alliance with Austria against her will under pressure between that country and Turkey as the latter was weak and doomed to destruction. The Bulgarian Army could in no case co-operate direct with Serbia, even if the latter voluntarily gave them the whole of Macedonia. He thought that Italy would come in only when both belligerent sides were exhausted, and then with three million men in alliance. When I asked him to account for that number of men, he replied that the formation of a 'bloc' was being attempted consisting of 600,000 Roumanians, 500,000 Bulgarians, 1,500,000 Italians and perhaps Greeks also.

On the 13th December, the following day, I saw Bourchier, the "Times" correspondent. He had a very fair but not quite accurate idea of what had lately been going on in politics. He told me the Triple Entente had actually proposed to Greece that they should occupy Macedonia with 40,000 men, and send another 40,000 to help the Serbians;

Mr. VENIZELOS.
(Greek Premier).

that Roumania had been asked to promise to attack Bulgaria if the latter attacked Serbia, and that Bratiano had refused. "Could anything have been more mischievous and fatuous?" he said. He told me that before replying, Bratiano had telegraphed to Athens, to make sure what were the views of Greece, and the man whom he told to go and see Venizelos on the subject, ran into the arms of the Representatives of the Entente just as they were coming away from interviewing Venizelos. Venizelos replied that that was the first he had heard of the proposal. Bratiano accordingly refused to give the guarantee on the grounds that he would incur Bulgaria's hostility by doing so, and might find himself involved in the fulfilment of that promise at a moment when the vital interests of Roumania demanded action in another direction. If Bourchier received a true account, Venizelos must have lied, as it was his suggestion that Greece should obtain Roumania's guarantee of Bulgaria's neutrality before doing anything. It is possible, however, that Venizelos merely replied to a query whether Greece had been asked to occupy Macedonia with 40,000 men, and send 40,000 to help the Serbs, whereas the representatives of the Entente had in point of fact asked Greece to send 80,000 men in aid of Serbia without mentioning Macedonia, and from Bourchier's account it would appear that Bratiano had been asked to guarantee Greece against Bulgaria before Greece had been approached on the subject. I am inclined to think that there must be some mistake in Bourchier's account and do not believe that Venizelos would have lied in the matter. In any case the idea of asking Roumania to attack Bulgaria in a hypothetical case was unfortunate.

On the 15th December, having occasion to go to the War Office, I made the acquaintance of a new Assistant to the Chief of the Staff, namely Colonel Jekoff (afterwards Generalissimo of the Bulgarian army). After a long conversation I asked him for information regarding the Turkish forces and he ended by sending for a junior officer who produced details of the Turkish Expeditionary force against Egypt, which I telegraphed home. The details were as follows: VI. and VIII. Army Corps, commanded by Djemal Pasha with the German Colonel Frankenberg as Chief of the Staff, 39 Battalions—39,000 rifles, 4 companies Machine Guns—16 guns, 27 Batteries, not Q.F., namely 14 field and 13 mountain—136 guns, 10 squadrons of Bedouins—1,500 sabres. Other details included pioneers, telegraph and medical detachments and some 18 depôt battalions of local militia. The total strength of the expedition was estimated at 55,000 to 60,000. The present position of the forces was not known but Djemal Pasha with his Staff had left Constantinople 22 days previously and reached Headquarters in 12 days. The fact that the Bulgarians gave me this information shewed that they were not hostile to us at that time, as was believed by some people.

On the 18th December there was news that German ships had bombarded some of our towns in Yorkshire and elsewhere on the North Sea. Also that the Serbians had gained a great victory, reoccupied Belgrade, and had taken a quantity of arms including 150 guns, some automobiles, and 50,000 prisoners. The same evening there was a big dinner at the British Legation to which Radoslavoff, the Premier, came. It was the first time since the war began, that he had entered a Triple Entente Legation, and there seemed to be a change in the official relations. Dobrovitch, as the King's Private Secretary, was also there, as well as the three Ministers of the Entente, their Military Attachés and Dimitrieff, a Bulgarian Foreign Office Official. The latter told me I could be of great use in talking to Generals and others, and preparing them for Bulgaria coming in on our side, but they wanted Monastir at once, some more of Macedonia afterwards, including Kavala, and as regards the Dobrudja, would be content with Dobrich and Baltchik.

The following day was the Czar's birthday, and everybody, including both Bulgarian and foreign bigwigs, were at the Russian Legation where the toasts of the Czar and the Grand Duke Nicolas were drunk enthusiastically.

On the same day a telegram arrived from the Foreign Office saying that Sazonoff, Russia's Foreign Minister, had telegraphed to Grey that there were disquieting rumours of an attempted 'bloc' between Italy, Bulgaria, Greece and Roumania, and that he thought Serbia should be included. I had already reported these rumours on the 12th inst., but the Foreign Office did not appear to know about it. The question of including Serbia was difficult, because the idea of the 'bloc' was that it should be independent of the two main groups of belligerents. Besides, according to Fitcheff, Italy wanted pretty well all the Adriatic coast including Dalmatia and Albania. On this day also there were rumours in the Austrian and German papers of a great Russian defeat. It had been reported to the Legation through O'Mahony, a celebrated Irishman who had spent much money and many years in protecting Bulgarian refugees, that Von der Goltz Pasha had been overheard, when travelling to Constantinople, to say that Germany's plan was to take Warsaw and Ivangorod, establish a defensive line in the Vistula, and then transfer every available man to the French front. I happened to be going to see General Savoff, the late Commander in Chief, that afternoon, and took the opportunity to sound him, without of course, making any suggestions. He said exactly the same thing as to Warsaw and Ivangorod, and as to not going beyond the Vistula, but nothing about bringing every available man to the West. I asked him whether he were really a Russo-phobe and he acknowledged that it was quite true that he did not like them. It was quite possible that the Germans might had confided to him something of their general intentions.

On the 23rd December, I wrote out a telegram to the Foreign Office that Bulgaria was expecting some thousands of rounds of field and mountain gun

CHAPTER FIVE.

ammunition, practically doubling her supply. Other items of supply included intrenching tools, boots, rifles, medical stores and telephones. These stores were coming from Germany, and Bulgaria had asked permission to transport them by the Danube from Orshovo, a port in Austria on the river. Both Serbia and Roumania had referred the question to Russia, who had mined the Danube, and objected. Roumania had suggested that Serbia should sink ships in the fairway. Meanwhile Sir Edward Grey thought the ammunition might be sent by the Danube, if Bulgaria gave a guarantee that she would not also pass stores on to Turkey. I suggested in the above mentioned telegram, that these stores might be sent, via the Mediterranean, to Cyprus or elsewhere, and be detained until Bulgaria had joined the Triple Entente. Sir Henry Bax-Ironside advised my first asking the Russians, as they might not like us to interfere. Accordingly I saw both the Russian Minister, Savinsky, and the Military Attaché, Tatarinoff, and found them both delighted at the suggestion.

On the 26th December, having heard at the club a few days previously some remarks by General Elias Dimitrieff (late Intendant General of the Bulgarian army) that the Russians could never advance into Prussia direct from Poland, I took the opportunity to go and see him at his house and brought some maps with me. I asked him to explain his strategical ideas. We took out my map and he proceeded to point out that Russia had only four railways approaching the line Bielostok—Brest—Litovsk. Beyond that, up to the line Kossow—Siedlitz—Lukow—Lublin, she had only three railways and beyond that again, to the line Warsaw—Ivangorod only two. In a country like Poland these two lines could not support an army of more than 1,200,000 men. I remarked that during the Japanese war, Kuropatkin had kept an army of 1,000,000 men at the end of a single line of railway, 7,000 kilometres in length. But Dimitrieff declared that that was no test as they supplied themselves with all the grain, fodder and bread they wanted in the country, and their meat came from Mongolia, close by, and that the provision of other things including war material, etc., only amounted to 1/3 of the total required. After some further discussion he went on to point out that the German lines of railway were two or three deep, encircling Poland, with strong fortresses and perpendicular lines of advance based on them. These permitted Germany to place a superior force wherever she liked. Russia had already tried twice to break through and had twice been beaten back. The only thing to do was to go through Roumania. That was for Diplomacy to settle, or for Russia to push through as Germany did through Belgium. The railways should be used as well as the Danube, and about 15 army corps of 40,000 men each would be sufficient. This would transfer all the enemy's strategical advantages to Russia, who would then have to advance on Vienna by that route, at the same time also advancing by the Carpathians. Then from Vienna the campaign against Berlin could be resumed. I asked what Bulgaria would do in that case. He said " of course the Russians could not move up the Danube without securing both banks of it." He had, I think, forgotten his animosity, in pursuing his strategical proposition, but he then remembered that he was himself a violent Stamboulovist and hoped that Russia would be beaten. On the other hand he is a great Anglo-phil, having been educated at the American Robert College at Constantinople, and declared he was sure that old England would have to do the work herself, without relying on Russia, and would come out on top in the end. I thought it worth while to telegraph these strategical views to the War Office. Although they doubtless knew all this, I thought it of interest as coming from a Bulgarian General of experience. Many of the senior officers of the Bulgarian army had received their higher military education at St. Petersburg, and were apt to judge the Russian army from its very inefficient condition in former days. But they did not know, any more than I did, to how great an extent the Russian army had improved since the Japanese war. I put the question, "Can the leopard change his spots?" Unfortunately Sukhomlinoff, the Russian Minister of War, had been Dimitrieff's instructor at St. Petersburg, and the latter answered "No—besides, Russia could not have another Skobeleff in the present day, as the Grand Duke Nicholas had crushed all initiative. Russian Generals too, were jealous of each other, and played for their own hand, witness the dismissal of Rennenkampf." Such were Dimitrieff's remarks on the capacity of the Russian, apart from the strategical aspects of the case. He had much greater respect for the Germans.

On the 27th December I heard from Tatarinoff that Djemal Pasha had telegraphed to Constantinople that he needed three or four months more, another 30,000 troops, and some Decauville light field railway material before he could march on the Suez Canal. He added that they were sending him 10,000 men immediately and another 10,000 were being sent to Bagdad. Also 37 waggon loads of guns had left Adrianople on the 20th December for Constantinople, intended for the defence of the Bosphorus or Dardanelles. The Turks were evidently much afraid of an attack on both these points. The position of the Turks at this time was :— 1st Army Corps, Constantinople; 2nd, Adrianople, and on the move to Constantinople and beyond ; 3rd, Rodosto, with two Divisions at Gallipoli; 4th, astride the Dardanelles, with one Division gone to the Caucasus or Syria; 5th, Across the Bosphorus, with two regiments at Erzeroum; 6th, On the move from the Dardanelles to the Russian frontier or Syria.

On the 30th December I saw General Fitcheff. He had nothing to say about the Italian "bloc" which appeared to have missed fire for the present. I asked what his Military Attaché at Vienna thought of the Austrian army, and he replied that according to him the Austrians were doing well. At the beginning of the war they had mobilized altogether

8TH DECEMBER, 1914—4TH JANUARY, 1915.

4,000,000 men; which was all they had. Their losses, up to date, were 700,000. But they were not able to arm or clothe all their men. This was being done by degrees. 6,000 rifles a day were being manufactured in the country, and Germany was sending her guns from Belgium. The morale was good, and Vienna was confident. Regarding Russia, according to his information, Russia had mobilized 7 millions, had lost $1\frac{1}{2}$ millions and consequently had $5\frac{1}{2}$ left. His estimate of Germany was 6 millions mobilized, losses over 1 million, and nearly 5 millions left. I then asked Fitcheff about the possibility of putting an end to the war by joining in with us. If Bulgaria and Roumania came in together, Italy would probably follow, but apparently the Triple Entente was tired of making proposals to Bulgaria. How would it be, I suggested, if Radoslavoff went to our Minister and told him frankly what Bulgaria wanted in return for active assistance against our enemies. Fitcheff said it might be of use. After work on the Budget was over, in four or five days time, they would have leisure to think the matter over. Had we not noticed a difference in Radoslavoff's attitude to us? I replied yes we had. "That was due to me," said Fitcheff. I thanked him, and suggested he should now use his influence to screw Radoslavoff into making an offer. What did he think was the price? He replied "the San Stefano Agreement. We can do without Salonika. All we want is Kavala, Seres, Krusha Planina and the other mountain ranges to the South of the Gomela Prestanka Lake, South of Lake Okrida, and to the North, Kumanova, and Skopie." A nice little slice! He did not think the Austrians would be able to undertake operations against Serbia under two months and two German corps could not be spared now.

On the 4th January I went to the Sobranie to hear Fitcheff introduce his war budget. He carried all his points, but was too verbose and egotistical, spoke for an hour and a half, with interruptions from the centre and left. The result was an increase on last

Military Attaché G.

year of about 7 million francs, and 10,000 men more on the peace establishment.

I went on to the War Office and saw Colonel Jekoff. A junior officer assured me that the Gallipoli Peninsula could be carried by a coup-de-main with one army corps of Bulgarian troops with twelve or fifteen c.m. howitzers, either from the direction of Adrianople, or from Gumuldjina.

In the evening I dined at the Greek Military Attaché's. Sir Henry and Lady Bax-Ironside were there, and several other Diplomats. I heard that an effort to bring in the Greeks had failed.

Chapter Six.

THIRD VISIT TO ROUMANIA — ROUMANIAN PREPARATIONS FOR WAR — CERTAIN THAT ITALY WILL FIGHT AUSTRIA — NUMBER OF MEN AVAILABLE FOR ROUMANIAN ARMY — GHENADIEFF'S SPECIAL MISSION TO ROME — BOURCHIER OPTIMISTIC REGARDING BULGARO-ROUMANIAN ALLIANCE — VISIT OF TREVELYAN AND SETON WATSON — ILIESCO SUGGESTS MAKING USE OF BULGARS — CONCENTRATION OF GERMAN TROOPS ON ROUMANIAN BORDERS — CONSEQUENT RELUCTANCE OF ROUMANIA AND BULGARIA TO FIGHT — UNFRIENDLY ATTITUDE OF GENERAL FITCHEFF — SERBIAN ATTITUDE TO BULGARS EXPLAINED — GERMAN LOAN TO BULGARIA — FAVOURABLE TIME FOR GETTING BULGARIA IN, NOW PAST — BULGARIAN OFFICERS OF RESERVE TO BE CALLED OUT — ADVISABILITY OF ACQUAINTING BULGARIAN OPPOSITION PARTIES WITH ENTENTE'S OFFER.

AS there was nothing much going on at Sofia in the evening of the 5th January I decided to go to Bukarest, and left with M. de Russi, the Roumanian Minister, and his Military Attaché. De Russi did not seem quite so clear or confident of Roumania going into the war as I should have expected, and seemed to think they would wait on Italy, but might go in first if they were quite sure that Italy would follow suit. The Military Attaché thought it was a long way to Buda-Pesth, and the distance between them and the Russians as allies would be great. De Russi hated the Bulgars, and spent all his time in abusing them. He could not understand how they hypnotised people like Bourchier and O'Mahony,* as they had no endearing qualities and no talents. I said they had courage, perhaps that was the reason. "But we all have courage," he replied. "No one spends their money at the expense of their own relations in order to help us, who are much nicer people than the Bulgars—We are full of courage too." When he had worked himself up into a war-

---
*FOOTNOTE—The O'Mahony had founded a Home for Macedonian Refugees of Bulgarian origin.

like heat, I suggested that now the Roumanians had a glorious opportunity of proving to all the world a fact of which I had not the slightest doubt, and then he came to the conclusion that I was "getting at him," and changed the conversation. We crossed the Danube by the ferry steamer in perfect spring-like weather, and there was no sign of floating ice, as is sometimes the case at this season. Giurgevo which is the Roumanian town opposite Rustchuk is a very considerable place, with clean, well paved streets in agreeable contrast to Rustchuk. We lunched there and reached Bukarest at 5 p.m. I put up at the Athenée Palace Hotel, a luxurious place after the hotels at Sofia.

On the 7th January, Christmay Day by the Greek Calender, I saw M. Blondel, the French Minister, who told me that the Roumanians would not wait for the Italians; they had gone too far. That was the most significant news I had yet heard. However, on the 10th, I met M. N. Filipesco, late Minister of War, out riding, and he did not seem very sanguine. He thought Bulgaria was in the same position as she had been months ago, that Roumania had made slight progress, but that Italy was playing a waiting game, and intended to throw in her weight on the winning side. I thought no doubt all the Balkan States were doing that, but did not say so. About this time I saw Colonel Semenoff who had his hands full with a Russian Mission under Prince Usupoff who was on his way to decorate the Allies. Semenoff told me of an impending increase to the Roumanian army. In addition to the existing five Army Corps, there were to be five Reserve Divisions, to be organized into two or three additional Army Corps. The increase to the army by the new formations would not be less than 80,000 men. Also there would be called to the colours in the next mobilization all those men who for one reason or another had not done any previous military service, and there would be no gradual mobilization, but the whole army would mobilize simultaneously. He also informed me that maps of Austria and Bulgaria had been served out to the troops. From our Consul at Braila I heard that the Roumanian troops had been served out with coloured prints of Russian and Austrian soldiers and with a map of a big Roumania shewing the national aspirations on ethnological grounds. It was also reported, on the authority of General Iliesco, that the Roumanians had ordered from Italy 50,000,000 loaded cartridges for small arms, and material for manufacturing another 50,000,000; there had also been ordered 60 motor lorries. There was a rumour that the Roumanians were getting some heavy siege guns either from Italy or Germany, and the Russian Military Attaché was suspicious that they might be used against his country instead of Austria. I thought his suspicions too far fetched, but he pointed to the fact that Austria was leaving the Transylvanian frontier unguarded, and that Iliesco had not informed him about the heavy guns. On the other hand the Diplomatists had no longer any doubts about Roumania and the war material had been ordered to be let through by our fleet. From France Roumania was getting 20 electric projectors, but not much else, whereas from Austria she was due to get clothing and field artillery ammunition, while ten days before, 78 truck loads of warlike stores were received from Krupps in exchange for petrol. It was not therefore surprising to find some doubt thrown on Roumania's intentions. I then saw the Italian Military Attaché and asked him if he thought Roumania could come in without waiting for Italy, purposely assuming that there was no chance of Italy coming in. Colonel Ferigo said he did not think they could do much without Italy, but asked why I thought Italy was not coming in. His personal opinion was that Italy could not possibly refrain, but would join us in less than two month's time. "Have a little patience," he said, " we have no quarrel with Germany, but we absolutely must fight Austria."

On January 14th, New Year's Day in Roumania, I wrote my name in all the Royalties' books and left cards on Court officials, Ministers of War and of

Foreign Affairs, Chief of Staff, Take Yonescu, Philipesco, and also on Russians, Serbs and Bulgars. The latter had a dinner party at the Athenée Palace Hotel where I was dining, but not with them. After dinner I had an interesting conversation with Samardjiew, the Bulgarian M.A. He said that up to the present the Triple Entente had done nothing in the Balkans. I replied "But our Minister is very pleased that you have not gone against us." I then told him that Radoslavoff had declared that Roumania's policy was perfectly clear to him, but that I myself did not understand it. What did he think? He replied "Roumania's policy is quite clear. She is waiting for the next great victory, ready to join the side that wins." "Well," I said, "according to Radoslavoff Bulgaria's policy is the same as Roumania's." "That is not true,—Bulgaria's policy is Macedonia. That is the beginning and the end of it." "But Radoslavoff does not say so" I replied. "Everybody knows it, what need is there for him to say so" was his rejoinder. The conversation was then interrupted by Radeff who came up to me with an invitation to lunch. Later in the evening I heard of a telegram from Sazonoff in Petrograd to say that the Greek Minister here was intriguing with Bratiano to form an anti-Slav "bloc." Later on Samardjiew gave me his figures about the Roumanian Army, shewing that the men available were :—

Active Army with its reserves ...	276,000
Second Line Reserves	349,000
Militia	124,000
Total	749,000

On the 17th January, at lunch with Radeff, the latter informed me that Ghenadieff, a prominent Bulgarian politician, had been sent on a special mission to Rome by the King and Radoslavoff, especially the former, to gather information. He would probably be away for three weeks, and had been promised a seat in the Cabinet (not the Ministry of Foreign Affairs) on his return. Radeff had just returned from an interview with Bratiano and said that things were going very well as regards a Bulgarian and Roumanian Entente in the interests of the Triple Entente. But he regretted the Entente had been so vague about Macedonia. That we had offered them in exchange for their neutrality the Vardar Line, and something in the direction of the Enos-Midia Line—not the Enos-Midia Line itself— I said, if it had depended upon me, I would have offered them everything for co-operation, but nothing for neutrality, to which Radeff replied that mine would have been the best policy for the Entente.

I met Bourchier, who had just arrived from Sofia and was in great hopes that the Bulgarian and Roumanian agreement would be accomplished. He thought, however, it would be necessary to give further satisfaction to Bulgaria's Macedonian aspirations, perhaps at the expense of Greece, otherwise Ghenadieff's mission might be directed towards delaying the action of Italy and therefore also of Roumania. I agreed with Bourchier that if one had to choose between Greece and Bulgaria, the latter was more valuable to us. Besides, the interests of Greece and Italy were opposed, and the great object was to bring in Italy.

The same day Trevelyan and Seton-Watson arrived from England. They appeared to be on some unofficial mission similar to that of the Buxtons, and I asked them to dinner, and introduced them to Russians and Bulgars, but they were more interested in the fate of Hungary's Roumanian subjects in Transylvania.

On the 18th January by order of the King I was invited to attend the Blessing of the Waters. The last ceremony of that sort that I had attended was on the banks of the Neva in 1906, when an attempt was made on the Emperor's life by a charge of grape shot from a battery firing the salute from the opposite bank. I had passed the battery when it was getting into position the day before, and had wondered why the officer in charge was so careful about the exact position of his guns. Here in Bukarest there was a kind of drain that flowed through the town—a stream, but very dirty, and much in need of a blessing. There also was no ice to break, and the scene was consequently very different, although the ceremony was the same. The King and the Crown Prince were both present. I noted that neither the Russian Military nor Naval Attachés were present, and heard that they had not been invited, so this was a special favour accorded to me.

On the 21st I had a message from General Iliesco to come and see him. He discussed the Balkan situation with me again. He declared that the Bulgarians wanted to occupy and hold the Vardar railway, promising to pass everything through to Serbia and Roumania. The Roumanians, i.e., Bratiano, would not take action unless the Bulgars were involved in a war somewhere or other. I asked if they could not make a separate engagement with the Bulgars. To this he replied that they wished to, on the condition that they did not cut the railway communication of the Serbs which was also theirs, namely the line between Negotin, Nisch and the Vardar railway. He suggested that the Bulgars might be asked to put 50,000 men into Bukovina between them and the Russians under the command of a Russian General. I replied that I was sure the Bulgars would not agree to that, but I thought it possible they might operate on the West of the Roumanians from the direction of Vidin with 100,000 men if the Entente permitted them to occupy the Vardar line now, with the promise of Macedonia up to the 1912 line after the war. General Iliesco said that would suit them all right if the Bulgars openly joined the Triple Entente. I thought the plan was worth trying, but the Serbs must be allowed to hold the railway until the end of the war.

However, just about that time it was reported that there were five Austrian Army Corps between Shabatz and Orshovo on the Danube, near the southwest corner of Roumania, the same troops that had not long before been badly beaten by the Serbs, but now completely refitted and brought up to strength. Also that 30,000 Bavarian Landsturm troops had arrived at Dornovatz in Bukovina, and that two more Bavarian Corps were coming into this theatre of war, and the chances of getting the Roumanians in on our side at this time grew less. There was also a rumour that 200,000 German troops would be used against Serbia, and in the direction of Transylvania and Bukovina. According to Captain Capitaneanu of the Roumanian artillery, a nice fellow who had been told off to look after me at some of the parades, etc., to which I had been invited, the reason why all the agitation against the Government and in favour of war had ceased, was because Bratiano had given his word of honour to Filipesco, Také Yonescu and other party leaders, that Roumania would come in on a certain date. The same authority informed me also that the actual combatant Roumanian army did not exceed 360,000, although the sum total of their contingents amounted to 700,000 or more. They could not equip more than 500,000, and if they had rifles for 360,000 that left a very small percentage over for a reserve. Also they had not got enough mountain guns, but were expecting enough for five regiments, although they had ordered many more from Italy, but had been unable to secure them. Altogether he appeared to be apologetic for Roumania not coming into action, and anxious to explain that she was not so strong as had been supposed.

On the 28th January I saw General Zotto, the Chief of the General Staff. He flatly denied that there were any movments of troops, concentration towards Craiova, or even reinforcements of frontier posts. He declared it would further complicate the situation if Roumania were to mobilize. He had information of German and Austrian troops at Bistritza, near the Bukovina frontier (Sir George Barclay had informed me that Bratiano had been very uneasy two days previously at hearing that there were 40,000 German and Austrian troops at Palanka

CHAPTER SIX.

half way up the Western frontier of Moldavia, and 60,000 at Bistritza). I asked General Zotto whether he meant that the Germans were capable of coming across and surprising them in the middle of their mobilization, to which he replied: "Of course. But the military situation depended on Bulgaria." If they were in accord with Bulgaria they would not mind the German concentration. This ended my interview with the Chief of the Staff. I had seen the Russian Military Attaché the night before, and he had declared that the Roumanian secret service in Transylvania was very faulty, and they did not really know what the enemy's movements were, although it was inhabited by Roumanians. I had also heard of a visit of a certain Prince Hohenlohe who appeared to have shaken the mailed fist in the face of the King or of Bratiano, and that, together with two German Army Corps in this direction, had been enough to stop all pourparlers with Bulgaria. There was one other difficulty, the army had been mobilized once already for several weeks, and it could not be mobilized for long again without going into action or without causing discontent. I concluded therefore there was no chance of any mobilization occurring in Roumania, and took the train to Sofia where I had to collect information regarding the Bulgarian railways. All sorts of proposals were now being made to bring the Bulgars in and induce the Roumanians to fight also, but I did not think they would be successful.

On the 31st January I heard that General Sir Arthur Paget was coming out to bestow decorations at Petrograd, and that he was being put off from visiting Sofia en route by the Foreign Office. I thought this was a pity, as Sir Arthur Paget had made a favourable impression on King Ferdinand some years ago when he visited Sofia on a special mission during my term as Military Attaché. He was now going to visit the Kings of Greece, Serbia and Roumania with verbal messages from King George. I could not see the point of rubbing up King Ferdinand the wrong way while still trying to negotiate with him. I also thought that, considering the Diplomatists of the Entente practically never saw the King, it was an opportunity which should not be missed, and I suggested telegraphing to ask the Foreign Office to reconsider it. This, however, the Minister did not approve of doing.

On the 7th February I saw Colonel Jekoff at the War Office. On his table was a map of Transylvania. He had evidently been studying the German concentration, and had marked troops at Bistritza and further South between Klausenburg and Vasarhely on the railway leading to Palanka, the centre of the Moldavian frontier. He told me that, judging from what he would do himself, he thought it likely that the Germans would attack Roumania rather than Serbia. If Roumania was forced to march with Germany, the same process, he thought, might be applied to Bulgaria who would be obliged to agree. He was most friendly and gave me some details regarding the untrustworthiness of the Bulgarian war budget which was cooked to suit the Sobranie, but the details were not very important. I then went to see Fitcheff, the Minister of War. He said much the same about the Germans and the Roumanian position, and then burst out indignantly at our having refused the Bulgars medical supplies while we were giving Roumania ammunition and all she wanted. He went on to talk about the cruelties of the Serbians to the Bulgars in Macedonia ; that the matter was now acute ; that we allowed that to happen, and then asked the Bulgars every day to join us. Was it likely? We should try and gain their sympathies first, by making the Serbians behave properly to Bulgarian subjects. On further enquiry I found that what had ruffled the War Minister was that the Austrians had taken 12,000 prisoners from the Serbs, among whom were 4,000 Macedonians, who were being returned to Bulgaria as Bulgarian subjects by way of propaganda. But they were diseased with typhus and cholera, and the War Minister was afraid of infection spreading to the Bulgarian troops. There were also some refugees,

CHAPTER SIX.

likewise diseased, from Serbian territory. I said we had nothing to do with prisoners of war from Austria but that I would mention the matter of the refugees to our Minister, but did not think that in time of war we could do much, although we had given evidence in the past of our humanity in that direction. Regarding ammunition, etc., we had offered to supply Bulgaria, but she now seemed to be an enemy. She was going to Berlin for money when she could have had it without any conditions from England. This referred to a loan to Bulgaria that the Germans had just brought off*. Fitcheff denied that we had offered the money free of any conditions but only on condition of her joining the Entente. He had seen the document. I said my Minister had told me the contrary only the day before, but he refused to believe it. Fitcheff was blustering and told me that Bulgaria was "not yet our enemy." I reflected that if Roumania had been suppressed by German threats, it was not at all unlikely that the Germans had told the Bulgars they would keep Roumania quiet, if Bulgaria would only go for Macedonia, and I thought that they might also attack Greece at the same time. Colonel Tatarinoff had told me a few days before that he thought the country was preparing for war against Greece. I could see they were certainly preparing for something. The school for Reserve Officers was full of students, and officers were being detailed to instruct them. I sent a telegram to the Foreign Office to inform them that the Minister of War, formerly friendly, was now menacing, which I attributed chiefly to the German concentration. In the evening I spoke to Colonel Kouchakovitch, the Serbian M.A. He was quite obstinate about the Bulgars, and said the utmost they could do for them would be to give up the Vardar line after the war. If any further concessions were made, they would have to be kept secret from the Serbian army, as, since the beginning of the war, the Serbs had drawn 100,000 men from Macedonia. They would already have

---
*—Vide Appendix A.

been beaten had it not been for these men. And the moment they heard they were going to be handed over to Bulgaria at the end of the war they would refuse to fight any more. As for the refugees, they were good for nothing and ran over the border to escape military service. If Bulgaria were to mobilise they would run back again into Serbia. No, the Triple Entente should not speak politely to the Bulgars, they only took it as a sign of weakness. He was sure they would do nothing and would not dare to attack Serbia, on which point I did not agree with him. At the same time he acknowledged that they were making rapid preparations for war.

It was announced in the paper the same day that a part of the reserve of officers would be called up for a month's training. At this time I was beginning to believe that it was hopeless to try and get Bulgaria on our side. The favourable moment had passed, and was, I thought, not likely to recur, unless the Triple Entente were to score another big success, especially in the Eastern theatre of war.

On the 8th February the Legation received an excellent telegram from Sir Edward Grey recounting his conversation with the Bulgarian Minister in London. He mentioned the loan which the Bulgars had just made from Germany, presumed there were conditions attached to it, and expressed sympathy for Bulgaria on the part of England. He declared that the Triple Entente intended to employ British, French and Russian soldiers in the Balkans before the war ended, and expressed the pious hope that we would not be obliged to fight the Bulgars. This was the first sign of a growl from the old British lion that we had shewn Bulgaria, and I hoped and believed it would do her good.

On the 11th February, I went to Philippopolis with Royaards, the Dutch Minister, nominally to shoot, really to examine the railway line. I found that Royaards still thought Germany would win, and that she was in a better position than before the war: in fact, he considered that the betting was now 6 to 4 on Germany. He said that the Germans had 60 submarines before the war and had built 40 since, of a better and newer type than ours. He thought Germans and Austrians were not at all uneasy about Italy, and had never suspected that she would go against them. Also that the Austro-Italian frontier was so difficult and strongly fortified that the Italians in any case could do them no harm. Royaards was an honest fellow and although not much of a sportsman, the spirit was willing. He wanted to go into the Rhodope mountains after bears, quite vaguely, but I could not spare the time, and so, after carrying out my purpose, we returned to Sofia. On my return I noticed that the Roumanian Military Attaché was more markedly polite to Germans and Austrians than he had been hitherto, and wondered whether he was a straw that shewed how the wind blew. On the other hand I liked Bratiano's recent language to Venizelos—refusing to put pressure on Bulgaria because he did not wish to encourage Serbia in her " non possumus " attitude towards Bulgaria. He recognized that Bulgarian and Roumanian interests were one ; and that our interests required an agreement between Serbia and Bulgaria as the paramount necessity of the situation. There was also no call for jealousy of a big Bulgaria, as the other Balkan States would also expand.

On the same day I saw Colonel Jekoff at the War Office. They had no information to give me regarding Turkish moves, but Jekoff was, as usual, very friendly. He said he thought the Bulgarian Government would join the Entente if they got the firm offer of the 1912 line at the end of the war, subject to no conditions as to whether Serbia did or did not get Bosnia, an outlet on the Adriatic, etc. I thought, if he were right, the thing was capable of arrangement, but that was not the way Fitcheff had spoken recently. Jekoff also told me that he did not think the Greeks were really going to have manoeuvres on the Bulgarian frontier, although they had been spreading reports that Bulgaria was preparing to attack them. At the same time he confirmed the fact that the Bulgarian officers of the reserve were going to be called out for training in two categories. As regards German and Austrian forces, Jekoff's map marked roughly 100,000 men in Bosnia on the Serbian Western frontier, 50,000 near Orshovo, and 50,000 between Belgrade and Semendria; also 200,000, with headquarters at Temesvar in Transylvania, and an unknown quantity, perhaps 100,000, about Bistritza threatening Bukovina and Roumania. Total 500,000 men.

On the 12th February, when lunching at the Legation, I heard that Lady Bax-Ironside was returning to England on Sunday. I accordingly offered to escort her as far as Nisch, thereby hoping not only to see the railway line, but also to learn how the land lay in Serbia.

The following day I went to see M. Gueschoff, a party leader and former Prime Minister. He told me he did not believe there were any conditions attaching to the German loan to Bulgaria beyond the purchase by Germany of a quantity of Bulgarian cloth for uniforms. Although the Bulgarian cloth was excellent, it did not sound a sufficient reason to account for a loan. Another curious thing that Gueschoff repeated very emphatically, was, that he believed if a proposal were made by the Entente to give up to Bulgaria the 1912 line in Macedonia at the end of the war, the King would find it very difficult to refuse. It would, of course, be in return for Bulgaria's active assistance in attacking Turkey, and she would also get the Enos-Midia line. Gueschoff did not seem to be aware that we had already promised Bulgaria the Enos-Midia line as well as that of the Vardar in return for neutrality. This meant that Radoslavoff was keeping these offers up his sleeve without letting the opposition know that they had been made.

Chapter Seven.

VISIT TO NISCH—LUNCH WITH CROWN PRINCE OF SERBIA—CONVERSATIONS WITH PASSITCH, PRINCE TROUBETZKOI AND TCHAPRASCHIKOFF—DINNER WITH CROWN PRINCE AND POLITICAL DISCUSSION—RETURN TO SOFIA—SIR A. PAGET TO VISIT SOFIA—GENERAL PAU—BULGARO-GREEK RELATIONS.

ON the 14th February we heard, when assembled at the station, together with nearly all the Diplomatic Corps and some few Bulgars to see Lady Bax off, that a bomb had been thrown into the Casino supper-room the night before by some unknown people. The result was that the son of General Boyadjiew, the late Minister of War, and the daughter of General Fitcheff, the present one, were killed. Also three aeroplanes had been flown across the Danube to Lom-Palanka in Bulgaria, and there packed by the Bulgars into a train for Constantinople. They were said to be intended for the Suez Canal expedition, and there were six more aeroplanes at Orshovo awaiting transit. Colonel Tatarinoff now scoffed at the idea of Bulgaria ever coming in on our side. I went with Lady Bax as far as Nisch, which we reached at 7.30 that evening. Des Graz met us and we transferred Lady Bax and the party to a sleeping car on the Salonika line. Des Graz kindly put me up and dined me at the Club.

The following morning I went to the Serbian Foreign Office where I saw M. Grouitch, the late Minister to London, and asked him to arrange that I should pay my respects to the Crown Prince. He went to see about it, and returned in half an hour with an invitation to me to join a lunch party which the Crown Prince was giving that day to Sir Thomas Lipton. On arrival at the Prince's abode I was greeted by him in the most friendly manner and he

PRINCE ALEXANDER OF SERBIA,
NOW KING OF YUGO SLAVIA.

(Presented to the Author).

told me that he had received the letter which I had written to him from Bukarest some months ago, and would like to talk to me about it. Then Sir Thomas Lipton came in. He had brought his yacht, the "Erin," out to Salonika as a hospital ship with a large staff of hospital nurses to help the Serbs. M. Pashitch, the Premier, the acting Minister for Foreign Affairs, M. Grouitch, and Colonel Ostoitch, who had been my colleague at Sofia in 1908, were also there. Colonel Ostoitch had since been at the Serbian Court with the King and Prince Alexander and had attended them through both the Balkan wars and the present one. The lunch was a nice informal meal. Lipton sat on the Prince's right and I on his left. Grouitch sat opposite, and as Lipton did not speak French, did the interpreting for him. Lipton told of his yachting experiences and how he had been sailing, with King Edward on board, when the mast fell and nearly killed His Majesty. Another similar instance occurred with the King of Spain, so I warned the Crown Prince jokingly, that Lipton was evidently a dangerous fellow for crowned heads to associate with. After lunch we were all photographed in the courtyard by a cinema operator who had come out on the yacht, and Lipton said with glee that we should be in every illustrated paper in the world! I tried to take a back seat, but the Prince insisted on my standing level with him, and Lipton behind, for which I was sorry, as he evidently wished to be in the limelight.

I had some conversation with M. Pashitch and found him quite obstinate about giving up the 1912 line to Bulgaria at any time. He was sure that Bulgaria could do nothing and that Serbia would have the help of Roumania. I told him that Roumania could not and would not move unless we got Bulgaria in also, especially now, since the German concentration in Transylvania. Pashitch said that if they did not help the Serbs, it would be treason, implying that they had Roumania's definite promise. He went on to say that if the Bulgars attacked them, they would make peace with Austria and defend themselves.

Military Attaché H.

The Austrians had promised them half of Bosnia and a port on the Adriatic, Ragusa, if they made a separate peace with them, so in that way they would be able to get both that extension and retain Macedonia. He added that we could not reproach them, should they make peace with Austria, if we demanded the sacrifice of Macedonia. I replied that he was assuming that Germany and Austria would win the war when he said that they would not lose anything in that way. Also that the Bulgars had themselves been offered Macedonia by the Austrians. However, there was no use in my arguing any further with the old man, who looked if anything younger and fitter than he did in 1908, when I first met him at Belgrade during that critical time.

That afternoon I made the acquaintance of Prince Troubetzkoi, the Russian Minister, who questioned me closely as to my ideas on the situation. I said I thought it was not much use making Bulgaria an offer at the present time to come in with us, owing to the momentary retreat of the Russians from East Prussia, and the German concentration against Roumania. But it should be done the moment we next got the swing of the pendulum our way. Troubetzkoi suggested a bribe in one hand and a threat in the other (meaning Roumania) to which I agreed, but feared the Roumanian pistol would not go off, at any rate not unless Italy were joining in also. I explained Fitcheff's complaint about the treatment of Bulgars in Serbia and the difference between refugees and prisoners of war from Austria 'rescued' from Serbia, and all diseased. I had inadvertently called them Bulgarian subjects, whereas they were Macedonians. Troubetzkoi did not trouble about niceties of that sort, but considered all Macedonians as Bulgarian subjects. We agreed that there was nothing to be done, but when Bulgars worked themselves into a rage over this question it had some definite object, either bluff, or an excuse for a premeditated attack on Serbia. It was not safe to assume it to be mere bluff.

On the 16th February Des Graz took me to call on M. Boppe, the French Minister, an interesting man, and said to be a great authority on Turkey and the East in general. From there we went on to lunch with Prince and Princess Troubetzkoi. There was a family party of the members of their Legation, including the Strandtmanns, old friends from Sofia. I told Prince Troubetzkoi of Gueschoff's remark for what it was worth, that King Ferdinand would find it difficult to refuse an offer of the 1912 line, even if it were conditional on Serbian acquisitions elsewhere, in return for war on Turkey. After lunch I called on the Bulgarian Legation, saw the Minister, Tchapraschikoff. He bragged about "la neutralité stricte et loyale" of Bulgaria and was almost indignant at the idea of there being any conditions attaching to the German loan. That it was an engagement undertaken before the war, and the Bulgars could not have got out of it even if they had wanted to by borrowing elsewhere. The Germans were not in financial straits, and did not want to lose their bargain which included concessions regarding the working of the Pernik coal mines. I said I believed him that there were no fresh conditions because I knew the Bulgars had a talent for getting something for nothing. I had to tell him that this was meant as a compliment, as he seemed doubtful. In the afternoon came an invitation from the Crown Prince to dinner, after I had given up expecting a summons, and had thought that possibly Pashitch had warned him off me. There was no one else at dinner except two civilians whom I took for secretaries, Colonel Ostoitch, and another A.D.C. in waiting. Before dinner I had a serious talk with the Prince all alone, and this was continued after dinner. He said he could not accept the proposition to let the Bulgars across the Vardar in any circumstances. The 1912 line was, even conditionally on getting compensation in Bosnia and the Adriatic, out of the question. How could he go to his soldiers and eat his own words? They had fought and bled for Serbia for three years and he had recently told them that they would remain Serbian subjects. It was a very risky game to discourage the Serbs. And what would the Bulgars do in return? I said they would attack Turkey, and by joining the Entente would also bring in Roumania and Greece, possible also Italy. That the Entente did not urge this policy in order to favour Bulgaria, but that their side might win, and in the interests of Serbia herself who stood to gain or lose more than any of her allies. The Prince told me that the Serbian army now numbered 200,000 men, and had been 250,000 strong, and cross-questioned me about the Bulgarian and Roumanian armies. He was not very pleased when I told him that the Bulgars were quietly and methodically preparing for war. As for Roumania I had a good impression both of officers and men, but especially of the officers, and thought them amply equipped. The Prince evidently did not like this, because he made some remark about "your friends the Roumanians." Then we went into the attitude of these countries. He was bitter against the Roumnaians and had none of Pashitch's illusions about their coming in to help him. I said I believed they would, if Bulgaria joined us. The Prince declared that was only a pretext like all the others. Had I heard that they were now asking the Russians for part of Bessarabia as the price of joining in? That was also another pretext. Then, as regards Bulgaria, how was it that she managed to hypnotise all the Great Powers of the Triple Entente? King Ferdinand of Bulgaria had said that he held the Balkans in the hollow of his hand? But he only did so because of their hallucination. I thought it was due to Bulgaria's geographical position, which enabled her to play this game effectually. The Prince then told me very confidentially that Greece had refused to allow the English or French troops to land at Salonika. He had just received that information and was furious with the Greeks. I said I supposed we could force the Greeks, but that it was hardly consonant with our attitude as the protectors of the rights of small States with which we had gone into the war. Returning to the Bulgarian question, the Prince said it would be of no use to offer Bulgaria any amount of compensation, she would not now join the Entente as the Russians were retiring. I agreed to this but hoped that a proposal might be made to them at a more favourable moment. The unfortunate part of the whole affair was that the Bulgars had got an " idée fixe " into their heads and they meant to have Macedonia sooner or later by one means or another. I thought Serbia was in the position of a man who had been told by his doctor that he would lose his life if he did not have his leg amputated, and the Prince replied that he would rather die than lose his leg. " Even if he assured you that you would grow a finer and stronger leg?" (meaning Bosnia, Herzegovina, etc.,) and the Prince said " Even then." Pashitch would not agree and he was the most moderate of all Serbian Statesmen, so he would not be able to find a Government to carry out that policy. " Bulgaria " said he, "wished to impose conditions that were harder even than those the Austrians had demanded, and about which Serbia went to war." The Prince then bade me a most affectionate good-bye, and asked me to continue to write him. I asked him if he would permit me to be with the Serbian army in case I should obtain the consent of the War Office, and he replied that he would be delighted.

On returning home I told Des Graz as much of this as he cared to listen to. He was very interested in the Greeks refusal to allow us to land, which he could not believe to be true, but was bored at my mention of the 1912 line, as an interference on my part with his business, which he had cautioned me to avoid discussing. Of course I had not been able to avoid discussing it.

The next morning I left for Sofia which I reached safely at 8 o p.m. The first thing I heard at Sofia was, that, instigated by the Austrians, the Bulgars were trying to implicate Serbia in having thrown the bomb into the Casino. As regards the Entente, our Minister had received instructions to ask formally,

CHAPTER SEVEN.

in conjunction with our Allies, on what conditions Bulgaria would join us. Bax-Ironside did not approve, and hoped that his "chers collègues" would jib. Personally I was of the opinion that it was not a favourable moment and I would rather have made them the offer of the 1912 line, as Gueschoff had suggested, with perhaps Kavala thrown in, and have let the opposition know that the Bulgars must take it or leave it; and if they left it, that we should assume they intended to belong to the opposition camp, and we would make arrangements to meet the situation. But as is was so difficult to get the three Powers to agree on any one step, I would not have raised objections if the others were agreed. It would do no harm to hear whether Radoslavoff had anything to say. He would probably be driven to make some impossible demands. A day or two later, Bax-Ironside, with me, called on the War Minister to express condolences on the murder of his daughter. Nothing was said regarding the instigators of the bomb outrage. Fitcheff remarked, as he had done before, that he could not see the outcome of the war, or the length of time it would take, and that small States were well advised to remain neutral. On our taking leave of him he asked me to come and see him again soon.

On the 20th February I saw by the paper that Fitcheff had seen the king just after our official call of condolence. So I thought I would go and see him again as he had suggested. I got to the War Office at 10 a.m., to find that the Austrian Military Attaché was already with him, so I went away and returned in half an hour. He then to my astonishment at once began on the advisability of forming a "bloc" between Bulgaria, Roumania and Greece. At the same time he said that Roumania was evidently intending to do nothing. He suggested that Bulgaria might get something out of Greece, say Kavala; and a bit of the Dobrudja from Roumania —including Baltchik; and the 1912 line in Macedonia from the Serbs. I told him that the

Serbs would not agree to the latter, as they did not wish to discourage the Macedonians in their army, on which he suggested it should be done secretly. I then asked him what he thought of the rumour that had appeared in the Press of an English landing at Salonika. He thought it was not true. I said we had no confirmation of it, but did he dislike the idea? He said " No, not if you are strong enough, and can spare the troops for a secondary theatre of war." I mentioned that the present time, when Russia was retiring, was a bad moment to expect Roumania to come in, and without Roumania a great deal of the value of Bulgaria's assistance would be gone. Fitcheff brushed this aside by declaring that Russia's check was only temporary. He then rather hurried me away, and I found the French Military Attaché, who very seldom saw the War Minister, in the waiting room. We compared notes afterwards and I heard that Fitcheff had said the same thing to him, only omitting all mention of Macedonia, which he would probably have done with me, if I had not asked him. The French Military Attaché took exception to Kavala, as the Greeks would not give it up.

I was puzzled. The whole tenor of Fitcheff's discourse was so different from what it had been even a day or two before, that he must have had orders from the King. The question was " Was this a sincere desire of Bulgaria to throw in her lot with the Entente after getting all the money she could out of Germany, and the result of the King's conviction that we were going to win the war? Or was it a trick to embroil us with Greece?" Bulgaria was supposed to be preparing to fight Greece. She may have thought Kavala the line of least resistance. Or regarding our promises of Macedonia as sufficient in that direction, she may have seen a chance of getting Kavala also. One thing was certain, that Fitcheff was not concerned with details, and that the Bulgarian Goverment did not like being regarded as having gone over to the Germans.

CHAPTER SEVEN.

A telegram arrived the same day from Petrograd, that Sazonoff thought our Foreign Office had made a mistake in not letting General Paget see King Ferdinand, and he hoped Paget would see him on the way back and tell him what the Russian army was like. This was rather a triumph for me as I had already protested against his not being allowed to come to Sofia. Now, on Sazonoff's telegram, the Foreign Office gave way and sent instructions to Paget to come to Sofia.

On the 24th February I dined at the French Legation to meet General Pau, en route to Petrograd, to decorate the Russians. He was a charming old man of 66 with only one arm. I sat opposite to him and the way in which he waved the stump of the other arm about as he was talking fascinated me. His Aide-de-Camp told me that counting Indians and Colonials, the British army had then 680,000 men in France. He also said that the French soldiers, notwithstanding all their losses, numbered over four millions, were very fit and absolutely confident. The King did not receive General Pau, but M. Panafiew, the French Minister, had not asked for an audience lest he should get a rebuff. He, M. Panafiew, told me that the Greeks had refused to allow Entente troops to land at Salonika. This confirmed the Crown Prince's news.

In the Chancery a discussion had taken place between the Minister and the First Secretary, O'Reilly. The latter had suggested that Bulgaria might be of use against a recalcitrant Greece. Bax-Ironside sent for me and put forward the suggestion. I proposed interviewing the War Minister, to which he agreed. But on arrival at the War Office, I was only able to find General Teneff, the Chief of the Staff, who was not accustomed to discuss such questions, and took a long time to grasp my meaning. This was that we should greatly deplore any quarrel between Bulgaria and Greece. The latter we considered to be more friendly to us just now than Bulgaria, and if such a deplorable event were to happen, Greece would probably declare herself on our side, and in this way Bulgaria would become our enemy. But if on the other hand Bulgaria were to forestall Greece by joining the Entente she would then win our assistance and would probably get Kavala without fighting for it. In any case we should not be against her. He denied that anything had been arranged in the shape of manoeuvres on the Greek frontier. Bulgaria was, however, preparing for war in all directions, he said. It was the Greeks who had begun the idea of manoeuvres and had increased their troops on the Bulgarian frontier, which the Bulgars had not done, although they had made certain preparations.

Later on I saw the Russian Military Attaché. He was quite agreed as to the idea of using Bulgars against Greeks, but knew no more than we did what line our Governments, who had always been so Hellenophil, were taking. He also confirmed the Greek's refusal to permit the landing of troops, although it was originally a Greek suggestion.

Chapter Eight.

FOURTH VISIT TO ROUMANIA—THOMSON APPOINTED MILITARY ATTACHE IN ROUMANIA—SUEZ CANAL EXPEDITION—AUSTRO GERMAN TROOPS NEAR ROUMANIAN FRONT—EXPERIMENTS WITH BULLET-PROOF SHIELD—PROGRESS IN FORCING DARDANELLES—RESULT ON BULGARIA—ARRIVAL OF COL. THOMSON—FAREWELL AUDIENCE WITH KING OF ROUMANIA—CONVERSATION WITH FILIPESCU—ARRIVAL OF GENERAL SIR A. PAGET—DINNER AT RUSSIAN LEGATION—FAREWELL AUDIENCE WITH QUEEN OF ROUMANIA—CROWN PRINCE.

ON the 25th February I again left Sofia for Bukarest, after another interview with the War Minister. This time he professed the most peaceful intentions. He did not think the Greeks really meant to attack them, although they had mobilized some troops at Drama, near their frontier. At the same time he told me it was his intention later on to carry out a partial mobilization of about 60,000 men for manoeuvres, in order to exercise the higher commands, and the place he had chosen was Kazanlik, south of the Shipka Pass, which was a menace to nobody. That was true, but I reflected it was also a central position whence troops might be moved against Serbia, Roumania or Turkey.

On arriving at the Legation at Bukarest, I heard that General Paget when passing through Roumania on his way to Russia, had been annoyed at not having had a Military Attaché at the frontier to meet him, and had supported Sir George Barclay in asking the War Office for a separate one for Roumania. It was necessary by this time to have a Military Attaché for each country. When I left Bukarest the last time, the Legation had not been informed of General Paget's visit, and I had been obliged to travel in Bulgaria. Meanwhile other information was required from Bukarest necessitating the presence of a

Military Attaché there at the same time, and the War Office had decided to send Col. C. B. Thomson, who was already on his way out. In some ways I regretted this, for, although it was very hard work trying to serve in the two countries, still, Diplomats and their Staffs were usually confined in water-tight compartments, and beyond the interchange of telegraphic information, generally very incomplete, there was no personal liaison between neighbouring Ministers. In the present instance, when it was so desirable to endeavour to promote better relations between two countries, who were so necessary to us as well as to each other, and the special object was to bring about a military alliance, it had been certainly advantageous to combine the two jobs.

At the Roumanian War Office I obtained some useful details about the Turkish expedition against the Suez Canal. The total "ration" strength of the force at this time was 120,000, and combatant strength not more than 75,000, including 51 battalions, 9 squadrons and 25 field and one howitzer battery. German engineers were with the force to sink wells, but they did not always find water, and the expedition was experiencing great difficulties. In Europe, and about the Bosphorus and Dardanelles, were 5 army corps, making a total of 135 battalions, of which 44 were Redif (Reserve).

I also heard there were mixed German and Austrian troops near the Roumanian frontier, and some 300,000 near Temesvar. On the Serbian frontier were three Austrian and one German Corps. Von dem Busche, the German Minister, had just left, and the Germans were asking the Roumanians every day why they did not come in on their side.

The Bulgarian Military Attaché told me that the Roumanians were less warlike than ever.

On the 28th February I lunched with the Russian Colonel Semenoff and Arsenieff, the first Secretary. The latter was now leaving, owing to his report against Poklewsky. Semenoff considered him a great patriot who had sacrificed his career because in his opinion (Arsenieff's) he (Poklewsky) had not carried out his instructions. The Czar had wished to have Poklewsky removed, but Sazonoff intervened, and Arsenieff had, of course, to go, but there was nothing of the nature of an intrigue. His reports were shewn to Poklewsky before being despatched. I regretted Arsenieff's departure as he seemed a fine fellow. With the party was a Russian correspondent who told me a great number of interesting things, if they had been all true. One was that the Bulgarian Exarch had ordered prayers to be said for the victory of the Entente, that Ferdinand wished to poison him in consequence, and the Exarch was obliged to cook his own food, or get a priest to do it for him.

I noted one curious fact. Semenoff had seen the same officer that morning at the General Staff that I had interviewed the previous day. When he asked for information about the Turkish expedition to Egypt he was told there was none. And yet he had given it to me the day before!

On March 1st I had a most interesting trial of a certain bullet-proof substance invented by a Greek called Ianopol. Shields of varying thicknesses were tried. The lightest was proof against a bayonet thrust, and weighed 3.3 lbs.; the heaviest was a slab of stuff as hard as a piece of solid metal, size 29.5 centimetres by 18 centimetres and 1.6 centimetres thick. It weighed 4.4 lbs., and it resisted a Mannlicher rifle bullet fired at a range of 10 yards. I was much pleased with the result.

On March 2nd I saw Radeff and with him the Mayor of Sofia. They told me that the progress we had made in forcing the Dardanelles would soon force Bulgaria to join us. The news was that we had taken the forts at the mouth, and cleared of mines 4 miles of Straits, and our ships were now inside bombarding the forts higher up. The Mayor said the present Government would go, and Malinoff, Todoroff and Lutzkanoff would form a National Party. But there did not seem much prospect of Roumania joining in. They now thought the Carpathian mountains very difficult ; that Transylvania had only belonged to them for a short time, since the 15th century, and it was not certain that the inhabitants who were more advanced than the Roumanian peasants, wished to come under the Roumanian Government. A former Minister of Roumania at St. Petersburg, an old friend, was very insistent that it would do our cause no good if Roumania were pushed into action when she did not feel capable of defending herself properly. Also the question of Constantinople passing into the hands of Russia was quite enough to put them off, and even turn them against us if they saw a good opportunity. From their point of view, the prospect of Russia in possession of Constantinople and the Dardanelles would be quite fatal to Roumania.

On 4th March I saw the Greek inventor again, and asked him how he first got the idea of making bullet proof shields. He replied that more than 20 years ago when out shooting he noticed how a bullet flattened against a tree. I thought possibly there might be some kind of wood fibre as well as metal shavings in the composition. The proportions of the mixture were not the same in the different classes of shields, but all had the same ingredients. The lighter shields looked and felt more like papier-mâché and the heavier like solid metal, but he maintained that no metal plate existed of the thickness of his shield, viz, 1.6 centimetres, capable of resisting rifle bullets at that range. Hearing that Sir Arthur Paget was expected shortly, I hoped that I would be able to induce him to witness a trial. Meantime I telegraphed details to the War Office and their reply was that they would only consider it if the inventor could produce something one foot square that weighed not more than 8 lbs. and would resist the German rifle bullet. The War Office had evidently not taken the trouble to work out the relative value of kilograms and centimetres to English measures. Had they done so, they would have found that it satisfied their own conditions, the bullet-proof substance in question weighing 8 lbs. to 149 square inches instead of to 144; the Mannlicher bullet could not be very different from a Mauser bullet, and the range was 10 paces. However, I let the matter rest for the moment, hoping to enlist the General's and my successor's interest in the matter.

The same day I saw Colonel Semenoff who estimated the total possible force of Germans and Austrians directed against Serbia, Transylvania and Bukovina at about 400,000 men, whereas the Roumanian estimate was 630,000, which latter was doubtless exaggerated. He also informed me that the Roumanians had recently received 50,000 projectiles, some quadrants, telemeters, etc., from Erhardt and Krupp in exchange for 200 cisterns of petrol and 190 waggon loads of beans.

On the 6th March Thomson arrived. I introduced him to the Military Attachés of the Entente at once. He seemed a very smart good-looking fellow with a great gift for conversation. At the same time he was careful to note what other people had to say, and I thought he was likely to be a very efficient Military Attaché.

On the 7th March I had an audience with the King. His Majesty was quite friendly and not at all nervous as on the previous occasion when I had the honour of being presented. His manner was, in fact, almost jocular. I had heard from the Aide-de-Camp a moment before, that Venizelos had resigned. This was most important news but the King did not mention it, and I did not refer to it. But I did say that I believed His Majesty was more inclined to believe in the success of the Entente than when I first came. He would not commit himself, but I had the impression that he was now on our side. He said "You will still have a great deal of difficulty in forcing the Dardanelles, and it is a pity the Bulgarians do not declare themselves." He had noted that the King of Bulgaria had not received General Pau, although he had sent an Aide-de-Camp to the station to meet him, and had had every opportunity of doing so. The King then said with emphasis that England was the only country that had not pressed Roumania to come in. This seemed to please him very much. I remarked that it was not because we did not want them, quite the contrary was the case, but I presumed that our Government thought each country should decide for herself. At the same time England was confident in her own strength and had the resources of the whole world to draw on. I tried to point out, however, that there was a moment when Roumania might have come in, and have brought in all the other neutrals, but he was so very pleased that they had not done so, "althought certain people in the country wanted it," that he would not listen. I ventured to ask him if he saw his way clearly at the present juncture what policy Roumania should pursue. But he shied off, and said things were still too complicated. His Majesty then wished me a pleasant journey and hoped that I should have some regrets at leaving Roumania. I frankly assured him they would be many, and expressed my grateful thanks for His Majesty's extreme kindness in permitting me to see so much of his army.

On the same day I secured an interview with Nicolas Filipesco. He was disappointed that I had not obtained an opinion from the King about Greece's attitude as affecting Roumania, but I was sure the King would not have told me. Filipesco himself did not at all like Greece's attitude and was apprehensive of her obtaining possession of the common line of communication for Serbia and Roumania through Salonika. I said that personally if we had to choose between Greece and Bulgaria, the latter was more important to us, and Fitcheff had latterly turned in our favour. Now, that the Greeks were veering towards the opposite camp, was too good an opportunity for Bulgaria to miss. Filipesco intended to egg the Bulgars on in his next edition of the " Epoca " (a Roumanian newspaper) by dangling Kavala before their eyes. I thought that if Greece became hostile to the interests of our ally, Serbia, we should declare war on Greece in the last resort.

CHAPTER EIGHT.

On the 8th March at 8 o'clock in the morning, Sir Arthur Paget arrived from Russia, and we all went to meet him at the station, including the Minister, who had unfortunately caught cold, but was otherwise fit enough. The evening before, Thomson had told me that the Government had big schemes for the Balkan peninsula. I feared that possibly Thomson in the first flush of his popularity with the Roumanians might easily be led to place undue confidence in them. I accordingly sent a telegram through the Minister deprecating any premature confidences either with the Roumanian or the Bulgarian Governments lest they might reach our enemies. When he heard of this, Thomson was furious and said that Sir Arthur Paget was much annoyed, as he represented Lord Kitchener, and was the only person capable of sending a telegram while he was here. I did not agree that anything could interfere with the Minister or any of the Minister's Staff, and I was glad that the telegram had gone. I then saw Captain Glyn, the General's Aide-de-Camp, and eventually spoke to the General and explained that I was referring particularly to a scheme of Thomson's. If it was the case that General Paget had thought of communicating some scheme or other to the Roumanians, he was very nice to me and did not shew annoyance.

On the 9th March we all dined at the Russian Legation with the Russian Minister, Poklewsky. My neighbour was M. Psycha, the Greek Minister, a very nice man. He was most distressed at the retirement of Venizelos and attacked me for having espoused the Bulgarian cause. When he went so far as to say he could not understand how any honest Englishman could encourage the idea of robbing the poor Serbs of their territory, when they had been shedding their blood for our cause, I gave him the benefit of the Bulgar's point of view, namely that the Serbs had quite recently robbed the Bulgars of the territory in question. As for the shedding of blood, it was we who had shed our blood for the Serbs, not they for us, and if there were a question of our choosing between one brigand and another I preferred the one who was capable of being most useful. We did not take offence at each other's plain speaking, but Psycha appeared to be rather apprehensive that we might rope the Bulgars in at the expense of Greece. If we did, I thought that Greece, or rather her King, deserved it.

About this time I had my farewell audience with the Queen, who was very interesting. I ventured to remark that I had seen a marked improvement in the King's political views, and that he was much more favourable to us than before. The Queen said that she was very careful never to tell him anything that she was not sure about, and avoided a woman's natural impulse to jump to conclusions. Little by little she was beginning to win his confidence as an adviser and informant, but it had been very uphill work, and she had to be frightfully careful of what she said in public. The other day she had said to Poklewsky, " Hurrah! now we have got through the Dardanelles." This was at once repeated to others and got to the ears of the Germans. She also said that she was very glad to hear that a smart young soldier (I had been singing Thomson's praises) was being sent here and would be able to help our Minister. The Queen then said she much wanted to know what King Ferdinand of Bulgaria would say to Sir Arthur Paget. I thought we could easily convey by cypher from the Legation in Sofia to our Legation here the result of the interview. She seemed very pleased with that arrangement and mentioned it to Glyn whom she saw directly afterwards. Glyn told me, however, that Paget would not communicate to us the result of his interview with King Ferdinand, and it would be worth while to send a letter by special messenger to the Queen. I thought this might be useful. After my audience with the Queen, I was presented to the Crown Prince and was pleased to note what a nice young fellow he was. We did not touch on politics. He had just finished 6 month's service with the 1st Guard Infantry Regiment at Berlin or Potsdam when the war

Military Attaché K.

broke out, and had been, of course, thoroughly imbued with German ideas. I was therefore delighted when he told me that since he had been in command of a Roumanian regiment, he had discovered that the Roumanian soldier as raw material was preferable to the German. He was now working in the General Staff. I noticed foils and trophies of the chase about his room. He was evidently a sportsman, and told me he wanted to go to India and shoot. I also heard from his Aide-de-Camp that he had started the Boy Scout movement in Roumania, so that altogether I was considerably impressed with his capabilities.

Chapter Nine.

RETURN TO SOFIA—EFFECT OF STORM ON RIVER DANUBE—PAGET ARRIVES SOFIA—HIS AUDIENCE WITH KING OF BULGARIA—PROBABILITY OF BULGARIA SPEEDILY JOINING ENTENTE ANNULLED BY LOSS OF THREE BRITISH SHIPS IN DARDANELLES—CONTRABAND OF WAR—DEPARTURE OF O'REILLY—POURPARLERS IN LONDON—WAR OFFICE REJECTS INVENTOR'S OFFER RE BULLET-PROOF SHIELDS—GREEK SUGGESTION FOR ENTENTE TO SEIZE DEDEAGATCH—BRITISH MINISTER'S REPLY — NECESSITY OF GRANTING RUSSIA CONSTANTINOPLE — SIR E. GREY SUGGESTS OFFER OF 1912 LINE—OPPOSITION OF FRENCH—INTERVIEW WITH SAVINSKY—WAR MINISTER APPROVES 1912 LINE AND PLANS CO-OPERATION.

THE following morning I started for Sofia in a blizzard, and when we reached the Danube the water was so rough that the steamer was unable to come alongside the wharf. The wind being dead against the current, and waves as big as in the English Channel, I was obliged to pass the night at Giurgivo. I heard that a fort was being constructed with a cupola to take one or more 21 c.m. guns with which to shell Rustchuk in case of war with Bulgaria. The wind changed during the night and blew down stream, consequently next morning the river was quite smooth and there was no trouble. A look-out was kept for floating mines but all was clear. We crossed the river at 11 o'clock in the morning but owing to endless dawdling on the Bulgarian side, did not arrive at Sofia till 2 a.m. on the 12th March. On reaching the Legation, I found telegraphic communication with Roumania was interrupted owing to the storm. The Minister had arranged for Sir Arthur Paget to have an audience with the King after some difficulty.

On the 13th March the weather cleared, and we heard that Paget was due to arrive in two days time. I also heard that unofficial efforts were being made by Bourchier and others to put Radoslavoff in touch with Sir Edward Grey via Hadji Mischeff, the Bulgarian Minister in London.

On the 15th March the Minister and I met General Paget at the railway station where we also found General Savoff on the part of the King. The General, who was looking much better, was accompanied by Captain Glyn. In the evening we had a big dinner at the Legation with Radoslavoff, Fitcheff, the Under Secretary of State for Foreign Affairs, and all the Ministers and Military Attachés of the Allied Powers. Bax-Ironside always did this sort of thing well. It was quite a good dinner and Sir Arthur Paget made a very good impression on the Bulgars.

On the following day I saw the Minister of War, General Fitcheff, who was in a very good mood. He had told me two days previously that he would welcome a co-operation between the Bulgarian and British troops. Nevertheless, on this day I had to remonstrate with him about the way in which the Bulgars were letting through mines and aeroplanes for Turkey. Fitcheff declared it would not happen again. On the same day there was a big luncheon at the Russian Legation. The Bulgars present included Radoslavoff, Fitcheff, Teneff (the Chief of the Staff), Gueschoff, Daneff, and Malinoff (Party Leaders). The Ministers of the Allied States and their Military Attachés were also there. Sir Arthur Paget sat between Radoslavoff and Fitcheff. I sat between Daneff and the First Scretary of the Russian Legation, M. Sabler. It appeared to me that Daneff was not kept very well informed of events, and that he was not aware of how favourable to us Radoslavoff now was, or at any rate pretended to be. General Paget was to see the King that afternoon. Glyn told me that Fitcheff's eyes nearly dropped out of his head when in reply to a question as to what route he would travel by on his return to Russia, Glyn said " By the Dardanelles and Odessa, as I do not expect to be returning there for another three weeks." That shewed that Fitcheff had not really believed we would force the Dardanelles without a regular campaign. Fitcheff had told me that very morning that he would prefer to land troops on the Asiatic side, had he been a British General, and disembark comfortably somewhere between Smyrna and Kum-Kale; that the Turks now had only 12 battalions at Kum-Kale, 50,000 men astride the Dardanelles, 40,000 in the neighbourhood of Keshan (between Enos and Rodosto), and 100,000 in and around Constantinople. We could then march on the Chanak forts and the straits would be ours, he said.

After lunch Guranesco was trying to persuade Malinoff that the Dardanelles were already as good as ours. Malinoff did not believe in the existence of a British disembarkation force, still less in the possibility of the Russians sending troops by the Black Sea, but he was struck all of a heap by the list of German refugees from Constantinople who were looking for houses in Philipopolis, and filling the hotel at Bukarest. I thought that if it were true that Radoslavoff was already on our side, the thing had come with such a rush, namely the success of the fleet, that the opposition leaders such as Malinoff had been left standing, and the Government was hardening its heart for the fatal leap. They saw that we were not going to waste time with Greece, as we had occupied the islands and had already landed 72,000 men at Lemnos, only they did not quite believe that all this was true. Much depended on Paget's interview with the King. Colak Antich, the Serbian Minister, professed to know the King well and declared he was very impressionable.

On the 17th March Sir Arthur Paget left Sofia. He saw the King for over an hour on Tuesday evening, and was very pleased with his audience. The King was most cordial and said he could not express what good it had done him to see and talk with his old friend Paget. I knew that the King was gradually becoming a morbid recluse, and I could quite imagine how he enjoyed seeing a man of the world, and a soldier like Sir Arthur, and listened with the greatest attention to everything he had to say. The General told me that he avoided touching the political compensation question, but appealed to the King's vanity, and the magnificent opportunity that he now had to step into the alliance in the place of Greece, what a position that would give him, and what claims he would have to our regard and support in the eventual settlement of the Constantinople question. That there was all the difference between coming in now, and after the Dardanelles had fallen. Every now and then the King's head would droop, but when Paget talked to him in this sense, up went his head and he became a different man. I thought that the General was perhaps a little too confident about the immediate result of his audience, but there was not the least doubt that he had favourably impressed everybody, not only by his fine soldierlike appearance, but also by his frank open manners and the pains he had taken to be particularly nice to everybody. Even the way in which he disposed of champagne in tumblers, and the stories told of his fabulous wealth, had an effect upon the frugal-minded and sober Bulgars. I had no doubt he had been able to open the King's eyes as to the strength of the British, French and Russian armies, and perhaps to hint that we were prepared to use our strength in this direction, but up to the evening of the 16th, the King had not sent for Radoslavoff, and it had been intimated to me at the War Office here that the Enos-Midia line alone, would not be enough to induce the people to commence a war against Turkey, and that it would be difficult to mobilize the army without some definite reason being given. I had often been told that before, but personally I thought, (as events subsequently proved) that they could mobilize their men whenever they chose, and that naturally enough they were holding back to get the best bargain possible, especially as they had been already offered the Enos-Midia line in exchange for neutrality, from both sides.

On the 17th March, General Paget on leaving Sofia, sent a telegram to say he would be very much surprised if Bulgaria did not join us in a fortnight's time, barring some great defeat of the Entente. Since then the Russians had taken Pshemysl, and we had lost three or four ships in the Dardanelles, which completely changed the situation. I saw Fitcheff on the 23rd, and he had quite veered round. He said they had already discounted the fall of Pshemysl, but now they were not sure we were going to take the Dardanelles. That it was a long war, and they were going to remain neutral until they saw more clearly who was going to win. That whenever they came in, they would still be badly wanted. I said he was talking like a Roumanian; that if the Bulgars had decided which side they wanted to win, (he confessed it was the Triple Entente, but perhaps he lied) they could hasten their desired result, and make it doubly sure by coming in. This would bring in Roumania, Greece and perhaps Italy also. He was doubtful about Roumania, and said many people were of opinion that Roumania would go against us. I reassured him on this point and left him, after quoting the parable of the men working in the vineyard, and said it was very exceptional that labourers who came at the eleventh hour likewise received their penny.

Meanwhile there had been a great row about contraband of war passing through to Turkey. I had sent a telegram a few days before, reporting that the Bulgars had detained ten waggons at Rustchuk as suspect, and that there had been several barges on the Roumanian side loaded with contraband. This was on the authority of the Russian Military Attaché. It had stirred up Sir George Barclay and the Roumanian authorities with the result that the Bulgarian and Roumanian authorities had jointly examined these barges, and found no contraband. One had to accept that for gospel. Nevertheless, I was glad that the Foreign Office ordered us to have these railways and canals continuously watched by native agents, and this was done.

The Minister saw Radoslavoff at this time, and was told by him that Bulgaria would remain neutral. On the other hand Bourchier came to see me, and

CHAPTER NINE.

was triumphant at the favourable way in which things were going, and hinted that Radoslavoff was intentionally reserved. I had heard that General Pau, who had returned from Russia that morning, was to be received by the King, which was also a good sign. Moreover, there was news that the Germans were stopping all Bulgarian medical stores and munitions of war.

I was very sorry to hear that our first Secretary, O'Reilly, had just been recalled by the Foreign Office. I presume the reason was, that he had a German wife who was on visiting terms with the enemy. I knew that Morris, a young Naval Officer incapacitated from service, and at that time acting as private secretary to the Minister, was staying with them, and that, apart from anything else, was sufficient proof to me that they were absolutely discreet. O'Reilly was a very clever fellow and it was a misfortune his going at this moment as he kept in touch with Bourchier. Bourchier was an asset of great value, especially if kept under control and used judiciously.

A telegram arrived yesterday ordering us to send copies of all military information to General Sir Ian Hamilton, commanding the Allied troops at Lemnos. He had been my guest here for three days in 1908, shortly after my first appointment to Bulgaria and Serbia, so he knew something about the country, and I hoped I might have the opportunity of seeing him again.

On the 29th March I went to see Fitcheff at the War Office. I began by asking if he had any Turkish news, but there was nothing fresh except that South of Demotika they were fortifying against the Bulgars, and had built a tête-de-pont at Kuleli Burgas with the same object, which I had heard before. It was armed with six 15c.m. guns from Adrianople. He then told me very secretly that Radoslavoff's declaration in Parliament yesterday in favour of neutrality was a blind. Pourparlers had been going on between Sir Edward Grey and Hadji Mischeff the Bulgarian Minister in London, and he thought that a satisfactory solution had been arrived at, and the Bulgarian Goverment was now going to frame their offer. I was not to tell anybody this and I promised accordingly. I then spoke to him about a report I had heard from my French colleague, Count de Matharel, to the effect that he himself had seen several guns on a siding at Gorno Orekhovitza (the junction for the railway passing South from Rustchuk). The waggons contained one anti-aircraft gun and two others of about 10c.m. calibre, all bearing the Turkish arms and quite new. There were several waggons covered with tarpaulins in one of which were white boxes that must have contained ammunition. The waggons were labelled to Harmanli near the Turkish frontier and bore the inscription in Bulgarian "despatched under the surveillance of the customs." Fitcheff declared it was not true, was most indignant and said that if the French Military Attaché maintained this story, he would find himself in a very delicate position. Fitcheff had seen the Director of railways with whom de Matharel would be confronted on the following day. I told the General that the Military Attaché merely stated what he himself saw and that if the War Minister simply said he had told a lie, there would be trouble with France and that would be a pity, as negotiations were going on so nicely in London. Fitcheff then said "There has evidently been a misunderstanding, we have some Turkish guns since our war with Turkey, and they must have been going to the fortress of Shumla." It was difficult however to account for the custom's notice on the waggons. Fitcheff said it was only the day before that the Goverment was discussing the expediency, of also stopping the export of foodstuffs to Turkey. I then took my departure.

Arrived at my house, I found de Matharel, who told me he was going to see the Minister of War together with Morphoff, the Director of Railways, on the following day. I told him the result of my interview, and he said that he could not swear that the Custom's notice was on the waggons containing

CHAPTER NINE.

the guns, but it was certainly on the waggons which he believed held ammunition. I said, in that case I thought it would be better to give them a loophole and say he might have been mistaken about the guns, and as he had taken the numbers of the other waggons, he could ask to have them examined.

About this time I also had information that the Bulgars had placed some stacks of hay along the railway at Sarambey and Tatar-Bazardjik. This was significant, because there are roads leading South from these places towards Kavala.

On the 1st April, the Bulgarian papers contained rumours of negotiations borrowed from the Milanese paper " Stampa," that the Entente had offered Bulgaria territory in Macedonia up to the Vardar line at the end of the war, besides the Enos-Midia line. These rumours may have had their origin in London, but nothing was known about them here. At the same time I noticed in the local papers that Gueschoff had had another audience with the King, and I heard from Bourchier that the Bulgarian Government had ordered that no rolling stock should leave the country which might be a preliminary measure to mobilization. Another informant told me of a quantity of railway waggons being massed at Stara-Zagora.

About this time Garnett, the new secretary, arrived in the place of O'Reilly, and Fitzmaurice also arrived as supernumary with the rank of 1st Secretary. The latter was for many years Chief Dragoman at the Embassy at Constantinople and had an unrivalled knowledge of the Turk and of Turkish affairs.

On the 3rd April I heard from Bukarest that the War Office had declined to take up the question of the bullet proof shield. The inventor had asked for £500 down, £500 on arrival in London and £1,000 compensation if the invention were not taken up, which did not sound extravagant terms. But after two reminders from my successor, the War Office replied " nothing doing," and the inventor went to Constantinople to try and dispose of his invention.

I was very much disgusted at this, as I thought the Germans would get hold of a good thing. Seeing was believing in my case, and, added to the evidence of my own eyes as regarded the shooting test, my sprained wrist still gave me twinges to remind me that I had bent a sword bayonet in trying to pierce the lightest of the shields. This was before anything had been heard in this part of the world of steel helmets, and I often wondered what became of this Greek and of his invention.

On the 4th April the O'Reilly's left, taking a Foreign Office Bag. There had been a regular battle the day before, between Bulgarian comitadjis and Serbs in the direction of Strumnitza. There was a rumour that the line had been cut and that the Bulgars were regular soldiers. I was asked what I thought and I said it was certainly not the work of the Bulgarian Government which had no immediate interest in attacking Serbia. Had it occurred in Greek territory, that would have been another story, but it might have been due to Turks or Germans who could always hire comitadjis. There had also been a heavy snow storm, so the prospect was not alluring for the O'Reilly's journey.

On the 5th April a telegram arived from Athens, where the Ministers of the Triple Entente announced to their respective Governments in concert, that Dedeagatch was the best place to land, and that the Bulgarian Government should be asked at Sofia for permission to land there, refusal to be considered a hostile act. I quite understood the Greeks making that suggestion, but not that it should be seriously considered by the Entente Ministers. How could one expect Bulgaria to do this, apparently for nothing, when she was determined to profit by the present war, to make good her losses suffered by the treaty at Bukarest? She knew we were not strong enough to force a landing and smash Bulgaria, which was doubtless what the Greeks wanted us to try and do. But why on earth our Government did not clinch the bargain with the Bulgars while there was yet time, I could not conceive. What was

Macedonia or Serbia or Greece to us, compared with the necessity of beating the Germans? And why could we not combine an act of justice with our own interests by granting Bulgaria the 1912 line regardless of Serbian threats and objections, by order, without asking the Serbs for their permission? Then Serbia would yield to "force majeure and would not sacrifice her "amour propre." That combined, with a hint to Bulgaria that the Entente would favour the Bulgars' subsequent claim to Kavala at the close of the war, and the promise of a share of the war indemnity (Fitzmaurice's suggestion) would, I hoped, bring Bulgaria in. Fitcheff was itching to have the job of marching on Turkey in co-operation with the Entente troops, and, in that case, they might let us land at Dedeagatch, if that were really the best place, but we knew what a very poor landing that really was.

On the 6th April our Minister interviewed Gueschoff, and then despatched a telegram in reply to the one from Athens above mentioned, in which he pointed out that Bulgaria would not be satisfied with less than the Vardar line and Kavala, as a reward for coming in. He ignored, and rightly so, the possibility of demanding permission to land troops in Bulgaria without any adequate "quid pro quo." I thought it was not the time to haggle about the Vardar or the 1912 line now; that if Serbia could not realize that she would be wiped out altogether if the Entente did not win, and that she was handicapping us very heavily by her "non possumus" attitude, the thing should be arranged over her head. In the papers it was said that Serbian troops had been attacked by Macedonian bands, and fifty Serbs killed, the station at Strumnitza burnt, and two Serbian guns had been captured, but were subsequently retaken. The aggressors were local Turks and a few Bulgars and they were suppressed after heavy fighting. The papers attributed the rising to the reign of terror inaugurated by the Serbs in order to force the Bulgars into taking action against them, as in 1913, and in this way to bring upon them the vengeance of the Triple Entente. "But," commented the papers, "this time the Serbian intrigue will not succeed."

It was reported to me that the Bulgars at this time had been making some important defences at Eski-Jumia in support of the fortress of Shumla on which they had also been working. It was sad to note that both Roumanians and Bulgars were now beginning to fortify against each other after I had spent several months in my puny efforts to bring them together. I could only hope that perhaps they had not been altogether wasted, and that at any rate, neither Bulgaria nor Roumania had joined the enemy. Now that the War Office had practically told me that we were going to let Russia have Constantinople and the Dardanelles, it was more important than ever for Roumania to make friends with Bulgaria, and vice versa, in order to save themselves from both being swallowed up. But this was a point of view on which one could not discourse at this time, seeing that one was obliged to assume complete confidence in one's great Ally. The British Government, I heard subsequently, had had no choice in the matter of promising Constantinople to Russia, as the Czar had announced in no ambiguous terms that Russia had no interest in continuing the present war other than the prospect of obtaining Constantinople, and presumably with it the free passage, if not the control of the Dardanelles.

The "Utro" reported on this day the gist of a public lecture, given by a certain Professor Kavalevsky at Petrograd to the effect that Russia would never be satisfied with the neutralization of the Dardanelles, and that the unconditional surrender of Constantinople could alone guarantee a long European peace. Also that according to the "Russkoe Slovo" there had been negotiations between England, France and Russia, in which the Allies had acknowledged Russia's right to Constantinople and the Dardanelles. In exchange, Russia had acknowledged England's right to Egypt, Arabia

CHAPTER NINE.

and Mesopotamia, and France's right to expand in Syria. I reflected that the Balkan States would have no more doubts as to the fate of Constantinople if we won, and that our task would become correspondingly more difficult.

On the 7th April Fitzmaurice told us, during a discussion, when lunching with the Minister at the Legation, that if we wanted the Turks to destroy all the Embassies and St. Sophia and then sack the town, the way was for the Allies to attack them, which would prove a slow and lingering process. But if we wanted to save all that, then we should bring in the Bulgars. The Turks having got it once in the neck, now had the fear of the Bulgars in the marrow of their bones. Once they heard the Bulgars were coming in, they would have no time to sack the town, as they would be only thinking of how to save their own skins, Fitzmaurice also thought it was unwise for the Bulgars to ask for Kavala, which would fall to them anyhow later on.

According to the Serbian Military Attaché no post had reached Bulgaria from Austria for seven days, which he attributed to the rumour that the Austrians were transporting their troops from the Italian border to the Serbian, some 300,000 men. The inference was that Austria had somehow squared Italy, and there would be a combined Austro-German attack, which would commence from the direction of Sarajewo in about three weeks time. If this was true it was bad news, implying that Italy was lost to us. We were now three days over the fortnight within which General Paget had expected that the Bulgars would join us. The day before our Minister had gone to see Dobrovitch and had told him that until now, he himself, had been satisfied with Bulgarian neutrality, but that now he considered it was time for her to come in. What was her price? Dobrovitch had promised to speak to the King and had at the same time let out that some vague pourparlers had been going on between Sir E. Grey and Hadji Mischeff in London, to which he did not attach any particular importance.

So the War Minister had not deceived me after all the other day! I hoped that the rumour about Italy was not true, otherwise it would spoil everything.

On the 10th April I took Fitzmaurice to see the Minister of War, who continued to be most friendly, and on returning to the Legation, we found a telegram from Sir Edward Grey which we thought ought to do the trick. At last he had given way about the 1912 line, including Monastir, which was to be offered to Bulgaria by the Entente Ministers, who were to take care that the Opposition heard of the offer. It was to be conditional on Serbia getting Bosnia, etc., and an outlet on the Adriatic in return for Bulgaria joining in the war. But already I heard there were discordant opinions. Each Minister of Foreign Affairs of the Entente Powers had his own pet scheme, and each representative Minister here seemed to have his, so I feared that between them they would upset the apple cart if they possibly could, and I thought I would give my unsolicited opinion in support of strictly adhering to Grey's instructions.

On the following day it turned out as I feared. The French had always been down on the Bulgars and it seemed that M. Delcassé had another plan. In order to avoid giving Bulgaria a part of Serbia, he proposed to wait until Italy came in, or something of the sort. As soon as I heard this, I dashed off to Savinsky and told him that I thought this offer would go a long way towards bringing in the Bulgars and that it would be a great mistake to stave it off in favour of some other plan. There was a suggestion apparently from the Russian and British Ministers, he told me, that it was useless to make this offer, and that it would be better to force the situation by carrying out a landing of the allies at Burgas and Dedeagatch. I said it would do no harm to try Sir E. Grey's plan first—in fact it was a necessary preliminary to the second plan. Supposing we had made this offer and it had been refused by the Government, we should then make it public, wait a few days to see the effect, and then if it had not

CHAPTER NINE.

worked sufficiently, carry out the landing. We should then have already won the sympathy of the whole country, especially the very powerful Macedonian party, and there could be no opposition. Savinsky saw this. I told him the War Minister was on our side, naturally he wanted the job of commanding the army in the field and he knew they would not readily fight against us. Savinsky promised to see Panafiew, the French Minister, and talk to him. Then I saw Count Matharel and reiterated the same idea. Fitzmaurice lunched with Savinsky and I believe backed up this suggestion. So I heard the next day that both the Russian and French Ministers had telegraphed to their respective Governments asking permission to join our Minister in making the 1912 proposal.

On the same day, 11th April, I saw the War Minister and had a very interesting conversation which I telegraphed to the Foreign Office. It was to the effect that the proposals in London to Hadji Mischeff, both by Grey and Lloyd George, although slightly different, were each acceptable in the opinion of the War Minister. He would not tell me what they were, but I gathered that the 1912 line without Kavala might do, but it would depend on the Bulgarian Government. He added that the Bulgarian army could not begin to mobilize before the end of April old style, and that the mobilization would take two weeks. The army was still lacking in uniforms, tents, etc. The General then gave me a further list in detail of all the Turkish troops available for Constantinople and the Dardanelles. He asked me whether the Greeks would attack Bulgaria. I said certainly not, if Bulgaria were our ally, as we could suppress her at once by sea. All the same he said he would leave three Divisions to watch that frontier, and that before marching against the Turks it would be necesary to make an arrangement with Roumania, which would take time. I replied that we knew that Roumania was ready to cede Dobrovitch and Baltchik and that it was no use asking for more, but that could be fixed up in 24 hours. I then asked if we could count on the Bulgars to help us if necessary at once with a few divisions as he could not carry out a full mobilization in time. I was asking these questions in view of the possibility of my going to Lemnos to see our General Officer commanding who would be sure to want such information. Fitcheff said no—if they went to war at all, they would go with their whole force and not piecemeal. I then asked him whether he would be ready to carry on against Austria after that, as soon as we had finished with the Turks, and he replied " of course, once in this war we shall go through with it, with all our might." Fitcheff also said that the Bulgars had only got three months supply of ammunition and that as soon as matters were arranged she would begin to ask us for ammunition. I recommended the Government to agree to this at once but not actually hand over until she were irretrievably compromised on our side. I decided to leave the following night for Dedeagatch, the Bulgarian Government supplying me with two motors. This expedition was to combine a visit to Sir Ian Hamilton at Lemnos with escorting Lady Bax-Ironside on her way out from home, from Dedeagatch to Sofia.

Chapter Ten.

VISIT TO LEMNOS — INTERVIEW WITH SIR IAN HAMILTON — CONFERENCE ON BOARD STAFF TRANSPORT — SUGGESTION FOR LANDING IN GULF OF SAROS — RETURN TO SOFIA — WAR MINISTER READY TO CO-OPERATE IF POLITICAL NEGOTIATIONS SUCCEED — NEWS OF LANDING ON GALLIPOLI PENINSULA — GREEKS ENDEAVOUR TO QUARREL WITH BULGARIA — NEWS FROM GALLIPOLI POINTS TO A LONG CAMPAIGN — BULGARIAN CABINET IGNORES ADVICE OF WAR MINISTER AND PREFERS TO REMAIN NEUTRAL — RUSSIAN DEFEAT IN GALICIA — FITZMAURICE ADVISES OFFER OF 1912 LINE — ITALY DECLARES WAR ON AUSTRIA — BULGARIAN ARMY RECOVERS ITS SPIRIT — CONSEQUENT DANGER OF WAR WITH SERBIA — BAD NEWS FROM GALLIPOLI — FORMAL OFFER OF 1912 LINE BY ENTENTE MINISTERS — FALL OF PSHEMYSL — RUSSIAN MILITARY ATTACHE DESPONDENT AND ITALIAN MINISTER DEPRESSED — VISIT OF CAPTAIN AMERY-FITZMAURICE'S INTERVIEW WITH WAR MINISTER — FRICTION BETWEEN BULGARIA AND TURKEY — VISIT OF SIR MARK SYKES — IMPROBABILITY OF NOW SECURING BULGARIA'S AID.

AT the last moment Fitzmaurice decided to come with me. We sent a telegram to ask Admiral de Robeck to send a boat to Dedeagatch to take us to Lemnos to see him and General Sir Ian Hamilton. That night there was a dinner at the Roumanian Legation to ourselves and the Italians. Rather suggestive that! I went straight on from the dinner to the station in de Russi's motor at 11 p.m. We got to Haskovo on the railway at 7.30 the following morning, found a War Office motor car and lorry waiting for us and started off.

The road, which had been constructed, or at any rate very much improved, by the Bulgars since their recent acquisition of Gumuljina, was fairly good as far as Kirjali, and very good from there to Gumuljina, where we arrived at 5.30 p.m., and came in sight of the sea. But the wet weather, combined with the newness of the road, made travelling difficult and we had great trouble in passing several fords, while some of the bridges were distinctly bad. In the mountains the zig-zags were rather sharp and there were no parapets. We were obliged to stay at Gumuljina on the night of the 13th April and continue our journey by train at 4 o'clock the following afternoon, reaching Dedeagatch that evening. Here we were met by the British Consul, and we found H.M.S. Agamemnon outside the three mile limit, and a boat was coming ashore to take us off. We had been half expected the day before. Admiral de Robeck was an old friend of Fitzmaurice and perhaps it was to that we owed this civility. But in any case the idea of sending a first class battleship to pick us up was an excellent one. Captain Fyler, in command of the battleship, had improved the occasion by inviting the principle officers of Dedeagatch to come on board and look over the ship, and gave them a salute of nine guns. The whole thing made an immense impression. It was the first time any battleship had visited their coast. They were at first afraid of a bombardment, and afterwards delighted. Both salutary!

Arrived at Lemnos on Thursday morning the 15th April, we found that Admiral de Robeck and Sir Ian Hamilton were starting out on a reconnaissance of the Dardanelles, and we had to spend the day hanging about, but we visited the Queen Elizabeth, a magnificent sight, lunched there with Captain Hope and the officers, met the French Admiral Guepratt, and visited the Captain of the Russian ship Askold. Then we boarded the Staff Transport and met Major General Braithwaite, Chief of the Staff, Colonels Ward and Doughty-Wyllie, respectively G.S.O. 1 and 2 for Intelligence; Colonel Williams, G.S.O. Operations, and General Hunter Weston, commanding the 29th Division. Captain Fyler then shewed us over the Agamemnon which had been in action on the 25th February, and had been hit in sveral places without being seriously damaged. Howitzers did more destruction than anything else, the shells going through a couple of decks, one very near the magazine. In the evening the Admiral and General Hamilton returned in the

CHAPTER TEN.

Triumph, which had a pretty hot time, being hit more than once. I slept on board the Staff Ship so was able to see the General after dinner. I gathered that he did not think the Gallipoli Peninsula was a nice place to attack, and it was a thousand pities that we did not have a Division of British troops ready to disembark when we swept up the Dardanelles so triumphantly in March. I told him that Col. Jekoff (Assistant Chief of the Staff and subsequently Commander in Chief) advised landing either at Melexler or Ibrije and marching on Keshan, but that the Bulgars were not in a habit of doing things by halves, and they were pre-supposing that we had a force of 200,000 men. Hamilton told me he had not got more than a certain number between 80,000 and 90,000, (as far as I recollect, for I purposely did not record the figure), and had to be careful of his ammunition.

The next morning, 16th April, we were up early at 6 o'clock. Lemnos harbour was a magnificent sight, almostly completely land-locked, and containing about seventy big ships, including men of war and transports, together with innumerable smaller craft. I had hoped to see the men practising landing from what the General told me, but unfortunately nothing was to be seen from our ship except a few men in boats rowing haphazard as far as I could see, but the harbour was immense. Later on Fitzmaurice and I were summoned to a conference on board the Staff Transport. The Admiral, Sir Ian Hamilton, Captain Keyes and others were there. Our suggestion was whether it were possible to postpone operations until we could tell what the result of the present negotiations with Bulgaria would be. Fitzmaurice's object was to induce the Admiral or General to telegraph home that the Bulgar's aid was indispensable, and that Fitzmaurice and I considered the offer of the 1912 line coupled with a friendly demand from the Tzar of Russia, for Bulgaria's acquiescence in a landing at Burgas would bring them in. I, however, demurred at this combination. I thought the 1912 line should in any case be offered, but I was doubtful about the landing at Burgas. That was a very delicate matter and I had not even ventured to moot it to the Minister of War. I had sounded the Russian Military Attaché and he also had not thought it practicable. On the other hand Radoslavoff had privately invited Savinsky to do it without asking, and both the Russian and French Ministers were in favour of it. Remembering in past years the extreme jealousy that Bulgaria had always shewn whenever there was a question of Russia even making a coal depot at Burgas, I stuck to my opinion that Bulgaria ought to be given a chance of coming in herself on the 1912 line in Macedonia with the Enos-Midia line thrown in, quite apart from the Burgas landing question. Then if that failed, and the Opposition could make no headway with the King, It would be time to insist on a landing at Burgas and adopt coercive measures generally. For the Tzar to make a friendly demand was not the same thing from Radoslavoff's point of view as doing it without asking. This difference of opinion annoyed Fitzmaurice who had not previously discussed this point with me and gave Hamilton the opportunity to say it was quite clear that Bulgaria was not coming in until the Allies had done something in the direction of the Dardanelles, and that he was going ahead with his plans independently of the Balkan States and their affairs. I suggested to Fitzmaurice that he should telegraph to the Foreign Office himself as he had told me he was privileged to do, but to this he would not agree. The conference terminated.

I had mentioned to Doughty-Wyllie what Colonel Jekoff had said about landing either at Melexler (between Enos and Ibrije) or Ibrije where there was deep water, on the North shore of the Gulf, and suggested telegraphing it home. Wyllie was delighted. Hamilton asquiesced but said that he did not want to see the telegram. Then when I gave Wyllie the telegram, the latter suggested that it would carry more weight if Hamilton backed it, I told him that the General preferred me to do it independently. But now that it was in cypher, thanks to Wyllie, I had no objection, quite the contrary, if he could get Sir Ian to back it. He tried. The result was that the General forbade me to send it from the ship at all. I accordingly told him that I would send it myself as soon as I got to Dedeagatch. Wyllie then gave me a private wire from himself to FitzGerald,* Lord Kitchener's secretary, to despatch at the same time in which he requested FitzGerald to draw Lord Kitchener's attention to Colonel Napier's number so and so to the Foreign Office. Fitzmaurice and I then left the transport, called on the French Admiral and went on board the Dublin a fast cruiser which took us back to Dedeagatch.

After steaming through the night at 7 knots without lights, we arrived at Dedeagatch, where we found Lady Bax-Ironside arrived from England and waiting for us. I sent my telegrams, and we started for Gumuljina, where we found the Bulgarian War Office motors at 11 a.m. We managed the return journey very comfortably. The road was in good order, having dried up, and repairs were being carried out very rapidly. Miles of stones were being laid, and a steam roller was at work. After sleeping the night at Haskovo we took the train and arrived at Sofia on Sunday afternoon the 18th April.

On the 20th April I saw the War Minister and urged him to hurry up. He said that we could land at Dedeagatch (the Bulgars had never had any jealousy about that, as they knew we had no designs of a permanent occupation), and that he would co-operate from Demotika, but all depended upon the success of political negotiations first. I wired to the Foreign Office accordingly. De Russi came to see me, likewise the Serbian Minister, both equally curious to know what had passed, but I did not enlighten them.

On the 21st April the Minister of War saw me. I told him that the Allies would not wait a month or more for Bulgaria, in response to his statement that

---

*FOOTNOTE—" On meeting FitzGerald a few months later, I ascertained from him that these telegrams were duly received, but it was not possible to pay attention to every suggestion which came to hand."

however the negotiations went, the Bulgarian army could not be ready before the last week in May. Although Bulgarian aid was not essential, it was always better to have timely co-operation in war. I asked him, supposing negotiations were concluded very quickly, could he not aid us by at least mobilizing the Bulgarian army? Even the commencement of a mobilization threatening Turkey would draw off troops. He promised to speak to Radoslavoff about this, and repeated that as soon as Bulgaria came in, we could use the port of Dedeagatch and the railway and that he had a plan for co-operating by placing the Bulgarian army at Demotika. He was glad to hear that the road I had come along from Gumuljina was in good order, as it would be needed if the railway broke down. He added that the work was going on on the road via Ksanti. I drafted a telegram containing the gist of these remarks, but it was not sent. The Minister said he was afraid it would give Sir Ian Hamilton a false impression that the Bulgars were coming in. I replied that it would be a good thing if he were to add a rider to my telegram to counteract that. I only discussed the military side of the question and if the Entente did not settle the political side, of course the army would not move.

The Minister said " You know as well as I, that the Government is hostile. You have seen all the telegrams." I replied that the Bulgars had never yet had a serious offer approaching to what they had always stated unofficially to be their price. Once that was done, and it was clear that they would not come in or force the King and Government to change their attitude, then we could take whatever measures were necessary to coerce her, but I did not think it was fair to say the country was hostile until it had been put to the proof. I therefore, declined to alter my telegram and eventually induced him to add a very satisfactory rider that until they got an offer, the situation could not be cleared.

In the afternoon I saw Morphoff, The Director of Railways, having heard that he had just returned

CHAPTER TEN.

from Constantinople. He told me that he had gone there in order to force the Turks to disgorge 200 waggons which should have been in use on the Dedeagatch portion of the railway. He had some difficulty, but they eventually gave way, and he had got eight locomotives in addition. This left the Turks with only 900 sound waggons in Europe. The number in Bulgaria was between 4,000 and 5,000. Morphoff then gave me some details of the disposition of the Turkish forces, both in Europe and in Asia, and said that Djemal Pasha was coming back and his expedition to the Suez Canal was regarded as a complete failure. The Turks were very mistrustful of the Bulgars, and Halil Bey had gone to Europe two or three weeks previously on a special mission to induce the Germans and Austrians to send an expedition against Serbia, and in order to keep the Bulgars from coming in against the Turks.

On the 26th April I heard that the Russians had again postponed making Bulgaria the offer of the 1912 line or something approaching to it, on the grounds that it would be better to wait until Italy came in. I reflected that here we were unable to judge of the situation as a whole, because we did not know what Italy was doing or what troubles they might not be having at home over the Dardanelles question, but our troops were still waiting in their transports, and Greeks, Turks and Roumanians were all working hard to embroil us with Bulgaria. None of these powers liked the idea of Bulgaria coming in with us, and I suspected Russia of the same sentiments, although she pretended otherwise.

On the 29th April there was good news from the Admiralty that our troops had successfully effected a landing on the Gallipoli Peninsula, and it was reported to-day that 29,000 men had landed.

The Greek and Russian Military Attachés came to see me. The Greek wanted confirmation of Bulgarian conferences with the Turks at Adrianople, and the Russian said it was possible they had been invited to meet the Turks and could not refuse in order not to disclose their attitude prematurely.

I told the Greek that his Government was not doing the Entente a good turn by trying to pick a quarrel with the Bulgars. If the Greeks really thought that Bulgaria was likely to commence an attack on Greece without provocation they must have got this idea from the Greek Legation here. If these apprehensions were sincere, their best safeguard would be to join the Entente openly at once, but I was afraid the real truth was, that the Greeks were not sure which side was going to win. He acknowledged that, and said the German Emperor's recent telegram sent openly to the Queen of Greece was quite genuine, saying " Woe to those who go against me! I guarantee the final victory of Germany."

About this time a very interesting man arrived from Constantinople, by name Fraser. He had had had to leave Constantinople, as the American Government had discovered that he was using an American passport on the strength of having been born in the United States, although of British parentage and being a British subject. He had begun the war as an officer with a special commission, and was an interpreter with the Indian Corps, speaking English, French and German like a native of each country. In Constantinople he had been hobnobbing with German naval officers and gave me information as to where aerial attacks on Constantinople should be made. He said that until a fortnight previously, German officers had worn fezzes and Turkish uniforms, now they wore German uniforms. This did not sound as if the Germans had lost the confidence of the Turks as had been reported to me from another source. He also said that they were much afraid of an attack from the Bulgars, but otherwise did not fear the Entente as they considered 300,000 men would be needed to carry the Straits, and they did not believe, and rightly so, that we had anything like that number. But as regards the Suez Canal expedition his information was contradictory to that reported to me by Morphoff, for he declared that the Suez Canal expedition was going steadily forward, and that its light railway would be finished in seven weeks time, which would enable them to bring heavy artillery against us and attack us again with much greater chance of success. Another piece of information from Fraser was that German Officers in Constantinople, were daily expecting the arrival of two submarines, and I presumed that they must be coming by the Danube, as they could not come by rail through Bulgaria. I now heard confirmation of the submarines from the Russian Naval Attaché as having passed Gibraltar, doubtless accompanied by a neutral ship which kept them supplied with petrol. (I was subsequently to learn from sad experience that the German submarines carried sufficient petrol on board to enable them to voyage from Hamburg to Pola without replenishing their stores.) It was reported also that an Austrian submarine had blown up the Leon Gambette, a French cruiser, on the 27th April, 20 miles from Santa Maria de Luce.

On the 4th May our news from the Dardanelles continued to be satisfactory, although it seemed likely to be a long operation before the Peninsula could be captured. I saw the Minister of War, who had just returned from a tour of inspection. He told me that he had informed the Cabinet that Bulgaria ought to march with the Triple Entente, and he added that the Entente should make a definite offer of the 1912 line in order to arouse the enthusiasm of the nation before mobilization. On the other hand, Sir Henry Bax-Ironside had reported that the Cabinet Council a few days previously had come to the conclusion that Germany and Austria would win, and that Bulgaria should therefore remain neutral. This was very disquieting because, if true, it meant that the Cabinet was ignoring the advice of the War Minister, and that the situation must be critical. I did not believe in a neutral Bulgaria. The army was for use and not for show, and I thought if they were not with us, they would be against us before very long. I had drafted a telegram about my interview with the War Minister, but had decided not to send it as I had been officially warned by the War Office to be very careful about reporting such semi-political conversations with the Minister of War. I now, however, sent my telegram, because if the Minister's information were correct, the offer of the 1912 line should no longer be delayed, and that it was the enemy's game to spread mistrust of Bulgaria amongst the Allies. Regarding Italy we could form no opinion as to whether it were necessary to wait for her or not. We had to look at the question from a local point of view which was our "raison d'etre" so my estimate necessarily had reference solely to the Bulgarian situation.

On the 8th May according to the Bulgarian papers, Filipesco had publicly announced at Bukarest that Italy had joined the Triple Entente. A telegram arrived from Sir Edward Grey instructing the Minister to inform the Bulgarian Government that up to the present we had been able to decline any conditions that conflicted with the just aspirations of the Bulgars, but we were also negotiating with other neutral Powers, and that this state of affairs could not long continue. This excellent hint that Bulgaria might outstay her market produced from Radoslavoff a definite quotation of conditions under which Bulgaria would come in. They were rather heavy, namely the 1912 line including all the disputed zone together with Kavala, Seres and Drama. Also the Enos Midia line in Thrace.

On the 12th May three classes of reservists were called out in succession for three weeks training, continuing up to the 8th July for the last, the 1912 class. Reserve officers were called up for one month's training from the 1st May to the 1st June. They probably amounted to about 2,000 officers.

On the 13th May the public telegrams reported a great Russian defeat in Galicia with the loss of 143,000 prisoners. It was extraordinary that whenever we had managed to get the Entente near to a decisive offer, something happened to give us a set back.

CHAPTER TEN.

On the 17th May as the result of an enquiry from the Foreign Office as to Fitzmaurice's views on the situation, he gave it as his opinion that in spite of Russia's recent defeat in the Carpathians, the offer of the 1912 line should be made to Bulgaria.

On the 20th May the Italian Commercial Attaché informed me that it was a certainty that Italy would join the Entente. A telegram arrived from the Foreign Office in which Sir Edward Grey authorized the Minister to make the Bulgars the offer of the line Egri Palanka, Sopot, Koprulu, and Ochrida, including all the part of Macedonia, between that line and the Greek frontier. Also the Enos-Midia line, which could be occupied immediately, while the Macedonian territory could only be had after the war, and then contingent on Serbia obtaining Bosnia and Herzogovina and an outlet on the Adriatic. The Entente would also endeavour to secure Kavala for the Bulgars. This was good news. The Russians and the French after some palaver agreed to join our Minister in making this offer, but a short delay was necessary because the wording of the Russian instructions differed a little from ours. They offered Kavala outright to the Bulgars, ours said we would try to get it for them. The Russians eventually agreed to our wording. Then came another blow, the French Foreign Minister did not agree to make any offer until the Greek elections were over, on the chance of Venizelos coming back.

On the 23rd May according to the public telegrams, Italy declared war on Austria.

On the 26th May I saw the War Minister who said that the Bulgars were getting more inclined for war every day, and there was a great change in the army which had quite regained its old confidence and was keen on fighting. I had also noticed this myself. The recovery had been remarkably rapid and was largely due to a popular song which commenced with the words "Soyuznitzi, Razboinitzi," meaning "Allies, robbers" and referred to the events of the late war of 1912-13 when the Serbs and

Greeks conspired to rob the Bulgars of the fruits of their victory over the Turks at Adrianople. The words had been set to a good rousing tune, probably by the Germans. The schools took it up, followed by the army and the man in the street. It thus became an easy task to fan the flame of hatred of the Bulgars against our Allies, and proved a clever piece of propaganda on the part of our enemies. General Fitcheff, referring to Italy, now said he did not think her participation would shorten the war owing to the difficult nature of the terrain in which she would have to fight. As for the Gallipoli Peninsula, he declared that the Turks had 100,000 men there and he declined to believe that there was the slightest chance that the defences would soon fall. The gist of his remarks pointed to the fact that, although Italy had come in, the Entente still had as great need of Bulgaria as ever, and that therefore the latter could afford to continue sitting on the fence, without the danger of losing her market. I left him with the conviction that they would rather see Roumania come into the war first, than take the plunge themselves at present. I suggested to Bax-Ironside that it was improbable that Bulgaria would now jump at the Triple Entente offer, but would prefer to continue bargaining, and in view of that I drafted a telegram suggesting that the Bulgars should be given a time limit of one month within which to attack Turkey, failing which the offer would no longer hold good. The Minister did not, however, approve of this, so I did not insist on my telegram going forward to the Foreign Office, which would have been useless under the circumstances, but I asked him to put the idea before his colleagues and ascertain what they thought. Fitzmaurice, I found, also did not approve of my suggestion. I then went to see Morphoff, who had just returned from a visit to Bukarest and Buda-Pesth, which had been successful, as he had been able to release some 300 waggon-loads of wheel bands and seventeen waggons of medical stores which had been hung up in Austria. This was rather significant of better relations with Roumania, as hitherto, she had not permitted the passage of these stores. But it also shewed that Austria had equal hopes with ourselves of obtaining Bulgaria as an ally.

On the 27th May I saw De Russi. Radeff had arrived from Bukarest that morning concerned with the question of ceding territory to Bulgaria in the Dobrudja. De Russi had consequently been told not to interfere in the matter. But I gathered from his conversation with reference to the Kutso-Vlakhs in Macedonia, some 400,000 in number, and considered as Roumanians, that there would be further complications and delays in making any arrangement with Bulgaria, and that these two countries would not be likely to settle their differences without the interference of the Entente.

The French had now at last agreed to our proposals regarding the formal offer to Bulgaria. Meanwhile the Triumph and the Majestic had both been sunk; we had news of the presence of four enemy submarines in the Dardanelles and Sea of Marmora and feared perhaps the Gallipoli expedition would have to be abandoned.

On the 29th May the Ministers of France, Russia, Italy and Great Britain went in a body and communicated the offer of the Entente to Radoslavoff in writing, adding verbally a request for a speedy reply.

The following day I saw the Minister of War at his private residence. He hinted that further demands in the direction of Kavala might be put forward by the Bulgarian Government. I was afraid that a second refusal from Bulgaria might put the Entente off altogether and the other Balkan States would get their chance. He then said it was very important to please the peasants by letting them get their harvest in first. That would mean a delay until the middle of July, after which a fortnight would be needed for mobilization. I said that I imagined our Government gave the preference to Bulgaria because she was on the spot and they thought she could move the quickest, but if this were not so, perhaps they would not be so anxious for her assistance. He then said it was not absolutely necessary to wait for the harvest, but in any case they could not move for another month. He would mobilize ten divisions of three brigades plus one Macedonian division of two brigades. He would also put six regiments of militia into the Gumuljina district to keep the Mahommedan population quiet there. This time he would pass Adrianople on the West side. (It was Fitcheff who had planned the campaign against the Turks in the last war when they had passed Adrianople on the East side. There were roads that could be used in the summer time which would enable him to concentrate a big force south-west of Adrianople for operations in the direction of Gallipoli, while another force marched on Chataldja.

I then took my leave. I was much afraid that negotiations between Roumania and Bulgaria could not be settled without the direct interference of the Entente which might cause much delay. I therefore addressed a telegram to the Foreign Office saying that if there were any further negotiations, I strongly recommended the Entente to put a time limit of say one month on their offer, otherwise Diplomats would go on talking interminably. However at Fitzmaurice's request I held back this telegram.

By this time my wife had joined me from England, and on the 4th June we arranged to take a short railway trip with M. and Mme. Morphoff. As Chief Director of the Bulgarian railways, Morphoff had a whole waggon to himself complete with kitchen, saloon and sleeping apartments, so we were very comfortable. Our first halting place was Philippopolis from whence we passed through Stara Zagora, where we heard that a landslip had occurred in the night and that the railway to Tirnovo was impassable. At a wayside station beyond Stara Zagora we were met by M. Shipkov, one of the richest rose-essence distillers, and he insisted on taking us in his car to see the rose gardens at

CHAPTER TEN.

Kazanlik, and the Shipka Pass, about twenty miles off. M. Shipkov proved to be a great politician and consequently a terrible bore. His idea was to get hold of me and convert me to the Bulgarian cause. After enduring the process of conversion for about two hours, I entreated Morphoff to tell him I had long since been converted, which, fortunately for my Bulgarophil sentiments, caused him to slack off. We drove through some fields of roses and saw the distilleries in which the essence is made. This industry had been going on here with native distilleries for about two hundred years but had only comparatively recently been worked on modern lines. To give an idea of the value of the industry, one kilogram of rose essence is worth about 2,000 francs. Work is only carried on for one month during the year when the roses are in bloom, but Shipkov is reputed to be a millionaire. Shipkov had some influence in the country and told me that two days ago, he had sent a long political telegram to the King urging him to stick to England.

As there was no possibility of going to Tirnovo owing to the landslip, we returned to Philippopolis and so back to Sofia. On our arrival, the fall of Pshemysl had just been announced and the Bulgarian Government issued a sort of unofficial notification to the Press, that Bulgaria would remain neutral, and I feared this was likely to be the case. In the afternoon I went round to the Russian Military Attaché and found him in very low spirits. He said the Bulgars would not come in now, even if they were offered unlimited rewards. He thought we ought to give up the Dardanelles expedition and concentrate on the main theatre of war. Russia was not able to spare troops for these diversions. The want of ammunition was very serious, because Russia could only manufacture 20,000 rounds a day. However, it was not, he said, necessary to open the Dardanelles on that account, as they could get all that could be made via Arkangel and the Siberian railway. Japan could supply a little, but at present the fact was we could not manufacture enough in

France or England or even America. Lack of ammunition was the cause of the " débâcle" at Pshemysl. He also gave me some information regarding the passage of contraband to Turkey.

On the 28th May 160 empty waggons had reached Dobrudja from Roumania for the Turkish railway. They were discovered to have double sides with ammunition packed in between. This was also confirmed by Fitcheff who told me that he had made the discovery and had sent Morphoff to examine the others, at the same time confiscating 21 of them which had come on to Sofia owing to the landslip on the Tirnovo railway.

Cucchi Boasso, the Italian Minister was also very depressed at this time, and much annoyed that Roumania had not come in together with Italy. He also told me that a constant flow had begun of Germans, chiefly officers, artisans and engineers to and from Turkey via Roumania and Bulgaria, and this in spite of all remonstrances regarding the laws of neutrality.

On the 5th June Captain Amery, M.P., arrived from England bringing a Foreign Office Bag, and asked me to present him to the War Minister. But having had no instructions from the War Office, and Fitcheff being engaged, we put this off until he should return from Bukarest in a few days. The same day he showed me a telegram which he had drafted to the Government at home, the gist of it being that it was hopeless to try and bring Bulgaria in. I reserved my judgement on that, but agreed with his concluding sentence that it was useless to base any plans for the near future on the assumption of Bulgarian co-operation.

On the following day, two Englishmen, residents of Constantinople, who had arrived the night before, gave me some interesting but disagreeable information regarding the strength of the Turkish position generally, and their confidence that the Dardanelles could not be forced. The one, a Mr. Kingham, was a Director of the National Bank of Turkey and

Military Attaché M.

I was bound to credit his information, which I telegraphed home without comment.

On the following day I took Fitzmaurice to see the War Minister as he wished to complete his conversion. He wanted a good innings, and I suggested half an hour. As a matter of fact, he talked to Fitcheff for two hours and a quarter. They both looked exhausted in the end and Fitcheff was delighted when I at last dragged Fitzmaurice away. But the conversation was very interesting. Fitzmaurice explained point by point the details of our offer, how it placed three keys in the hands of the Bulgars to unlock the doors of the Dobrudja, Macedonia and Kavala. But he spent at least half an hour on trivialities as one would in dealing with an oriental in order to get him into an agreeable and receptive frame of mind. Fitcheff ended by saying that nothing could be done without a Balkan alliance, with Roumania, Serbia, and Greece and much as he hated all of them, he would be ready to put aside his private enmities for the sake of a great cause.

The worst of having to approach the Bulgarian fortress by regular sap like this was that it would take endless time. It was perhaps necessary under the circumstances, but the offer to Bulgaria of a little or a big piece of each of her neighbours was bound to put them all against her which was sufficient to prevent her from moving. My original plan had been to induce Bulgaria to make friends with Roumania first and then get Macedonia from the Serbs, leaving the Kavala question alone. That would have left them with one enemy only, who was already fully occupied and they would thus have been able to attack Turkey without incurring the enmity also of Greece, but as the war has gone on, it shewed up more clearly the great strength of the Germans and the inability or unwillingness of the Balkan States to look at the war from anything but a purely Balkan and individual State point of view, and I much doubted our ever getting the help of the Bulgars until we no longer needed it. About this time there was an increase in the passing of contraband of war through Bulgaria to Turkey. Several aeroplanes flew over the Danube from Orshovo to Turkey, and two or three of them had to land in Bulgaria and the driver was allowed to go on to Turkey. I also heard from the Russian Military Attaché that two aeroplanes which the Bulgars confiscated nearly two months before had now been sent on towards the Turkish frontier.

On the 11th June I saw the War Minister and tackled him about the contraband. He gave fairly satisfactory answers, but there was no doubt that some members of the Cabinet, notably Tontcheff, Minister of Finance, would do anything to help the Germans, and it was he who gave orders for petrol landed at Varna to be loaded up for Turkey. Fitcheff said the Government had given orders to stop it. I asked him about the Entente Note and he replied that the answer of the Bulgarian Government would reach us in a day or two but he could not give us the contents beforehand though he implied that they were settled. I then sounded him about the supposed negotiations between Bulgaria and Turkey. He told me that the Bulgarian Government was demanding from Turkey the unconditional surrender of the Dedeagatch railway line, and that he did not anticipate that the Turkish Government would give way, the eventual result of which might be a war between Bulgaria and Turkey. I did not altogether trust this frank statement but thought it probable that Bulgaria would accept the Turkish offer which I knew the Germans were urging Turkey to make in exchange for Bulgarian neutrality. One thing was clear however, that the Bulgars were determined to have this line.

On the 16th June Sir Mark Sykes arrived from home. He told me he was an officer " de liaison " regarding the affairs in Turkey, and that the question began at Sofia and ended at Hyderabad; four totally different departments dealt with it, namely the Foreign Office, the Fleet and the Expeditionary Force of the Dardanelles, Cairo, and the Viceroy of

India, and that he would be the connecting link between them. He asked me what was going on at the Dardanelles and whether there were any grounds for the optimistic speeches of Winston Churchill and Runciman. Of course, I knew nothing, but promised to wire to Sir Ian Hamilton and try to find out, as it would be useful for this Legation to know also. I doubted if Hamilton would be pleased at getting my telegram, and this turned out to be the case. His reply, however, that he could not answer such a question convinced me that we had no good news to expect. But of course, this reply took some days to arrive. Meanwhile I telegraphed home my summary of the present situation here. It was to the effect that Bulgaria would not come in at present, first because the offer was not definite enough, secondly guarantees were not good, and that they believed they would have to fight another war with the Serbs in order to get what we were promising them for this one. Thirdly they were not satisfied that we were going to win. We were in a worse position than we had been in for many months. The Russians had had a severe defeat in Galicia and there was every probability that Lemberg would fall and the Russians be useless to us for some time to come. It was also uncertain whether Italy could influence the war to such an extent as to render another invasion of Serbia impossible.

The only thing to do at present was to try and define our offers of territory and to make sure that Bulgaria would get what was promised to her.

A conversation which I had at this time with the Aide-de-Camp to the War Minister when waiting in the ante room, was rather significant. The A.D.C., remarked that Russia was bearing the whole brunt of the war and was losing thousands while the French and ourselves were losing tens and hundreds. At Gallipoli he heard, doubtless from the Germans, that we were making no progress. He considered the Roumanians were " regular artists " at avoiding the war. They had been shouting all the time for the Entente and had promised Italy to come in with them. Meanwhile Italy had come in and there they were still neutral. I refrained from telling him that I thought Bulgaria was no mean artist either, lest I should dry up a source of information.

Further troubles at this time occurred regarding contraband, in spite of our urgent remonstrances, especially with regard to the passing of aeroplanes and hydroplanes.

A letter also arrived from Thomson very pessimistic about Roumania, and saying that if the Russians had offered them what they were offering now they would have joined the war at the beginning of May. Certainly if we could have made our negotiations with Bulgaria coincide with the entry of Italy and Roumania I thought we would have had the game in our own hands and the Russians would not have been driven out of Galicia. How the Powers had bungled this Balkan question!

Chapter Eleven.

CHIEF OF STAFF'S VIEWS REGARDING POINT OF ATTACK ON GALLIPOLI REPEATED—BULGARIA'S NON-COMMITTAL REPLY TO ENTENTE OFFER—ARRIVAL OF O'BEIRNE—DEPARTURE OF SIR H. BAX-IRONSIDE—ENTENTE MINISTERS SUGGEST OCCUPATION OF MACEDONIA BY BULGARIAN OR BY ENTENTE TROOPS—ARRIVAL OF SIR V. CHIROL—I ADVISE DESPATCH OF 100,000 ENTENTE TROOPS BASED ON SALONIKA IN PREFERENCE TO O'BEIRNE AND CHIROL'S PLAN FOR OCCUPATION OF PART PROMISED TO BULGARIA—SAZONOFF OBJECTS TO OCCUPATION OF MACEDONIA—O'BEIRNE PERSISTS—CHIROL GOES TO NISCH—GANTCHEFF'S MISSION TO BERLIN—CHIROL GOES TO BUKAREST—RUMOURS OF GENERAL FITCHEFF'S RESIGNATION—INTERVIEW WITH DANEFF—ENTENTE REQUEST TO SERBIA—SERBIA SUMMONS SPECIAL COUNCIL TO CONSIDER REQUEST—GENERAL JEKOFF REPLACES FITCHEFF AS WAR MINISTER.

ON the 27th June, the Chief of the Staff talked to me about the then state of affairs and said that Bratiano had that very morning telegraphed to the Bulgarian Government to say that Roumania was satisfied with Russia's concessions and was prepared to go in with the Triple Entente. The Chief of the Staff thought there would be no great trouble between Roumania and Bulgaria but that the latter would demand all that part of the Dobrudja that she had lately lost except Silistria and a perimeter of about 5 kilometres to the south. He then repeated what I had already heard and mentioned to Sir Ian Hamilton and telegraphed to the Foreign Office, that in the opinion of the Bulgarian General Staff who had had a recent practical experience of that theatre of war that we would not be able to take Gallipoli for a long time, if at all, unless we landed a force of about 200,000 men somewhere on the mainland coast of the Gulf of Saros between Enos and Ibrije. He calculated that the Turks could at most bring 150,000 men to meet such an attack, even though reinforced by the troops from the Caucasus and

Syria. That the permanent fortifications at Bulair were not capable of resisting an attack from that direction. Once we got our army ashore and organised with the necessary transport, etc., it would not take more than three days to reach Bulair.

The Bulgarian reply to the Entente offer was non-committal. The Bulgars did not think they had a real guarantee for securing the part of Macedonia offered and they were curious to know what compensations exactly would be given to Serbia upon which the offer of Macedonia was contingent. In so doing they evinced a certain jealousy of Serbia increasing her territory so largely and thereby upsetting the balance of power in the Balkans.

On the 26th June our rejoinder to Bulgaria reached the Legation, and contained, I was glad to see, a hint as to the time limit, in which Bulgaria had to say " Yes," or " No," though the exact date was not given. The Entente had wisely not asked anything definite from Greece which was due to Venizelos who had pointed out that in that case he could not carry the country with him and there might ensue a Greco-Serbian war against Bulgaria. This reply was at the time only in the form of a telegram to Petrograd and the other Entente Capitals, submitted for approval with the reasons for not offering anything more precise to Bulgaria at that time.

On the 28th June Bax-Ironside informed me that he would shortly be leaving Sofia and that O'Beirne was coming from Petrograd to take his place. He gave me to understand that he was unable to change his views of the impossibility of getting Bulgaria in, and he had all along been opposed to that policy. But that if it was thought that we had to continue our efforts and that somebody else might be better able to carry it out, he would not stand in the way. I thought the choice of O'Beirne who was Councillor at Petrograd (where he had remained ever since I left in 1907) and knew Sazonoff the Russian Minister for Foreign Affairs extremely well, could not have been bettered, and if anyone had

CHAPTER ELEVEN.

been capable at this juncture of securing the Bulgars to the Entente it would have been he. Bax-Ironside also told me that Sir Valentine Chirol was shortly arriving at Athens on his way here from London. On the same day I received a telephone message from M. Grube who had just arrived at Sofia from Petrograd. It was a great surprise meeting him here. We were old friends from Teheran days when he was a Director of the Russian Bank there, and one of our most capable opponents before the Anglo-Russian agreement about Persia came into being. I had since then met him in Petrograd as Director of the National Bank. He was a very able man and had been sent out here nominally as head of a great oil trust but really with a diplomatic mission to clear up the "impasse." I had some talk with him during which I raised the question of indemnifying King Ferdinand against the loss of his Hungarian properties in event of our beating the Germans. He caught on to this eagerly but the puzzle was how to approach this very unapproachable Royal Sphinx. I arranged to ask Fitzmaurice to meet Grube and talk the matter over and the meeting took place that evening, but no progress was made regarding the knotty question of how to approach the King. Grube had to return to Petrograd the following day with the intention of coming back to Sofia later on.

A day or two later I saw the War Minister and subsequently sent off a telegram to say that the Bulgars were very anxious here to know what the Entente rejoinder would be to their reply, and that they would be very disappointed if there were no change, especially as regarded Kavala. I suggested that the following addition might be made to the Entente offer. That if within 15 days of Bulgaria's entry into the war as an ally of the Entente, Greece had not joined also, Bulgaria should be definitely guaranteed the valley of the Struma up to the watershed of the Ktusha Planina and Beshik Dagh, and the Entente should guarantee Bulgaria against an attack from Greece. I added that the

Bulgarian General Staff still thought that we ought to land a force of 200,000 men on one side or other of the mainland, and that a time limit, coupled with the rumour of some such landing force, would be advantageous. I knew that my suggestion about defining the Hinterland of Kavala in the event of the Greeks not coming in would not be welcomed at home, but after all, Greece was the only country upon which we could really put the screw, and if Bulgaria became our ally and Greece attacked her as Venizelos apprehended, we could surely have no further scruples as the champion of the rights of the smaller states. I thought that asking Bulgaria to refrain from insisting on a clear definition of what we meant by Kavala because of our interest in Greek historic traditions, as the Foreign Office said, was rather playing the fool at a critical moment. At the same time I did point out to the War Minister that it was foolish of Bulgaria to ask for something from each of her neighbours simultaneously as that was likely, even certain, to induce them to try and combine against her which made our task much more difficult.

On the 8th July the funeral took place of the Bulgarian Exarch, the highest Church Dignitary in the State. He was a great loss to the Entente as he had been advocating Bulgaria taking part in the war in order to help Russia, out of gratitude, even if Russia were losing. This old man had perhaps done more than anybody towards creating the Bulgarian nation by using religion as a political force.

The procession in which all the Diplomats took part, was most imposing. On leaving the building from whence the procession started I noticed that the German and Austrian Legation Staffs with a formidable array of military uniforms, had obtained a leading place in the procession just behind the Ministers of the various foreign countries. They were followed by the Staffs of the Entente Legations. The Ministers of all the foreign nations were leading, the British and Austrian being side by side. From a spectacular point of view this did not signify

CHAPTER ELEVEN.

as regards the Ministers who were all in much the same diplomatic uniform, but I thought the effect of the German and Austrian military uniform strutting along in front of the British, French and Italian all through the town was most undesirable. So, as soon as a favourable bend of the road came in sight, by gradually edging up we were able to insert ourselves in front of the Germans and Austrians, which must have annoyed them considerably. This manoeuvre was, however, not in time to stop several cinematograph operators who photographed the procession at the start and doubtless only those samples eventually reached Berlin.

At this time I saw the War Minister and taxed him with the Government having let 8 aeroplanes through to Turkey. He declared he knew nothing further about them, having had them stopped once. We should ask Radoslavoff. He argued that it was impossible to stop contraband, and if Greece and Roumania let stuff through to Serbia, and Roumania, who professed to be our friend, sent contraband to Turkey, why should Bulgaria worry? Bulgaria, who had not declared herself anybody's friend! There had also been a case of contraband having been sent from England to Germany. I said each belligerent Power did what it could to stop it. We had had to declare a blockade of Greek ports for that reason. If Bulgaria were taken " en flagrant délit" sending on aeroplanes that she had already confiscated, it would create a very bad impression, and I should be very glad to be able to deny it if he could prove that such was not the case. He then said * "After all, what is the passing of a few aeroplanes if we can get the Turks to give up the Dedeagatch line!" But I reminded him that he had only just told me that he considered that Turkey would not yield an inch of ground in that respect. He replied that was his personal opinion only. He then told me that the Turks had formed a new, sixth army, of two army corps of three divisions, with headquarters at Keshan and quartered at Keshan, Kuleli Burgas

---

* Vide Appendix A.

and Adrianople. He also said that the Turkish losses up to date were 100,000, of which 40,000 had been killed.

During these days there were a number of farewell dinners to Bax-Ironside. O'Beirne arrived on the night of the 7th July and Bax-Ironside left on the 9th. In the papers of that day there was a detailed account of an Austrian offer to Roumania which did not sound pleasant. The Central Powers had one great advantage over the Entente in the fact that with them diplomacy went hand in hand with military measures. They did not wait till they got a severe blow before making an offer but chose the most favourable moment and gave a time limit.

On the 17th July I heard that the Entente Ministers had come to the conclusion that Bulgaria would certainly not move unless she were given actual occupation of at any rate a part of Macedonia, and therefore it would be useless again to ask Bulgaria what she wanted to induce her to come in, which were the latest instructions from home. They suggested that the line of the Vardar should form the limit of actual occupation. They also suggested that troops of the Entente should occupy the portion eventually to be handed over to Bulgaria, and there was an idea of sending them there via Dedeagatch. A telegram had been sent to this effect the day before without my having been aware of it. I thought the latter a ridiculous notion and might well make confusion worse confounded. Supposing the enemy made a push on Serbia, or the Balkan States quarrelled amongst each other, and communications were cut at Salonika, what a humiliating situation we should find ourselves in, unless we went there in force and kept the communications open to Salonika! Diplomats seem to have no idea of the need for lines of communication and think one can just dump a force down anywhere and let them live on the country. The idea of sending them via Dedeagatch was to avoid Greece, but whether they were intended to march there or go by train via Turkey or via Seres I did not know. What

CHAPTER ELEVEN.

made matters worse was that I was quoted in the telegram as confirming Chirol's information that the military situation in the Dardanelles was so critical that it was a matter of supreme importance to get the Bulgars in. Perhaps this was so. I had been urging it, at first almost alone, for 10 months, but Sir Valentine Chirol had not yet arrived, but was only due that evening on a special mission from the Foreign Office. I had seen Gregory of the Foreign Office who was travelling with him as part of the mission, and had spoken with him and quite shared the views that he said Chirol entertained, but I had given him no authority to quote me, still less through the Minister, and in connection with other matters about which I had not been consulted. O'Beirne explained that it was an oversight, but I was obliged to send another telegram to qualify it lest I should be taken to task by the military authorities for assuming an inside knowledge of the operations, our resources and military plans which I did not possess. I also thought we might be playing the enemy's game by trying to make Serbia give up part of Macedonia immediately. A war between Serbia and Bulgaria would suit the enemy better than anything else, and there was the risk of that unless we could occupy it in force.

It was an unfortunate time for O'Beirne and Chirol to arrive with the intention of making the Bulgars march—now that there seemed a great chance of Warsaw being evacuated or cut off, and a Kingdom of Poland declared by the Germans. However, by this time it was neck or nothing.

On the 20th July I saw the War Minister and he told me that all parties were agreed that they would not march without being given some part of Macedonia in hand. I invited him to shew me what part of Macedonia they wanted, but he declined to indicate it. I had always told Fitcheff that it was practically a hopeless thing to ask for. He said nothing more about Kavala which he was very keen about a short time before. When I asked him whether Bulgaria would dare to come in now against

Turkey with the risk of having Germany on their back, he said " Yes." It would take the Germans some time to crush Serbia, and he could put 150,000 men of the 2nd line troops into fortified positions on the Western front of Bulgaria, while attacking Turkey with 250,000 of the 1st line. In spite of this declaration I was not sure whether he were not egging us on to make this offer of immediate occupation which they would perhaps try and obtain for nothing just as they had been doing lately with the Turks regarding the railway to Dedeagatch. It would, of course, have been good policy for the Serbs to have surrendered it voluntarily or with a good will, but that, I feared, after my interview with the Crown Prince, was not likely to occur. Fitcheff then alluded to a telegram which had appeared in the daily bulletin that morning emanating from the Wolff Bureau at Berlin, to the effect that the British Military Attaché at Athens had declared that the Greek army, supported by 50,000 British troops, would march through Bulgarian territory against the Dardanelles and force the Bulgars to join them. He knew there had been some talk of this as a Greek General Staff plan some months ago. I said we had no official confirmation of it, but I purposely did not throw cold water on the scheme as we sadly wanted some competition for the Dardanelles job. Fitcheff said that we could not imitate the German invasion of Belgium after all our declarations about the rights of nationalities, and, of course, the Bulgars could not let a force through without breaking their neutrality, and would be bound to attack them. This was unfortunately true, and effectually put a stopper upon any such plan without Bulgaria's assent.

On the 22nd July, Chirol, together with O'Beirne called on me, and we had a talk about possibilities. I was not encouraging. It was comparatively easy to frame a programme that would satisfy the Bulgars, but I thought it impossible to get the Serbians to agree to, or even tacitly accept, an immediate occupation unless we ourselves sent at

CHAPTER ELEVEN.

least 100,000 men, based on Salonika, to hold the Vardar line. O'Beirne and Chirol had suggested our sending about 4,000 men via Dedeagatch to occupy the territory in Macedonia promised to the Bulgars by way of guarantee that they would get it after the war. Fearing that they did not agree with me, I wrote an official despatch on the subject and presented it to O'Beirne on the following day.

On the 25th July, it was evident that the proposal of the four Ministers here, backed up by O'Beirne's telegram, had caught on at home. Grey had apparently brushed aside my objection to sending a small force and said 1,000 men could be spared from the Dardanelles. I was afraid that the home Government would jump at the idea of doing the job with a small force. Meanwhile we heard from the Russians here that the Tzar was more Serbophil than ever, and that Prince Troubetzkoy had told them so when he passed through to resume his post at Nisch. Also Sazonoff's reply to the suggestion of the four Entente Ministers sounded a note of despair. He said "je m'y perds," and that we should cause a Serbo-Bulgarian war. In spite of that O'Beirne, Fitzmaurice, and Chirol meant to carry the thing through. O'Beirne had just telegraphed to suggest that if Sazonoff would not approach the Tzar, Sir George Buchanan should be instructed to do so, and to ask him to demand this sacrifice from Serbia. I told O'Beirne again that in my opinion the extreme limit of safety had been reached when we offered Bulgaria the 1912 line at the end of the war and that, with Kavala, etc., would have been enough at almost any time during the previous 10 months. But now I did not think they would go, and 1,000 men would be no guarantee unless the Bulgars were allowed to occupy something themselves, quite the contrary in fact, as they would prove a red rag to the Germans and a splendid opportunity for inflicting a humiliating blow on the Entente. However, the situation at Gallipoli must have been pretty desperate as the Government jumped at the idea. Even with a larger force it

M. PASHITCH.

meant winning the Greeks over to us by some means or other, and they were at present furious with us. I hoped we would not merely succeed in putting all the Balkans against us.

On the 26th July, O'Beirne lunched with me and met the Serbian and Russian Military Attachés. Our conversation had to be guarded. On the same day a telegram arrived from Buchanan to say that Sazonoff did not see his way to asking the Tzar to intervene personally with the Serbs to make them give their consent. Although in my opinion O'Beirne had arrived in Bulgaria too late for this drastic treatment, I could not withhold my admiration for the way in which he stuck to his programme through thick and thin, and only hoped he would be successful. Chirol left the same day for Nisch. The Bulgarian papers were following events very carefully. They noted that Savinsky had motored over to Nisch a few days before and had seen Prince Troubetzkoy and Pashitch. There was also a protest by the Bulgarian Government addressed to our Legation against our having blockaded Dedeagatch to stop contraband going to Turkey. Finally there was a report that Turkey had ceded to Bulgaria the Dedeagatch railway.

On July 31st, I heard that Chirol had gone to Kraguevatz to see the Crown Prince. The Diplomats were busy going ahead with their offers of Serbian territory and a telegram from home outlined what we were proposing to the Serbs, namely an immediate occupation by the Bulgars up to the Vardar (no notice had been taken of my objection to the actual Vardar line as giving the Bulgars practical control of the railway), or if they did not like that, then an occupation by the Allies of the same territory. On the same day, I happened to be at the War Ministry discussing a contraband question, when Fitcheff took occasion to intimate to me that he was opposed to a policy of adventure for a small State, and that unless the situation changed either by the Russians beating back the Germans from Warsaw, or by the capture of the Dardanelles, or

CHAPTER ELEVEN.

by a definite offensive in the West, he would advise the Cabinet to sit tight. This without reference to the particular terms offered, about which I did not say anything. It was the intention, when the Entente got something like a tacit assent from Serbia, then to put on a time limit and leave Bulgaria to accept or reject the offer.

On the 1st August there came a very lengthy telegram from Chirol, who was at last beginning to realize what we were up against in our endeavours to make Serbia give up Macedonia unconditionally and at once.

The day before, Colonel Gantcheff, a very capable Bulgarian, who had formerly been my colleague in Serbia, and had since been at Berlin as a Military Attaché was seen going off by train in plain clothes in the direction of Berlin. The fact was suspicious, as officers did not generally wear plain clothes, and he was trying to hide himself. He was at this time Chief of the Staff of the Sofia Division and pretended he was going to Tirnovo. As a matter of fact he did go to Berlin on a very important mission.*

About this time Grube returned from Russia. We discussed the situation, and he was inclined to think with me that all efforts to make Serbia agree to an immediate occupation were futile and dangerous. We thought it better to complete the offer that had been made, and Grube suggested that if the Bulgars did not accept it we should withdraw our four Legations. I thought we should at any rate try to avoid giving them an ultimatum at the moment of the fall of Warsaw, if it were to fall.

On the 6th August Chirol and Gregory who had returned from Serbia, left for Bukarest. I asked Chirol if he had found matters as difficult in Serbia as I had predicted, and he said " quite as difficult." They looked rather depressed, but on one point he ought to have been pleased because our Government had taken up O'Beirne's and his proposals with the most extraordinary vigour, and on that very day

---

* Vide Appendix A, page 251.

all four Entente Powers through their rulers, Emperor, Kings and President, had sent identic notes to Serbia calling upon her to give up Macedonia to the Bulgars in the common interest. There was a scare that Bulgaria contemplated going against us. I thought it had been started by the Russians but did not believe it was imminent. However, the presence of Colonels Jekow and Justoff at Constantinople whither they had gone three or four weeks before to negotiate about the cession of the railway, and of Gantcheff in Berlin, gave some reason to infer that a military convention between Germany, Bulgaria and Turkey was brewing.* That evening I met Strandtmann who was here for a few days from Nisch. He thought Pashitch was as unyielding as ever. He described Prince Troubetzkoy as being a very good Minister. He himself had just been appointed to Rome.

On the following day the Russian Military Attaché, Tatarinoff, told me he was much perturbed at Fitcheff's attitude. Fitcheff had declared that he had been kept in ignorance by his own Government of the terms of the Entente offer to Bulgaria and that he knew absolutely nothing about Gantcheff's mission to Berlin. The latter had been sent without his having been informed or consulted in the matter.

On August the 8th it was reported in the paper that Hakki Pasha had seen Radoslavoff the day before, and had left for Berlin immediately after the interview. The Roumanian Minister here was being told by his Greek and Serbian colleagues that Bulgaria was on the point of attacking Serbia, but he did not believe the news. Meanwhile there were signs in the papers that Serbia was beginning to consider the Entente proposals. There was to be a special Council which the King and the Crown Prince were going to attend. At the same time Greece was perfectly furious at the idea of being asked to give up Kavala and declared she would never consent, but would defeat the Bulgars first.

---

* Vide Appendix A, page 248.

Military Attaché N.

There were even said to be cries in favour of Kaiser Wilhelm in the streets.

As regards Russian news, the very alarmist reports on the situation in Poland which had been rife were not confirmed, and the prospect of their being cut off in their retreat from Warsaw was no longer imminent. So I went to the War Office to see the Chief of the Staff, General Boyadjiew, recently War Minister, and, as I thought, a more simple and straightforward soldier than Fitcheff. I first asked about the supply of officers and found the training of the cadets was proceeding apace and that 1,200 would soon have been instructed. Also 800 officers of reserve out of about 1,400 candidates would receive their commissions about the 15th September. Ten Divisions of three brigades would be mobilized in case of war, and an eleventh, a Macedonian division, 35,000 strong would be called up for training shortly. I then asked the General what he thought of the situation in Poland and how it bore on Bulgarian politics. Boyadjiew remained of the same opinion that he had expressed on previous occasions, namely that Germany was a long way off and Bulgaria could settle Turkey before the Germans and Austrians could finish off the Serbs. In his opinion present conditions had not altered this. Russia had not suffered any great disaster and would come on again at once, if a large number of the enemy troops were withdrawn. That being the case I could not understand Bulgaria's attitude, if the Cabinet and Radoslavoff went by the opinion of its military advisers. She had a unique opportunity. By a great effort we had induced the four Powers to agree to give Bulgaria the chance of getting all she wanted as the price of coming in with us. The reason we wanted Bulgaria was because our diplomats had a scare about the Dardanelles and that we should not be able to go on with our operations in the winter owing to bad weather. I believed personally that we were quite comfortably off at the Dardanelles and could prolong our campaign there right through the winter in spite of bad weather. Boyadjiew said yes, of course there was no bad weather to speak of in those parts. I did not think it necessary to go into the question of enemy submarines with him, but gave him the idea that there was a false scare about the difficulties of the Dardanelles, and in reality the Turk was very sick and very hard up for ammunition. Then I said Bulgaria would be a perfect fool not to take advantage of the present moment. It would not last very long. At present we were trying to get the immediate occupation of Macedonia for them, and ultimate possession of Kavala. But if we could not realize this and the Bulgars still insisted on impossible conditions, the moment would pass and we would get on somehow without Bulgaria. The General then expressed the same fears and suspicions of Roumania that have been noted previously, but I assured him that Roumania would not go against us except under direct menace of a large body of German troops being concentrated against her. If that was impossible, as he believed, I could guarantee her behaviour. Of course, if Bulgaria joined the other camp, that was another question. As regards Greece, who was protesting so loudly, we could of course suppress her by a display of naval force but we probably would not do that owing to our principles of safeguarding the right of small nations.

But if Greece attacked an ally of ours such as Bulgaria would be in the event of her attacking Turkey, we would not be long in settling our account with Greece. I then left the General, went to our Legation, and shewed O'Beirne a Bulgarian paper called "Utro," a Germanophil rag, in which it appeared that the Germans were threatening Roumania with an economic war if she did not allow munitions to pass into Turkey, and that she would not buy her surplus grain, also that she would permit Bulgaria to occupy Macedonia, and the prospect of a big Bulgaria joined to a big Turkey would force Roumania to change her double-faced policy. I thought this language satisfactory as shewing that the Germans were at that time able to threaten by words only, instead of by a shew of actual force.

Owing to rumours that General Fitcheff was going to resign, I went to see him on the 12th August. He denied the truth of the rumour, but owned that there had been intrigues against him on all sides, emanating especially, he hinted, from the King. Politicians were jealous of him and accused him of being Anglo-phil or Russo-phil. They did not understand the situation. He, Fitcheff, was against a policy of adventure as he had told me before. He knew this was going to be a long war and that the Russians were not yet "hors de combat." I hoped that I had really succeeded in impressing him with the fact that we were only just beginning to fight in earnest, that we should have conscription, and that the Germans were merely fighting for the best terms they could get. They could not hope to win. Anyhow, Fitcheff said he was going to occupy himself solely with army matters and not proffer his advice any more. He also said that the Bulgarian negotiations with Turkey had been broken off and Colonel Jekoff had been ordered to return. He had always thought that the Turks would not give up the railway. There were rumours that General Markoff or Colonel Justoff might be appointed Minister for War. The former had just returned from Berlin as Minister and was not suited to the post of Minister of War. If he were appointed I felt sure that it would mean the country was going against us. I next saw Tatarinoff, who told me that the King, ten days before, was jubilant over the impending fall of Warsaw (which actually fell on the 5th August) but that now he was gloomy and dissatisfied with the progress the Germans were making. He added that the Bulgars intended to occupy Macedonia with the new Macedonian Division and the 7th Division which together would form one army under General Toshew. He also thought that they would move against Serbia with some of the Danube divisions which were busy changing their draught transport into pack transport. On the same day I had myself inoculated against cholera, so as to be ready against all eventualities. My doctor, a Bulgarian, said he had heard that Bulgaria had signed a convention with Germany two days before, but added that he did not believe it.* He was strongly pro-Entente and abused the King as the "fons et origo mali." He also said that the Government was afraid to mobilize in order to help the Germans, because the peasants would say "Let us first get our rifles in our hands, and then we will tell you in which direction we mean to march."

That evening Daneff came to dinner with me after having spent two hours in conversation with Radoslavoff. He confirmed all that I had heard from Fitcheff and told me to advise Fitcheff to stick to it, and not allow himself to be turned out, even if the King were against him. There had been a moment when the Bulgars had thought of going for Macedonia, but that had now passed. The Russians were not knocked out. Also the Hungarians had been favouring the Serbs because they did not wish Austria to conquer Serbia, in which case a very large Slav element would overshadow the Hungarians in the Austrian Empire, whereas if Russia were to win, it would be counted to them for righteousness that they had not permitted Serbia to be crushed. Count Tisza had been and still was opposed to a campaign against Serbia. Daneff was very anxious to know whether the Serbs would consent to the Entente note. Their consent was absolutely necessary, but it did not matter so much about Greece or Roumania. He thought that an occupation of Salonika would go a long way towards making Bulgaria march, and if the Dardanelles began to fall, King Ferdinand would himself beg to join the Entente. He added that according to a Bulgarian engineer who had just come from Turkey, things were going well for us in the Dardanelles. Daneff had also spoken to Radoslavoff about the

---

*Vide Appendix A, page 251. The Convention must have been signed about this time.

negotiations with Turkey. They had been broken off, but the Turkish Minister, Feteh Bey, had come back to Radoslavoff who intended to renew negotiations omitting the town of Lozengrad (Kirk Kilisse), which the Turks would not give up. He spoke of the importance of getting through railway communication, and said the Entente knew of and did not mind their negotiating, as they wanted Bulgaria to have the railway to avoid contraband passing to Turkey. But Radoslavoff was not hopeful of success. He would not offer neutrality which the Turks would not believe in anyhow, and which would get him into hot water with the Entente. He had said nothing about seizing the railway by force, but Daneff did mention some idea of the Turks putting up a shew of resistance to try and hoodwink the Entente into the belief that they were at loggerheads. It seemed to me that the Turks did not trust the Bulgars and were not likely to give up anything without fighting. I expressed apprehension that if we let the Bulgars into Macedonia first, they might not fight the Turks afterwards. Daneff thought that we ought not to do that until we had the definite engagement of Bulgaria, and that the occupation of Macedonia by the Allies with an ultimatum to Greece, was the best arrangement.

On the 16th August, a secret report from Adrianople shewed that the Turks were preparing to blow up the railway bridge over the Maritza and abandon Adrianople. They had recently been fortifying it, so this information pointed to their intention to oppose the Bulgars, but that owing to recent losses in the Dardanelles, they no longer had sufficient troops to defend Adrianople.

Chirol and Gregory had now returned from Bukarest and reported that the Roumanians were not letting any more ammunition through, and could be relied upon to resist the pressure from Germany to do so, so at least the Queen had told Gregory.

On the 19th August I went to see General Fitcheff. He was very depressed, told me that he was on the point of being turned out, and that

General Jekoff was to be his successor. He knew that intrigues had been going on, and certain people were dissatisfied with him. But he had always done his duty as a Bulgar and had nothing to reproach himself with. He wished now to go into the English Army. I was afraid that was against our regulations, and he could speak no English, as he acknowledged, but he seemed serious. The King had accused him of having been misled by Generals Paget and Pau into a false idea of the excellence of the Russian army. Now that the Russians had retired to the Brest-Litovsk line, and that Kovno had fallen, the King was having his revenge on him for having given wrong advice. He had been against a policy of adventure either with the Entente, or with the Germans against Serbia, but on the whole he had favoured the Entente. I suggested his going into the Russian army, but he said General Radjko-Dimitrieff was there, and I understood that they were not friends. I knew he disliked the French, but as he had been educated at the Turin Military School I thought perhaps he might find employment in Italy. At any rate he would be a great loss to the Bulgarian army. He was Chief of the Staff during all the brilliant operations of the Bulgarians against the Turks in 1912 and only left the army when they decided to go against their own allies in which he proved himself to be right. Now, he declared, he would prove to have been right again. General Jekoff, he said, was good, having been a pupil of his own, but he had not enough experience. I thought Jekoff's health was worse than that of Fitcheff, who was now nominally retiring on account of ill-health. Jekoff had a feeble constitution and was, I thought, inclined to be nervous in consequence. Otherwise he struck me as a cautious man, and perhaps better fitted to be a diplomatist than a commander in the field.

Fitcheff's removal created a great stir as it looked as if the King had decided on a definite pro-German and pro-Turk military policy. The King had treated Fitcheff abominably, had refused to see him for the past three months and now had turned him out without telling him anything. He was probably the last man in the Cabinet to know of his dismissal. Jekoff had also been educated at the Turin Military Staff College, and did well as Chief of the Staff of the 2nd Army in the late war.

On the 20th August the Russians were very depressed, as it was evident that the Brest-Litovsk line had been broken through. Fitcheff said they would be finished if we did not make an offensive in the West, or carry Gallipoli.

On the 22nd August I had my final inoculation, so now I was presumably proof against both cholera and typhoid fever. The doctor told me an interesting story of the cause of Doctor Grätzer's sudden dismissal. Doctor Grätzer had been the King's physician for many years. He was a German by birth, but thoroughly identified with Bulgarian interests and Bulgarian society. When attending the King a few days previously for an attack of gout, the King was seated at his writing table, and while occupied in removing his foot coverings, saw, or thought he saw, Grätzer glancing his eye over the correspondence on the table. The King was furious and said he would not have a German spy about him! Grätzer replied that if anybody else had accused him of spying he would know how to answer him, and left the room. If true, this was important, as shewing that the King had not yet burnt his boats. In my diary of the 3rd September, I noted that this story had been confirmed.

Chapter Twelve.

INTERVIEW WITH JEKOFF—SERBIAN REPLY TO ENTENTE NOTE
—DISGUST OF O'BEIRNE—INTERVIEW WITH BOYADJIEW—
O'BEIRNE'S AUDIENCE WITH THE KING OF BULGARIA—
FURTHER DETAILS OF SERBIAN REPLY—VISIT TO VRATZA FOR
BULGARIAN MANOEVRES—O'BEIRNE TAKES UP SUGGESTION
OF LANDING FORCE AT SALONIKA—FINAL OFFER OF 1912 LINE
BY ENTENTE—VISIT OF DUKE OF MECKLENBURG TO SOFIA—
BOURCHIER SANGUINE AS TO ATTITUDE OF OPPOSITION—
RUSSIAN OFFICERS REPORT ON GALLIPOLI — OPPOSITION
LEADERS INTERVIEW WITH KING — INTERVIEW WITH
GUESCHOFF—SECOND VISIT TO SIR IAN HAMILTON—BULGARS
COMMENCE MOBILIZATION—JOURNEY TO IMBROS AND ANZAC—
CONVERSATION WITH SIR IAN HAMILTON—RETURN TO SOFIA.

ON August 23rd, the thirty-first anniversary of of my first commission in the Army, I saw the new Minister of War, General Jekoff, the same aged man as myself. Two months before he was Colonel and Assistant to the Chief of the Staff. He was then appointed to command the 8th Division, and had hardly taken up his command a fortnight, before he had to go off to Constantinople to take part in the negotiations between Bulgaria and Turkey for the cession of the railway. He looked young, had not a grey hair, but also looked ill and liverish, and had suffered from pneumonia and rheumatism. I began by asking him what he thought of the present condition of Russia. He replied " serious but not desperate. Still, unable to take the offensive before the Spring." He did not think Petrograd was in danger. "That being so, what was the policy of Bulgaria?" "Still one of expectancy" said he. He disbelieved in the Entente being able to re-form the Balkan "bloc." Regarding Turkey, she was better organised than at the beginning of the war, and had formed several new units, he did not know how many or what they were. The Germans had helped the Turks in the

matter of ammunition of larger calibre than 15 c.m,
and they were short of big gun ammunition. Then
he asked me my opinion. I said we were bound to
take the Peninsula some time or other, if for no other
reason but that some day they would run out of big
gun ammunition. Besides, we had good news about
our fresh landing, and now that the Italians had
declared war, we might expect their aid also. Once
Gallipoli had fallen, we should make short work of
Constantinople, even without the help of Bulgaria.
He demurred at this and said the Turks considered
that there would still remain great powers of resistance before Constantinople fell. I asked him
whether he was still of opinion that Bulgaria could
finish off Turkey in a short space of time, and he said
"Yes." "In spite of the new style of trench warfare?" asked I, and he still said "Yes." Then I
touched upon the negotiations with Turkey. I
opined they had come to nothing. He made some
evasive answers, so I said of course they could not
give up the line now. Any concession would be
regarded as a sign of weakness. He agreed to this
and said the Turkish Government had to keep up
their prestige. They pretended that all was going
well, but in reality the Dardanelles fighting had
caused them many qualms, although they had been
able easily to make good their losses in men.

I then harked back to our negotiations, and asked
him whether he thought Bulgaria would have the
courage to attack Turkey, supposing that we were
able to secure for her all the concessions that we
had promised. At first he tried to avoid answering
by repeating that he was sure the Serbs and Greeks
would not give way, but I pinned him to the original
proposition, and he then replied with some sign of
heat, that the Entente had let a whole year go by
dallying with this question. Why had we not made
the offers we were making that day months ago, when
we were in a good position? "Now you come to
us when your position is precarious and your success,
to say the least, doubtful, and you ask us to take the
risk of being on the losing side!" I told him that

it was said he was in favour of attacking Serbia. He answered "on principle I am in favour of attacking each and all of our neighbours, but I am not able to do so." I said "Quite so, I suppose you would require to arrange with Greece and Roumania first and you would have to consider that you would then have the Entente against you, and if they should after all happen to win the big war Bulgaria might cease to exist." We were quite friendly over it all, and some time during the conversation I touched upon the German danger. Jekoff, I knew, was a Russophobe. But in endeavouring to escape that danger Bulgaria was running to meet a greater danger. To this he agreed, but consoled himself with the thought that in that case many other States would be in the same boat. Before leaving, I asked him whether he would continue to let me have information about the Turkish army, and he said yes, I could get it from someone in the War Ministry. Just as I was leaving, the A.D.C. brought in the cards of the German Minister and one of his secretaries. I had left the Serbian Military Attaché in the waiting room as I went in. He had told me just before, that he thought the Bulgars would attack them in Macedonia.

On the 28th August I took Colonel C. B. Thomson, who was returning to Roumania from leave in England, to see General Jekoff. Thomson's news from home was that we had then 50 infantry divisions in England, and 15 in or around the Dardanelles. Altogether we must have had about three million men under arms. Besides trying to impress Jekoff with the idea that England was only beginning this war and would have to go on until she beat Germany, we wanted to convince Jekoff that Roumania was not a danger to Bulgaria if the latter attacked Turkey. If, on the other hand, Bulgaria attacked Serbia it was quite wholesome that he should regard the intervention of Roumania as not only a possibility but a certainty. During the conversation, Jekoff told us one or two interesting facts, notably that in the unlikely event of Bulgaria attacking Turkey he considered that the mobilization and concentration of the Bulgarian army would take from 20 to 25 days, and that they would be in Constantinople in 20 days from the crossing of the frontier, making 45 days in all. But Germany could concentrate a force of say 400,000 men against her within one month from the time that the offensive movement against Russia ceased. Of course, the behaviour of Roumania was of capital importance. I was afraid that Thomson had not made any more impression than I had been able to do as to the certainty that Roumania had no desire to attack Bulgaria. Her interest in the future was directed towards Transylvania and Bukovina, or towards Bessarabia, but not southwards. Jekoff still thought that, failing either of these, she might fancy a little more of the Dobrudja.

A telegram arrived from our Foreign Office showing that the Serbians were still uneasy about the Bulgarian manoeuvres. Of course they did happen to be coming off at rather a convenient time if Bulgaria wanted to bluff, but they were only following out the programme laid down on the 24th June for the exercise of the troops. They were to consist of small manoeuvres between the 28th August and the 14th September (new style) of regiment against regiment, and brigade against brigade, under the superintendence of the Infantry Divisional Commanders. Of course, those divisions which were adjacent to the frontier could not help holding these exercises in the vicinity of their own regimental and brigade headquarters, and therefore not much more than 30 miles from the Serbian frontier, but I did not see how we could ask them to go further afield and thus incur more expense, especially as they were not mobilized. The Serbian Military Attaché was especially solicitous about the 6th Division, thinking they might rush the Serbian fortress of Zaichar, in connection with a German movement to clear the Danube. I thought this movement had been too much advertised to be a danger at that time. Moreover, the Germans had not yet finished with the Russians and they would need at least a month to assemble a sufficient force, whereas these manoeuvres would be over in a fortnight. Besides, if the Bulgars wanted to co-operate without mobilizing, they could easily make a dart at any time without our knowing much about it. The Serbians had got 15,000 men in the North-east corner of Serbia. The danger was that if Roumania and Bulgaria connived, the Germans could seize this corner and rapidly fortify the line Milanovitz—Zaichar. With both flanks protected and in possession of Zaichar, they could hold it with 100,000 men and so open up the Danube from Orshovo to Lom. Otherwise, without the connivance of Roumania and Bulgaria, the Germans would have to invade Serbia by the Morava valley, which would need at least 300,000 men.

On September 1st, I saw de Russi who had recently returned from Bukarest. He told me that Roumania had got 280,000 men under arms, and that should she be attacked she would defend herself to the last man. This with reference to the advertised intentions of the Germans to open up the Danube from Orshovo down to Vidin. He scorned the idea of Roumania letting through any warlike stores to Turkey, and he entirely disbelieved the recent report of powder having been sent through to Turkey as paper. There was also a rumour of 300 waggons of ammunition being in waiting on the Austro-Roumanian frontier for permission to pass. Roumania was supposed to have given its consent to the passage, and its delivery to Turkey was said to be the price of the Dedeagatch railway annexation.*

At this time Bourchier returned from Roumania and told me there was nothing to be done either there or here. I had dined with O'Beirne the night before, and met Savinsky who was very cheerful, although, as O'Beirne told me confidentially, he was about to be recalled.

On the 3rd September, the Government newspaper, "Narodni Prava," had for the past two days contained articles against the idea of an Anglo-

---
* Vide Appendix A.

French occupation of Macedonia, and had reproached the opposition papers such as the "Mir" for encouraging such a move, stigmatising them as traitors. I had always thought this an impracticable suggestion unless carried out in overwhelming strength, and with the goodwill, at any rate, of Greece. We did not know at this time what Greece's attitude was since Venizelos had come in again.

The Serbian note in reply to ours had been received the day before. I was surprised they had given way so far. O'Beirne was disgusted at their not having given way entirely, and said we could not communicate their proposal to Bulgaria. They offered to give Bulgaria a line starting from a hill called Rusin, thence following the Drejalmitza down to its junction with the Vardar, then down the Vardar, then along the Cherna river, a tributary of the Vardar, including the Ovche Pole and Prilep in Serbian territory, and leaving Kochana to the Bulgars. Lower down, Monastir was given up to the Bulgars, but Okhrida was preserved as also a little strip of Greek territory. Nothing was said about immediate occupation by Bulgars or by Allies, or whether it was conditional on Serbia getting other things. Hitherto all these proposals had been, of course, conditional on Bulgaria attacking Turkey. I noticed what I thought a regrettable tendency on the part of Fitzmaurice to try and secure these concessions to Bulgaria in return for her neutrality only. I was entirely opposed to a policy of neutrality which I did not believe a fighting nation like the Bulgars would preserve for long.

On the 3rd September, the Roumanian Military Attaché told me they had then 300,000 men under arms, and he wished that the Germans and Austrians would provoke a conflict with Roumania as he hated the shilly-shallying policy of his Government. In his opinion, in which I thoroughly concurred, Roumania ought to have gone against Austria in November last. On this day I also saw the Chief of the Staff, General Boyadjiew, and asked him for permission to attend some of the manoeuvres near Sofia. There had been a great fuss made over these manouevres, so I thought if they let a Military Attaché go to see them, it might seem to neighbouring nations a proof of their good intentions. As a matter of fact, of course, Military Attachés can be easily isolated at manoeuvres and put out of harm's way where they cannot get to a telegraph office, or even know what is going on. I hesitated about asking to attend the 1st or the 7th Division which were both near Macedonia. He had no objection to either, so I then asked to go and see the 6th Division. This was manoeuvring in the North-west corner of Bulgaria and would have been the point of danger if the Germans had intended to force their way through Orshovo. To this also he had no objection. We then discussed the question of the Turkish negotiations. He told me that the Government was bargaining for a narrow wedge-shaped strip commencing from the Black Sea, about half-way between the actual frontier and Midia, and ending in a point at the present frontier north of Lozengrad; also for the country up to the Tundja and Maritza valleys including Enos. He did not himself believe that the Turks would give it up, but if they did, it would be in exchange for neutrality, and he asked me what our attitude would then be. I said I could not answer for my Government, but, speaking personally, I thought it probable that we would break off our negotiations with Bulgaria for them to attack Turkey. We could not, I thought, continue, on the supposition that Bulgaria might break her treaty with Turkey. "But," he said, "with a change of Government, might not Bulgaria then repudiate her agreement with Turkey?" Again, speaking personally, I did not think that our Government would accept that state of affairs. General Boyadjiew then asked me whether we would go against Bulgaria. I replied that if we withdrew our offer we would of course be free to negotiate with other people, but if Bulgaria joined the other side whom could she attack: would she come and fight

CHAPTER TWELVE.

us on the Gallipoli Peninsula? "No," he said, "we might attack the Serbians. Would you induce the Roumanians and Greeks in that case to attack Bulgaria?" "Yes," I replied, "we might." But I also declared that the Roumanians had no desire to attack Bulgaria, they much preferred to get Transylvania or Bessarabia. And Bulgaria had the greatest interest of all in keeping out the Germans, as they were on the high road between Germany and her Turkish colonies. He agreed to this, but declared that the Roumanians were false and unreliable, and really waiting for an opportunity to swoop down on Varna. The conversation was conducted on friendly terms and I was quickly informed that the King consented to my going to see the manoeuvres of the 6th Division.

On the 4th September, O'Beirne had an audience with the King. Radoslavoff was present. O'Beirne managed to converse on politics and laid great stress on the German peril to Bulgaria which appeared to have some effect, and to be rather a novel idea to the King. Altogther His Majesty was very cautious regarding Bulgaria's attitude. He sent messages to King George and translated a part of O'Beirne's discourse into Bulgarian for the benefit of Radoslavoff whose French was weak.

The same day another telegram came into the Legation giving the full text of Serbia's reply to the Entente note. Without going into minute details, the line that they offered in lieu of the 1912 one, which they considered was neither ethnographical, nor geographical, nor strategical, but was imposed on them by the threatening attitude of Austria and other circumstances, amounted to an offer of about half the territory demanded, and the conditions which they attached to its cession were as follows :—

1.—Bulgaria was to attack Turkey at once with all her forces.

2.—The Serbian Government to obtain a formal promise of Croatia with Fiume.

3.—Recognition as an ally and a voice in the ultimate Peace Conference.

4.—No further delay in the monthly allowance of 36 million francs till the end of the war.

5.—Communications with the Aegean Sea guaranteed for imports and exports including munitions of war.

6.—Aid of the Entente for securing the independence and sovereignty of Serbia.

7.—The cession of territory to take place only after the line had been delimited and after Serbia had entered into possession of its promised territories.

The Entente was to take the responsibility of Serbia having ceded territory on the right bank of the Vardar contrary to Serbian engagements towards Greece. Finally Serbia asked the Entente to preserve secrecy with regard to the above.

So there was a long way to travel between this and the Entente's proposal of the cession of the 1912 line at the end of the war together with immediate occupation of Macedonia to the East of and up to the Vardar by Entente troops, and still further distance between it and the Bulgarian idea of their own immediate occupation, at least up to the Vardar.

Even with everything thrown in, it was now highly improbable that the Bulgars would come in on our side, so the matter had almost reached the academic stage.

I thought the only thing to do at this stage was to confirm our original offer of the 1912 line at the end of the war and guarantee that we would force Serbia to give it up when the time came. Similarly with Kavala, and then either wait until the war took a more favourable turn, or if that were hopeless, give the Bulgars a short time limit and then declare the offer off. After that we could make friends with Greece again, which would be better than nothing.

On the 6th September I started for the manoeuvres of the 6th Division and railed to Vratza, from whence I rode for some miles to the Headquarters of the 6th Division where I found my

Military Attaché O.

friend, General Papodopoff, very pleased to see me. I was given a flimsy tent, with one centre pole, of the usual Bulgarian pattern. The weather was very cold and I was glad of a fur coat. The details of the manoeuvres were of no particular interest but it was useful to see the country which was admirably adapted for the Bulgars to put up a strong defence against the Germans trying to penetrate by this corner, if they were so minded. The mountains and hills form a succession of ridges running North-east and South-west with fine open valleys between them. If these people could have only come to an agreement with the Roumanians and Serbs to resist Germany it would have been too big a job for the Central Powers to attempt, and it was obviously in the interests of the Balkan States to unite, in order to preserve their independence. I told Papodopoff this and he agreed, but at the same time could not disguise his hatred of the Roumanians, who only a year or two ago had systematically raped all the women and young girls they came across when they invaded Bulgaria, denuded as it was of troops in that part of the country during the second Balkan war. In fact, the Bulgarian instincts of revenge against all their neighbours except Turkey almost entirely over-rode all other considerations. Papodopoff himself said "If the Germans do come here and crush Serbia 'nous sommes fichus!'" Papodopoff told me with perfect honesty that he had not been able to see any sign of Bulgarian preparations against Serbia. I told him I had heard that the divisions on the Danube, and notably his own, had been busy converting their wheeled transport into pack transport. He replied that they had found the need of that during their last campaign in Thrace, and it did not point particularly to a campaign in Serbia.

I returned to Sofia on the 11th September and saw a telegram to the Foreign Office from O'Beirne of that date strongly advising an occupation of Salonika by the Entente troops in force, and referring to a despatch of mine in that sense dated

July 22nd. Sir Valentine Chirol had then just arrived here, bent on his mission of bringing Bulgaria in. He came to see me with O'Beirne. I told them that there was very little hope of getting Serbia to agree to any cession of territory until the end of the war, and I strongly objected to his and O'Beirne's idea of sending a force of about 4,000 men to hold Macedonia by Dedeagatch. I put my ideas on paper after they had gone, and sent it in the form of a despatch. This was pigeon-holed as it did not agree with their views. Chirol went to Serbia a day or two later and took a Foreign Office bag. I found afterwards the despatch had not gone and was put away in the Chancery. I had insisted on it going but as another bag did not leave for a month I had telegraphed supporting the idea of an occupation of Salonika and the Vardar line, an idea which had been also advocated by a French ex-Minister, M. Cruppe, who had been travelling here, presumably on a similar mission to that of Chirol. But I insisted on it being made in force. Now that O'Beirne had failed diplomatically with Serbia, he had reverted to my plan, but it was probably too late. The Bulgarians seemed already to have almost crossed the Rubicon. I heard from the Bulgarian War Office that the Bulgars were going to get the Turkish railway in exchange for neutrality. The Chief of the Operations Section implied that it was only for that and not for going against us, so we ought not to mind. He did not know if the matter were really settled, as no military measures had yet been issued for the occupation. I remarked by the way, that it would be better for Radoslavoff to wait until the Entente had definitely made their complete offer before finally throwing in his lot with the Turks. Politics, he replied, were no concern of his, but no doubt my remark would be repeated to the Chief of the Staff, and I took the opportunity of expressing my thanks to the King and General Staff for their civility in permitting and helping me to attend the manoeuvres of the 6th Division.

CHAPTER TWELVE.

On the 14th September the four Ministers of the Entente handed in to the Bulgarian Government what I hoped was our final offer. It was to guarantee the 1912 line to Bulgaria, absolutely, at the end of the war, and our diplomatic aid in negotiating with Greece for Kavala and its vague Hinterland, and also our aid with Roumania for Dobritch and Baltchik, similarly rather vaguely defined in the Dobrudja. This must have been rather annoying to the Germanophil Bulgarian Government just as they were completing an agreement with Turkey for the Dedeagatch railway. Hitherto Radoslavoff had been trying to get this out of the Turks for nothing, but since the Duke of Mecklenburg had been here and at Constantinople, (he was back again here at this time) there had been articles in the papers, and hints as already recorded in my conversations with members of the War Office, to show that the Bulgars had given up this attitude and were now endeavouring to obtain the concessions in exchange for their neutrality towards Turkey. The Germans had evidently been hard at work in forcing the Turks to give up this railway and strip of territory. What a pity that we had not been equally successful with the Serbs! O'Beirne, Savinsky and the Katsikoanis', the Greek Military Attaché and his wife, had dined with us the night before. The Greeks were more friendly than they had been. But they evidently thought that we should be at war with Bulgaria before long, and said the Salonika railway was blocked with Greek troops going to reinforce their men on the Bulgarian frontier

On this day I went for a ride with Bourchier, and found him sanguine about the attitude of the Bulgarian Opposition. The various parties composing it had never been so united before. Ghenadieff, the head of the Stambulovist Party, had broken with the Government's Germanophil policy some months before, and had got a majority of the Stambulovists with him. This made him rather the master of the situation, unless the King and Government were able to suppress all opposition by martial law and by gagging the Press. Bourchier was busy distributing pamphlets which he had had printed. A society, headed by Schuster, in London, had given him £100 for this kind of work. He wondered, I thought rightly, why our Legation did not occupy itself more with such propaganda.

The same day I saw Morphoff, the Director of Railways. Nearly a fortnight previously we had news that Roumania had promised to send 30,000 tons of coal to Bulgaria on condition that Germany supplied her with 50,000 tons. It was suspected that this coal was destined for Turkey. I ascertained from Morphoff that the coal was not for Bulgaria. At the same time the Roumanians were also sending 10,000 waggon loads of flour to Turkey which was more urgently needed, and would take two months to transport. So I thought it was not worth bothering about the coal. We would be lucky enough if we could keep them from sending ammunition.

On the 15th September I heard that a commission of three or four Russian officers had passed through here a few days previously coming from the Dardanelles. They had been studying the situation there and their report was not very consoling. They said the expedition had been mismanaged in the general plan from the commencement. That the main attack was on the Kaba—Tepe—Suvla Bay front, and the demonstration was made on the end of the Peninsula, and yet we used 28,000 men on the former and 21,000 on the latter front. Far too great a proportion for a mere demonstration. The military situation of the troops was very bad because all the English and French positions were under the direct field of fire of the Turks. But the morale of the troops was excellent and our men were fighting very well. The French, not so so well, and said to be slightly despised by our men. The Australians were wild men, not very intelligent, but excellent fighters. The Gurkhas were the best of all and had the post of honour on the Suvla Bay front. The Turks had to economize ammunition, otherwise

CHAPTER TWELVE.

they would have swept us all into the sea on both fronts. The war was being conducted in the most gentlemanly and chivalrous fashion on both sides. We had 53 hospital ships, several of them being anchored close to the shore within range and in full view of the Turks, but the latter never touched them. Similarly, our submarines boarded their hospital ships, inspected them and let them pass on if all correct. Then followed in detail a description of the various fronts with the names of the Divisions, etc., occupying them. It was also said that the Entente officers were continually expecting the entry of the Bulgars against the Turks, and that the positions on both fronts were very difficult, and that of the Turks at Achi Baba was so impregnable that officers referred to anything in conversation which was considered impossible as being "Achi Baba." Such was the Russian report on the Dardanelles as communicated to me by Tatarinoff.

On the 17th September the Opposition Leaders had a united audience with the King. I saw Gueschoff, the late Premier, on the following day. He told me that the meeting had had a great effect on the King, and that Stambolisky, the Agrarian Leader, had been particularly outspoken, and had told the King that the people would hold him personally responsible if another catastrophe befell Bulgaria. Tzanoff, the Radical, also gave him some good advice. These two were in favour of neutrality, while Gueschoff, Malinoff and Daneff were in favour of joining the Entente, but all were agreed as to the great objection to attacking Serbia. All the Opposition Leaders had not been so united for very many years, as the King's policy had always been to keep them apart. Gueschoff said that a week or so before, the situation had been very dangerous. It was just a fortnight ago that he had become alarmed on hearing from Radoslavoff that the agreement with Turkey had been signed. He then arranged with all the various party leaders[*] to approach the King. He did not believe that the

---

[*] Vide Appendix A.

M. STAMBOLISKY.

Turks had signed the agreement, but it had been sent to Constantinople either signed or approved by the Bulgarian Government. He thought that now the danger of an attack on Serbia was past, at any rate for the moment. I then asked him what he thought of our last note. He said he did not exactly know its contents, so I told him. He was surprised, I thought, that we were offering the 1912 uncontested zone line without any reservations, on the sole condition of Bulgaria going into action. But he was very disturbed at hearing that we were going to withdraw the offer if it were not accepted in a few days, and begged me to tell O'Beirne that he hoped the Entente would not do this without first consulting the Opposition. I had recently seen the Minister of War and had again tried to dispossess his mind of the idea that Roumania would attack Bulgaria if the latter invaded Turkey, but that she might do so in defence of Serbia if Bulgaria attacked the latter. I had also again rubbed in the German peril. To that he had replied that he did not apprehend that the Germans would take possession of Turkey, the Turks having had enough of them already. This was rather significant coming from Jekoff who had so lately been in Constantinople. I had hastened to say that I also did not believe it, because I knew we were going to win the war. But if the Bulgars believed that Germany was going to win, it meant that Germany would not only take possession of Turkey but also of Bulgaria. During my interview with Gueschoff, the latter had asked me whether I had recently seen the Minister of War, so I told Gueschoff of these two points and he was much interested in both, namely, that we thought we could rely on Roumania's attitude being friendly to Bulgaria if the latter joined the Entente, and that things were going badly for the Germans in Turkey.

On the 18th September, in view of the critical state of affairs in Sofia, and the fact that Morphoff had hinted to me that something dreadful would happen if we did not manage either to take the Dardanelles or to occupy Salonika in force, I decided

CHAPTER TWELVE.

to go to the Dardanelles and see General Hamilton. It was true that Gueschoff's audience with the King in company with leaders of the various opposition parties had been encouraging. But I was anxious to see if it were possible to get some troops quickly for Salonika in case the capture of the Dardanelles still lay in the distant future. I left Sofia at 11.30 p.m. and railed to Rakovski which I reached early next morning. Morphoff had reserved a large first class compartment for me, and had ordered an excellent little swift motor car to be at the station, so that I arrived at Gumuljina at 3 p.m. Near the frontier the road was bad and bumpy, but after that excellent. I left Gumuljina by train at 5 p.m. Arrived at Dedeagatch by 7.30 p.m., and put up with Mr. Morgan, our Vice-consul. Here a telegram had arrived for me from O'Beirne to say that the Bulgars were commencing to mobilize. He left it to my discretion whether to return to Sofia or not. I decided to go on, and telegraphed to O'Beirne to that effect, saying that sometimes Balkan States mobilized without being sure on which side they were going to fight*. I thought anyway I could do nothing in Sofia, and it might be of great importance if I could see Sir Ian Hamilton. I also thought that if the Entente shewed any kind of weakness, it would be fatal. The only thing was to keep our offer open and at once send troops to Salonika before the Bulgars completed their mobilization. I sent a wire to this effect to O'Beirne and telegraphed to Imbros to ask for a ship to meet me at Dedeagatch.

On the 21st September, at 6.30 a.m., His Majesty's destroyer "Arno" took me off, and in two hours I was at Imbros. I saw Colonel Tyrrell the Chief of the Intelligence, and then General Braith-

---

* It was in my recollection that on my first arrival in the Balkans in 1908, Bulgaria was on the point of going to war with Turkey. I had been appointed Military Attaché for Serbia. The Serbs had begun to mobilize. The British Minister, Sir Beethom Whitehead, in acquainting me with the situation, said that the Serbs would fight. To my enquiry on which side would they fight, Sir Beethom replied: "I can't tell you. I don't think they know themselves." And Sir Beethom was doubtless right. The war was narrowly averted.

waite, Chief of the Staff, and was invited to accompany Sir Ian Hamilton to Anzac at midday on the "Arno." We arrived there in three-quarters of an hour, and landed at a little wooden pier. Firing was going on on both sides, but not very heavy, However, General Birdwood, who had come off to meet us, said that two men had been killed and five wounded on the beach where we landed, about an hour before. A sailing ship was lying half under water about 100 yards off, sunk by a shell the day before. On landing, I was lucky to find an old friend in the Base Commandant, Colonel Young, of the Bengal Cavalry, a very cheery fellow. He gave me lunch in his dugout, and told off a very nice fellow, Captain Butler, to show me round. There was a steep mud cliff facing a narrow sandy beach and the cliff was honeycombed with dugouts, communication trenches and roads. It looked as if with sudden and heavy rains, the whole affair might collapse. However, this was where the Australians lived, and a very busy spot it was. I noticed a trolley railway besides innumerable roads. Mules were dragging trolleys and Indian transport carts down by the beach, while higher up, pack mules were taking stores up to the trenches. I was taken first to the right, Sir Ian Hamilton having started on a tour with one staff officer and one A.D.C., to the left. It was not advisable to be a large party. One had to stoop at some places where there were no sandbags. The enemy's trenches were about 200 yards off. We then circled round by Quinn's Post and the Neck. Now and then I was told to take care when we passed some "unhealthy" spot. The Australians seemed quite undisturbed and imperturbable, mostly engaged in cooking, sleeping and resting in recesses in the trenches just big enough to take one man lying down. Most of the men were reading newspapers. Notices were put up at the corners of this labyrinth of trenches to direct one to certain points. Some snipers had little bastion positions run out towards the enemy to flank our line. The men in the firing line were few, and

CHAPTER TWELVE.

nearly all of them were using a rough periscope fixed to the rifle with a wire hanging from the trigger, invented by an Australian, so as to shoot over the top without exposing oneself. I looked through one of them, and noticed it already had two or three shots through it. Some field guns and a 60lb. howitzer were firing on the left of the Neck. At the Neck itself the enemy trenches were 50 to 60 yards off, and the intervening space was dotted with corpses and human remains, a gruesome sight, as there had been heavy losses here. We were very keen on getting the Western hills which lay between us and Kuchuk Anafarta. The line connecting this position with that of Suvla Bay was continuous as far as the nature of the ground permitted. It was all very interesting and I nearly missed the boat back. However, I was just in time, and managed to have some conversation with the General on the way back. Sir Ian Hamilton told me he had 14 Divisions, including two French ones. The nominal full strength of a division was 15,000 men or 12,000 rifles. The expeditionary force was, however, 55,000 men under strength. The General said the Turks were good fighters and brave men; he had known and liked Enver Pasha. He was very bitter against King Ferdinand of Bulgaria and hoped we would not keep our offer open to the Bulgars very long, and would not let them maintain a neutrality favourable to Germany. It would be better to attack them with two army corps at Dedeagatch. I suggested going to Salonika because we might then get the Greeks in too, whereas the Bulgars might turn us out of Dedeagatch, and would in that case certainly side with Germany. A force at Salonika might give them pause. Back to camp and dined with the Intelligence mess.

On the following morning a touch of dysentry prevented my visiting the trenches at Helles Point. Two or three aeroplanes came over the camp in the morning and dropped 8 or 10 bombs. The shooting with the anti-aircraft guns was very bad. Bombs were dropped all around the Commander-in-Chief's tent and also round a canvas aerodrome, a very conspicuous object containing a small green sausage-shaped flexible airship, built especially to hunt submarines. It could launch a bomb of 60lbs. weight which could be set to explode at any depth under water. The officer in command thought the enemy were bound to bag her before long as they had already dropped 30 bombs all round her. I had been trying to impress on the Headquarter Staff the importance of putting troops down at Salonika where I thought they might also establish a base for the Dardanelles and so serve a double purpose. The Chief of the Staff told me they were pretty sure to get reinforcements from France within a month, but declined to say how many. It depended on certain definite events there, which must have meant an offensive on our part. It might be more or less, according to circumstances, but would in any case be a considerable amount and enable them to make a push on the Dardanelles. I therefore wrote privately to General Robertson, then Chief of the Staff in France, explaining the urgency of the present crisis in the Balkans, and the post left on the following day. Unfortunately there blew a gale for 48 hours which prevented me from getting back to Dedeagatch. I received a telegram from O'Beirne on the 22nd September shewing that Bulgaria was apparently still hesitating. She had not yet occupied the railway in Turkish territory and mobilization orders had not yet been published.

On the 23rd September I was given a special destroyer called the "Grasshopper," and returned to Dedeagatch. The sea was very rough and I passed several unhappy hours quite prostrated by sea sickness.

On the 24th September I left by the passenger train. Mobilization had begun. Crowds of peasants in about 20 covered trucks with men inside and on the roof, cheering very faintly. Arrived at Gumuljina I found that my car had been requisitioned and also nearly all the hired carriages, but I succeeded eventually in securing a carriage with a

CHAPTER TWELVE.

miserable pair of ponies, and then found I could not leave without a permit. I went to the Commander of the 8th Division and found an old friend, General Kolev, who received me with great cordiality and invited me to lunch at the Officer's Club. This I accepted. They were all very polite; they had not an idea where they were going and would not relish having to fight us. I told them they were bound to lose whichever side won the war, if they went with the Germans, as they would be swallowed up by them if they were successful. "But what will happen if it is a drawn war?" they asked. "How can you ensure us getting Macedonia in that case, if the Serbs won't give it up?" I had to confess that that was a difficult question to answer. I got away about 3.30 p.m. The ponies were dead tired, but by walking up all the hills I managed to make some progress. Put up for a few hours at a guard house in command of a Bulgarian officer, and continued my journey at 2.30 in the morning. The mountain scenery was lovely under a full moon. I reached Kirjali at 10 a.m. and the railway at Rakovski at 9.45 p.m. The ponies got better and better the further they went, and finished up at a smart canter. Good stuff these little Bulgar ponies — even the leavings after mobilization. During my drive I had seen peasants walking and riding along the road coming in to their mobilization centres. They wore a very sulky look; the mobilization was evidently very unpopular, and they feared they might be sent against the Russians. The train was due at 10.30 p.m. but did not arrive until 5 o'clock the following morning. The railway officials were all most polite, but when the train arrived I found there was no room, so had to sit on my baggage at the end of the sleeping car full of German officers, and did not reach Sofia until 4.30 p.m.

Chapter Thirteen.

BRITISH LEGATION THINKS OF OFFERING MORE CONCESSIONS TO BULGARIA — FRENCH AND RUSSIAN MILITARY ATTACHES NOT OF THAT OPINION — SERBS SUGGEST ATTACKING BULGARIA BEFORE HER MOBILIZATION IS COMPLETED — INTERVIEW WITH MINISTER OF WAR — SERBS REFUSAL OF ENTENTE OFFER VERY DAMAGING TO OUR PRESTIGE — PROGRESS OF MOBILIZATION — ENTENTE MINISTERS EQUALLY DIVIDED FOR OR AGAINST AN ULTIMATUM TO BULGARIA — RUSSIANS ISSUE ULTIMATUM AND WE FOLLOW SUIT — O'BEIRNE IS OF OPINION THAT WE SHOULD HAVE REMAINED AND CONSIDERS WAR WITH BULGARIA DUE TO RUSSIAN MILITARY ATTACHE — DEPARTURE OF ENTENTE MISSIONS — ARRIVAL AT ATHENS — ATTACHED TO LEGATION — NECESSITY OF MAKING GREEKS JOIN ENTENTE — INTERVIEW WITH VENIZELOS — COLONEL CUNNINGHAME LEAVES FOR LONDON — GREEK HARVEST — INTERVIEW WITH GENERAL DUZMANIS, CHIEF OF GREEK STAFF — ENDEAVOUR TO FORCE HAND OF GREECE — RESIGNATION OF GREEK PREMIER — LORD KITCHENER VISITS THE DARDANELLES.

SEPTEMBER 27th. On my return I found that our Legation was terribly upset over the mobilization, and were racking their brains to make more concessions to the Bulgars, still trying to force the Serbs to give up Macedonia to the Bulgars at once. I saw my French and Russian colleagues and the Minister of War. I found the French and Russian Military Attachés agreed with me, that to ask Serbia to yield any more was both futile and dangerous, being proof of the weakness of the Entente. In my language to the Minister of War at an interview on the same day, I accused him, according to information received from the Russian Military Attaché and other sources, of having German officers working in the War Office, and German officers openly parading the streets in uniform; of planning a concentration with the Germans against Serbia or Roumania and of passing contraband. I implied that we had had enough of such dealings and that we would prefer to have an open enemy. The Minister of War asked me if those were the opinions of my Government. I said no, they were my own personal opinions, and he could take them as such. He was very civil, confused by my direct attack about Germans working in the war Office and eventually denied it. As for the officers in uniform, they had red crosses. He declared that Bulgaria was out to defend her frontiers, and not to concentrate against one particular enemy. That the Bulgars would not attack Serbia if the Serbs did not first attack them. That their neighbours had begun to mock at Bulgaria as being exhausted and worthless. Now they wished to make their value felt. Everybody else had mobilized. Why should not Bulgaria do likewise? Other people also were passing ammunition which was not against international law. I told him that we could not suffer the importation of ammunition from the point of view of military expediency. The best thing that Bulgaria could do if she wished to avoid the Balkans being made into a big theatre of war and to save herself from German domination, was to come to an agreement with Serbia and Roumania to defend the Peninsula, and make a friendly neutrality with us if she did not dare to come to our help. Jekoff was afraid that even if Bulgaria were an ally of the Entente and had exhausted herself in taking Constantinople, she would be liable to be attacked not only by Roumania but by Serbia also. It was evidently useless to continue the conversation and my interview terminated.

At this time the Serbian Government asked permission of the Entente to fall upon the Bulgars at once before they completed their mobilization. O'Beirne asked me for my opinion. I said that if the Serbs thought they had a good chance of success, they would have done so without asking our permission. It was true that they might put one Bulgarian division " hors de combat " and delay the mobilization of the remainder, but the ultimate result would be that they would be crushed between the Germans and the Bulgars. On the other hand, until hostilities actually commenced, there was a remote possibility that Serbia might cede the coveted territory in Macedonia and Bulgaria refrain from fighting. The Entente did not grant Serbia the permission asked for. The fact of our not having been able to make the Serbs agree to the concession had been a great blow to our prestige. But nevertheless I did not think that Bulgaria had any wish to fight the Entente.

On the 28th September I saw Malinoff, by appointment. He had asked for the interview as I met him in the street the day before. Protogaroff, the Macedonian leader, was with him at the time I arrived, but soon left. Then Malinoff told me that he had been with the King for four or five hours the day before. The King had sounded him on all sorts of questions, but while asking him to enter the Cabinet would give him no indication of the policy he intended to pursue. Malinoff had said "Your Majesty remains to me a sphinx, and I cannot go blindly into the Cabinet." So he refused. Then I asked him if the King did not give him any indication during a five hours' conversation of the general trend of his politics? No, no indication, but he had asked him about the dispatch of 150,000 men to Salonika, whether it were true, and whether Malinoff himself believed it. Malinoff replied that Savinsky had told him so and had also told the Prime Minister. So had O'Beirne. And they had also declared that it was with the consent of Greece. Malinoff then asked me whether that was true. I said "Certainly if they told you so." I had also heard that the Greeks were willing, besides it was not conceivable that they could resist us. I suggested the idea of favourable neutrality to him. He asked if the Serbs had not something more to give away. Could we not permit the Bulgars to occupy Macedonia at once. I replied that speaking privately I thought not, because the

Serbs would at once fight them. "That would be suicidal of them with a gathering force of Austro-Germans on their front." "Still," I said, "they would do it for certain. If some people were fools and mad, one must take them as one finds them, one cannot alter them; but Radoslavoff has our offer, and if he chooses to ask us to occupy the line of the Vardar railway, we might permit the subsequent occupation by the Bulgars up to the Vardar after the latter had taken Constantinople."

Then I left him and saw the Serbian Military Attaché who agreed with me that no immediate attack on Serbia was threatened. He also told me of a big French success, 20,000 prisoners having been taken, and a depth of 5 kilometres of trenches on the Western front, which we thought might make a difference here.

October 2nd was the tenth day of mobilization. The town was full of reservists. There was no enthusiasm whatever, and we heard of some cases of insubordination and that shooting had been resorted to in some of the outlying districts to compel obedience with the orders of the Government. It seemed that the army now consisted of 40 regiments of the line, 18 reserve regiments, 24 battalions of Macedonians and 22 depôt battalions. Each division was believed to have two regiments of artillery of which the first was composed of 6 batteries of four 75 mm. guns, and the second of 2 batteries of four guns (75 mm.) together with 3 batteries of 6 guns of 87 mm. non-Q.F. The infantry companies did not exceed a strength of 200 men each. A few days before the mobilization began, three German aeroplanes went to Turkey by rail.

Regarding militia, each division had 6 battalions. There were also here 3 batteries of 12 c.m. howitzers. The first regiment of cavalry and the horse battery quartered here had left for the Western front just before mobilization was declared.

Three squadrons of the Guard had been gone about two days and the field artillery had left Sofia the day before, on 1st October. It was also clear that the 9th Division from Plevna and the 5th Division were concentrating towards the Serbian frontier.

The political situation was extraordinarily complicated. The Russians and the French here had made up their minds that there was nothing to be done but to give Bulgaria an ultimatum to accept our proposals to march against Turkey or demobilize. Our Legation, on the other hand, still wanted to try and force Serbia to give up the 1912 line. At our Legation I feared that our Bulgarian translator might have had an inkling of what was going on without being correctly informed. But at any rate the Bulgarian papers of the 2nd October announced that we had some plan for landing troops at Salonika, not to fight the Bulgars, but in order to force Serbia to make concessions. I thought this kind of thing was fatal and might explain why we had not heard of Greece's permission for our troops to land. I hoped now that Greece would remain obdurate and that we should not have to fight a fresh campaign in the Vardar Valley. In July I had proposed the sending of a large force to Salonika in order to prevent the action which Bulgaria had now taken, but now that Serbia had only herself to blame, I thought it rather hard that we also should be involved. In any case we ought to have been able to choose our own theatre of war. I was at this time in favour of giving Bulgaria an ultimatum to join us or remain in a condition of favourable neutrality with partial demobilization. There appeared to be a duel going on between the Ministers of the Entente who were equally divided for or against an ultimatum. On this very day we were on the point of making an official declaration that if Bulgaria attacked our allies, we would support the latter. Radoslavoff could not receive our Minister at the moment, and a few hours later came a Russian communiqué ordering the Russian Minister to give an

Military Attaché P.

ultimatum to Bulgaria to join us or demobilize. The other Ministers had not received any instructions but a telegram from Grey indicated that we should probably agree to Russia's ultimatum. The evidence of control by German officers, although denied by the Bulgars, was strong enough to put the British Foreign Office against them.

On the 4th October, Sazonoff, having broken away from all control by Grey and the other foreign Ministers, sent a sharp ultimatum to the Bulgars, to break off relations with the Germans and Austrians with regard to their plan of campaign, and dismiss any German officers that might be with the troops within 48 hours. As far as we were concerned, we concurred with the above, but if the Bulgars were prepared to give us any substantial proof of their good faith, we would stay; otherwise we would go as soon as we could after the Russians.

The Greek Military Attaché had heard from the Austrian that we had landed a Division at Salonika with General Hamilton and his Staff. Rather significant, I thought, the source of his information!

By the time that O'Beirne saw Radoslavoff, the latter had received the Russian ultimatum, and was quite upset. It had apparently taken him by surprise. His tone was quite an injured one of astonishment that we should interfere in what he regarded as a little Balkan quarrel.

The same day a German aeroplane came down here owing to shortage of petrol. It contained two officers, who dined at a restaurant, in German uniform, and then resumed their flight.

It was with great reluctance that O'Beirne was obliged to follow the Russian lead in the matter of an ultimatum. He would have remained on and have endeavoured to keep Bulgaria neutral. That was, however, too undignified a course for Russia to pursue—Russia, who always regarded herself as the parent of Bulgaria. In fact, O'Beirne went so far as to say he considered this Tatarinoff's war. Personally I do not think it would have been possible at this time to restrain the Bulgarian army from combining with the Austro-German forces to crush Serbia.*

October 8th. The Bulgars returned a somewhat impertinent reply to the Russian ultimatum, denied that they had foreign officers, German or Austrian, in their War Ministry or employ, but that if they had, they were perfectly in the right as being an independent country. The reply to us was more civil, but the rupture was equally complete. We left Sofia about 7.30 p.m. The King had given us a special train, and we started from his private station, presumably so as to avoid any demonstration. There was a tremendous crowd on the train, with three Missions, French, Italian and ourselves, and various traders, journalists, and private persons. The Russian Minister, Savinsky, was unfortunately obliged to stop behind as he had recently undergone an operation for appendicitis. We subsequently heard that the King, who always loved to have a second string to his bow, and evidently was experiencing qualms as to whether he had really backed the winning side, visited the Minister's bedside daily after our departure.

The strip of Turkish territory about which they had so long been negotiating had just been taken over by the Bulgars, and we inaugurated its occupation, arriving at Dedeagatch at mid-day on October 9th. It was an unpleasant reflection for us that had we been as clever as the Germans and retained as much authority over our Allies as they had over theirs, we would not have been leaving Sofia. There was a good chance that had the Turks not

---

*Vide Appendix A. General Jekoff, during his trial on 22nd November, 1921, said he had advised Radoslavoff to postpone taking military action against Serbia until the result of the Austro-German operations on the Danube were known. But meanwhile the Serbs considered the Bulgarian concentration provocative and commenced hostilities.

CHAPTER THIRTEEN.

shown a timely compliance in this matter, the Bulgars would have turned their arms against Turkey instead of against Serbia.

At Dedeagatch we found an Italian boat called the "Roumania" waiting to take us off. There was accommodation for about 80 people whereas we numbered about 120. However, we managed to fit in somewhow and arrived without incident at Salonika, escorted by a French torpedo destroyer. A slight excitement was caused by a British warship which fired a blank shot to order us to stop, and a young officer came on board to examine us.

On arrival at Salonika at sunset, O'Beirne, after much hesitation, decided to continue the voyage on a French boat leaving at midnight, so we of the Legation Staff accompanied him and went on board the "Yarra," a Messagerie steamer. We heard that the French had recently landed 20,000 men and that Sir Ian Hamilton had landed with a few men but that the movement had been interrupted. Count Matharel was taken ashore by his Admiral, saw his General, and remained behind. I, having been unable to communicate with Military authorities, or even get ashore, went on to Lemnos. We started at daybreak for Lemnos where we were met by Captain Fyler, of the "Agamemnon," an old friend who had kindly put me up during my former visits and now offered to take me off to see Admiral Wemyss and ask him to send a telegram from O'Beirne to Athens and some for me to the War Office. Halfway we met the Admiral who had been trying to find us, but thinking we were on an English boat, had not noticed the "Yarra." The Admiral kindly sent two telegrams for me, one regarding the position of the Bulgarian troops, the other asking for orders to be delivered to me at Athens regarding my future movements. The Admiral told us that 50,000 troops were already in Lemnos and they were expecting 20,000 more. We left again at 4 o'clock on the afternoon of the 11th and had to mask our lights as a precaution against submarines, as many had been signalled. The "Olympic," the big Atlantic liner, left the harbour just before us. A sailor told us she had just escaped a torpedo by making a pirouette. She looked much too solid to do any such thing, but must have been very fast and handy also.

On the 12th October we reached the Piraeus after a fine night and smooth passage. We masked our lights again. A naval officer told me they reckoned the enemy had about 20 submarines in those waters, which was probably an exaggeration, but they did infest the line between Crete and Matapan Point.

On the 14th October a message came from London to say that I was to be attached to the Legation at Athens for the present. I met Major Samson on special service here under the War Office, and got him to send a telegram for me to the War Office in which I suggested that owing to the reluctance of Greece to help the Serbs, we should need a force of not less than 300,000 men at Salonika. Also that as the Gallipoli Peninsula was still our main objective, it would be preferable not to send troops into the heart of Serbia or even Macedonia, but effect a landing at Enos and attack the Turkish communications with the Dardanelles as our first move.

October 8th. Since my last telegram to the War Office, I sent two others to the Director of Military Operations via Major Samson. One was to the effect that the Greeks already had three army corps in the Salonika district and were probably sending two more. That the Foreign Office request to Roumania and Greece to come in jointly would be of no avail, as Roumania certainly would not come in now, and her refusal would also put off Greece. That we must therefore get Greece in first, especially as the latter country was in our power, and that it was most important for us to maintain an effective occupation of Salonika. My second telegram was to report that the Entente Ministers often met and decided on what policy

CHAPTER THIRTEEN.

should be pursued, but as at Sofia, never once was a Military Attaché invited to be present at such discussions. Consequently they came to decisions that were frequently contrary to our military interests. I also telegraphed that without the threat of blockade, Greece would not come in on our side.

The Military Attaché of this Legation, Colonel Cunninghame, was at this time at Salonika, and I was performing his duties for him at Athens. A telegram arrived from him that the 5th Army Corps had reached Salonika and was being posted between Nigrita and Orliak, and also between Orliak and Serres. It was also reported that the Bulgars had cut the Vardar railway south of Vrania and that General Sarrail, the French Commander in Chief, was sending up a division complete into the Vardar valley north of Doiran. A telegram arrived about this time for Sir Francis Elliot, the British Minister here, instructing him to offer the Greeks the island of Cyprus if they came in with us, but no threats were made. Fitzmaurice, who had remained here, suggested that we should take from them the Island of Corfu if they did not join us, which I thought rather a good idea. I saw the Italian Minister, Count Bosdari, whom I had known previously in Sofia. He said we could make the Greeks our victims but not our allies by the starvation process. However, his own Military Attaché and those of the French and Russian Legations also, were unanimous that that was the only thing to do.

On the 21st October news arrived of a great Serbian victory. It was not altogether confirmed on the following day, but the Serbs claimed to have put one-third of the German force out of action. I sent a telegram through Sir Francis Elliot to the Foreign Office suggesting an occupation of Kavala. It was with reference to news that had reached us that the Greeks were trying to buy large supplies of wheat from Bulgaria. The chief object of occupying Kavala would have been to embroil Bulgaria with Greece, which would take off some troops from pressing on Macedonia. At this time the Bulgars were neglecting the Greek frontier. I also thought we might tempt the Greeks to Porto Lagos and so along the littoral of Thrace and give us access by water to the oriental railway. The public telegrams reported that we had bombarded Dedeagatch, which I thought would have a good effect upon the Greeks by shewing that we had no intention of pampering the Bulgars any more.

As regards our policy towards Greece and her dependence on Great Britain for her very existence, I gathered that her daily needs in cereals amounted to between 1,000 and 1,500 tons, and that the whole country was living from hand to mouth, dependent on its imports, and with only two or three days supplies in hand. The total capacity of the harbour of the Piraeus which imported nearly everything required by Greece was only about 3,000 tons per day; so that in order to store grain say for one month, it would take a month to carry out, on the 1,500 tons basis. It would be only necessary to stop her supplies from America and Egypt for a few days to bring her to her knees.

On the 24th October I read a leading article in "The Times" of the 18th October which called upon our Government not to make the same mistakes as with Bulgaria, but to force Greece to declare herself without delay and not permit an alien Government to dispose of Greece in German interests. I knew that Sir Francis Elliot wished to wait until we had 150,000 men at Salonika. But before that time arrived, the situation, I thought, might have changed for the worse and the Serbian army be imperilled for its very existence. I would have preferred to put the question at once and if answered in the negative, to commence a blockade without necessarily withdrawing our Legations.

Meanwhile the concentration of the Greek army was proceeding. Four ships left the Piraeus on October 23rd with parts of the 1st army corps including field bakery, sappers, ammunition column and engineer park.

CHAPTER THIRTEEN.

On the 26th October I heard from Captain Sells, the Naval Attaché, who was very disgusted about one of our transports having been sunk, two days previously, in front of the harbour of Salonika. Captain Sells had frequently drawn the Admiralty's attention to the state of affairs in the Mediterranean and the inefficient measures for countering the enemy's submarines, but the patrolling of these waters was at this time in the hands of the French Navy.

At this time a telegram was received from Thomson at Bukarest to say that it would take 15 days to clear the Danube of mines. In that case it would take 3 weeks to a month before ammunition for the Dardanelles could begin to arrive from Germany. Consequently the ensuing three weeks was a very favourable time to assault the Dardanelles position, and I accordingly suggested that this might be done by some of the troops destined for Salonika, and that if the operation were successful, troops could be sent on to Salonika afterwards.

There was a rumour on this day that the Greek General Staff had informed the Greek Government that as the Germans were not capable of a great effort, it would be best to join the Entente. Venizelos was present at the meeting and had confirmed this news to our Minister. I wondered whether the Greeks were sincere or merely wanted more money in order to complete their own mobilization. I thought it would be well for me to see Venizelos myself, so telephoned to ask for an interview, and the reply was to come at once. As I had met him only once before, over a year ago, when I was on my way to Sofia, I expected him to have forgotten me entirely. But that was apparently not the case. He interrogated me closely about the numbers and formation of the Bulgarian army, which I answered to the best of my ability. I was careful not to give him any hint that I had heard his news of the day before about the General Staff nor did I broach the subject of Greek politics at all. But he volunteered the statement that he had great hopes that when the Greek concentration in the Salonika district was completed, public opinion would force Greece into the war on our side. "But," he added. "at a certain moment the Entente would have to put the question to Greece to decide for or against the Entente." He criticised our past policy in the Balkans very severely. We should not have asked Greece or Serbia to give away territory but we should have told Bulgaria that at the end of the war we, the four great Powers, guaranteed that Bulgaria would be put into possession of such and such territories, and then we should have given Bulgaria 15 days in which to accept or refuse our offer. The Entente should not have allowed Bulgaria to use such insulting language as to say "Bulgaria does not believe that you will be able to fulfil your promises when the time comes." We should in that case have told Bulgaria that we did not permit such language and have withdrawn our offer. We should also have shewn Bulgaria the reverse of the medal; that in the event of her refusing, we should negotiate with Greece, Roumania, etc., and she would then lose so much. It was refreshing to me to hear these views from Venizelos which coincided so closely with what I had so long been urging. Venizelos thought that if Russia could supply 200,000 men, Roumania would probably come in with us. Bulgaria would easily be beaten and the Greek and allied armies would then march straight on Constantinople via the Bulgarian littoral. After the fall of Constantinople we could then have all combined to attack the Austrians and Germans and the war would have ended in our favour. He was quite convinced that the Germans would eventually lose the war.

On returning to the Legation I found a telegram from Cunninghame to Sir Francis Elliot saying that the despatch of our troops to Salonika had been stopped; that we did not understand the attitude of the Greeks, and that he suggested going home himself to tell the Foreign Office and explain to them

CHAPTER THIRTEEN.

the position. Meanwhile I was to carry on here in his absence.

On the 29th October Cunninghame arrived. I talked over the situation with him and suggested that I should go home and explain the matters that Cunninghame wanted to put before the War Office. They did not seem to be very complicated and I could also be of use in questions that concerned Bulgaria. Cunninghame at first agreed, but afterwards thought it would be better to put the points forward himself. Sir Francis Elliot, after some consideration, decided to send Cunninghame, but also had no objection to my going as well if the War Office approved. Sir Francis thought I was inclined to threaten the Greeks and was therefore probably very mistrustful of my baneful influence. I did not think we should get them in by kindness and it was not very consoling to hear him say that they would come in when we had assembled an overwhelming force at Salonika. It would then be too late to save the unfortunate Serbs, although they fully deserved their fate for having been such idiots as to trifle with our last proposals. The Crown Prince had told me months before, that he would rather die than suffer amputation, when I put it that way to him about giving up Macedonia. But now when the moment had arrived, the Serbs were crying out to be saved. I had heard of a most pathetic scene between a Serbian officer and Generals Sarrail and Mahon. He had come through in order to beg us to make haste and come to their help. Of course we could do no such thing with the troops then available, namely two-and-a-half French divisions and one of English, which probably did not amount to more than 50,000 men.

There seemed to be some idea at this date of the Italians sending an expedition to Vallona. That was to be encouraged, even if only to arouse the competition of the Greeks; besides, if they could get to Monastir, they would be of some real use. Doubtless the Greeks hoped to get Monastir for themselves.

On the 30th October there was a reply from the War Office who had no objection to my going if Cunninghame stayed. But Cunninghame was on the point of leaving if he had not already started, so of course I remained. It was sad, to my mind, the way we were muddling through this war, and past belief. Everything we did was done too late, at any rate in this part of the world. Too late with troops for the Dardanelles, too late with proposals to Bulgaria, too late in landing troops at Salonika.

On this day I sent a telegram to the War Office pointing out that, according to the latest information, the Bulgars could, if they chose, bring up three complete divisions to attack our allied troops at or near Strumnitza. They would amount to some 90,000 suitably equipped men, knowing the country, who could be brought against our 40,000 or 50,000. If we had a set-back it would damage our prestige enormously. It was a question whether we had sufficient reinforcements on the road close enough to hand, and whether, given the equivocal attitude of Greece, it were wise to leave so few troops behind and thus relax our hold on Salonika.

I made enquiries about the harvest. According to newspaper information, the crop of that year amounted to 300,000 tons, but, according to experts, the correct figure, I was told, was about 200,000 tons. Greece imports about half her total needs, and this, according to our shipping people, amounted to not less that 1,000 tons, sometimes 1,500 tons daily. The question to be solved was to what an extent could Greece gather in her local harvest of wheat, barley, oats and indian corn at Salonika, to make her independent of imports for a time. I also heard to-day that the German Military Attaché, Captain Falkenhausen, accompanied by a Lieutenant Bülow, had arrived at Athens. The former was Military Attaché here and the latter a Military Attaché at Bukarest. The King received them on the same day. It was not usual for Kings to receive Military Attachés of other foreign representatives on the very day of their arrival.

CHAPTER THIRTEEN.

On the 1st November I visited General Dusmanis, the Chief of the Greek General Staff, not so agreeable a person as the Minister of War, General Yanakitzas, but, I imagined, much more influential and not at all a friend of the British. He was a little man, apparently about 55 years of age, neither smart-looking nor soldier-like, nor possessed of ingratiating manners. He owed us a grudge, however, for the series of pin-pricks we had been giving Greece for several months past. He was particularly bitter about our having taken a Greek General and Corps Commander, General Mavrocorditis, across to Mudros, apparently for examination in connection with our partial blockade. I said I thought that the latter was instituted against contraband and to prevent the establishment of submarine bases. He declared that the real reason was to influence Greece in our favour, but that it had the opposite effect. I said one could not call it a blockade because if we were really to blockade Greece she could not obtain enough food to live upon. He replied that England dared not do that, as it would be against the laws of civilised nations. I ventured to enquire whether he referred to Germany as one of the civilised nations. He replied that he had no concern with Germany, so I presumed he was relying on the generosity of England to which he replied "Yes, we know you can't do that." He then said that the British, after having treated the Greeks badly, and offered Kavala to Bulgaria, wanted to flirt with them again, but they had told us in April that Bulgaria would not join the Entente. They were perfectly certain, but we would not believe it, and now I could see that they were right. I replied that I still did not believe that it was a foregone conclusion. It was possible that Bulgaria might have had a treaty with Germany all that time, which I personally did not believe, but that in any case it did not follow that she would keep it. Her action had depended on events, and it was not until Russia was driven back by want of ammunition and Germany had gained great victories in consequence, that

GENERAL DUSMANIS.

King Ferdinand had made up his mind. The proof of that was when he threw over General Fitcheff. General Fitcheff had always told the Cabinet that if they wanted to fight they could only use the army to good effect on the side of the Entente. The reason for that was the necessity of enthusiasm in order to carry out a successful war, and the fact that the Bulgarian people's sympathies were with Russia. In 1913 Fitcheff had been opposed to the policy of attacking Bulgaria's allies and had retired from his position as Chief of the Staff rather than carry on a war which he thought would be prejudicial to Bulgaria's interests. In the present war Fitcheff had been reproached by the King for having deceived him about the quality of the Russian army. But the King's policy had been that of an embittered man with a grudge against Russia and against many other countries and peoples. He never saw any news or people during the war other than Germans, and he was not capable of judging the situation. He had thought that because Germany was in occupation of a great deal of foreign territory, she was therefore going to win. He had not taken into account the immense value of sea power; that the French army was not beaten; that the British army was not beaten, and was still growing; that the Russian army, although many times driven back, still was not beaten. He had not known that Russia now possessed a double track railway to an ice-free port in the North, and that her supply of munitions was therefore assured independently of the Dardanelles. He did not see, as we saw and knew, that Germany was already beaten, and was only fighting on for the best terms she could get. What was she going to do this winter? Was she going to dig trenches right across Russia? And if she did and were driven out of them, could she dig more trenches in the frozen ground? No, the Russian territory was an embarrassment to her, not a gain. General Dusmanis said it was still a question which side was going to win, and that we did not yet know. But I felt that he had been impressed and really agreed with me. He continued, "Our attitude had nothing to do with Germany. We are not afraid of Germany. We look on this as a purely Balkan question. Our interest is to destroy Bulgaria, and you say it is not the fault of the Bulgarian people, but of their King that they went against you. England is still favouring the Bulgars. When you bombarded Dedeagatch the other day you were damaging Greek property, not Bulgarian." I replied that once we were at war with Bulgaria she was our enemy, and we also meant to destroy her. Of course if the Greeks considered that the bombardment of Dedeagatch was an unfriendly act to Greece and not to Bulgaria the matter was hardly worth discussing. The Bulgars had not thought that.

He said "What are you doing at Salonika? It is too late to save the Serbs; they are finished. You ought to land at Dedeagatch." I replied: "General, you know better than I do that the road to Sofia is via Salonika and not via Dedeagatch." "But," he said, "you want to attack Turkey?" I replied "That is entirely a secondary consideration at present. We have got to succour our ally and yours, Serbia, and the best way to do so is to march on Sofia." "You can't do that," he said, "you have not got the men nor the material." I sand, "You are mistaken, we have the men and we can get the material if we decide to do it. But we are behind hand; I suppose we relied on the Greek army. Now I see we were wrong. But we have made you certain proposals for coming in. If, however, you don't think we are going to win this war, or if you prefer that Germany should win it, you will of course not go with us." The General said: "It is you who say that, not I. I did not say that we preferred that Germany should win. We are neutral. We simply look on this as a Balkan problem and nothing to do with the big war." "You cannot separate the two at the present time," I replied, "you know that if Germany wins, Bulgaria becomes a province of Germany and will receive an extension of territory as her reward, so also will

Turkey, and both at the expense of Greece. Bulgaria will obtain Kavala and perhaps Salonika, unless the latter is claimed by the Austrians or Germans." To this the General did not agree, asserting that Greece would keep them both. I opined that Bulgaria would seize Kavala on the first favourable opportunity and that was partly why we had advised Greece to cede it to Bulgaria, and offered Greece Smyrna. The General scoffed at the idea of our offering Smyrna, which was not, and would never be, ours to give away, and pooh-poohed Cyprus, which was ours, and which we had offered. as being a thing of no value. I said that as Greece had refused these things she would not bear us any ill will if we were now to think of offering Smyrna and Cyprus to Italy. To which the General replied that if we offered Italy all that we had offered Greece we would not have offered her much. Altogether the General was most unfriendly and rancorous. Venizelos, he said, was the only man in Greece who would give up Kavala to the Bulgars. We had not understood Greek policy or Greek interests. He was, however, emphatic that Greece could not go against the Entente. As for joining us, he evidently had no wish to do so, but said that he could not speak as to the future, it was a matter for politicians. It was quite clear to me that we had lost prestige very largely by the Dardanelles, and had gained much ill will by petty annoyances in the matter of blockading which had sufficed to shew that we would have liked to go further, but dared not in view of public opinion. The upshot was, that if we assembled enough troops to ensure our success in this theatre, Greece would come in and try to get all the profit she could, but it was evident that Germany had guaranteed her territorial possessions as they stood with regard to Bulgaria, and had probably promised her large slices of Serbia and Albania. At present they would have liked to get us out of Salonika altogether. Venizelos had been turned out by the King, according to the General, because he had given us permission to land without previously obtaining his Sovereign's sanction. It was clear to me that if we did not evacuate Salonika it would be necessary for us to send a lot more troops there.

On the 2nd November I saw the Italian Military Attaché Colonel Mombelli, and afterwards Erskine and Sir Francis Elliot, and then the Italian Minister, Count Bosdari, and suggested to each of them the propriety of an Italian expedition from Vallona to Monastir, and that we should offer them Southern Albania, including the part then held by the Greeks but not yet ratified by the Powers, also Smyrna and the Hinterland and the Island of Cyprus in return. This was calculated to force the hand of Greece if she contemplated waiting until the eleventh hour and then claiming everything. Count Bosdari said it did not matter about the compensations, that could be settled at the end of the war ; that it would not be necessary for Greece to come in at all, they did not want a powerful Greece. At the same time he also said that Greece would be useless to us as an ally because they were worthless people. I thought he could not have it both ways, but I merely pointed out that this was the moment for Italy when France was naturally very disenchanted with Greece.

On the night of the 3rd November there was a scene in the Greek Chamber of Deputies. The Minister of War had spoken in favour of an increase of pay to the officers on mobilization. A deputy had said he did not see why they should take blood from the people in order to feed the families of officers of rank. The Minister of War then, remarking that the Chamber was no place for him, walked out. On this Venizelos attacked the Minister of War for having shewn contempt of the Chamber and demanded an apology. The Prime Minister did not agree, and asked for a vote of confidence in the Government. Venizelos said that his policy was as different as the poles asunder from that of the Government, and that he was profoundly grieved to see that Greece was threatened by their eternal enemy (the Bulgars) who would turn on them after crushing Serbia. The name of the King was dragged in. Venizelos said that if they did not like to take a vote of confidence, and preferred that the Constitution should be suspended till the end of the war, they had only to say so. Venizelos went on to speak of his policy and said that the Serbs had actually placed 120,000 troops against Bulgaria instead of 150,000, and if Greece had come in, they would now be at Sofia instead of having to wait until the Bulgars had annihilated the Serbs and were ready to destroy the Greeks.

A vote of confidence was taken and rejected by 147 votes against 107. On the 5th November I heard there was a difference of opinion between the King and M. Zaimis about the parliamentary crisis, and there was a talk of fresh elections although the army was mobilized. Eventually the King had to accept the resignation of M. Zaimis and appointed an old man called Scouloudis as Premier, General Yamakitzas remaining Minister of War and being rewarded by the appointment of A.D.C. to the King. It had been thought that Zaimis would remain and be supported by Venizelos, but later on German counsels prevailed, and the new Government was formed. About this time one of our officers of the Naval Mission reported that six mines had recently been removed from the Arsenal in a Greek mine-layer to an unknown destination. Also a mysterious ship had put in during the night and was gone again before daybreak, and some suspicious red light signals had been made. Altogether the officers of the Mission had noticed a distinct change of manner and of attitude for the worse by the Greeks towards the foreigner. There was also the news on the 5th November of a Serbian victory at a place called Izbor, between Prilep and Uskub, a defile, out of which the Bulgars had been driven to be fallen upon by French infantry and British cavalry. The Serbian Legation treated it as a great victory, but it must really have been a small affair, as there were only about six battalions

Military Attaché Q.

engaged. There was also a report that two German officers had recently been on board a Greek torpedo boat examining our mines and nets at the mouth of the Salonika Harbour.

On the 9th November news arrived of Lord Kitchener's approaching visit to this theatre of war. I went to see Venizelos. The conversation turned on this visit. I asked him whether he advised Lord Kitchener's coming here. Venizelos thought a little and replied, "Yes, it would have a good effect if he were to see the King, and he could put matters pretty plainly to him in a nice way. Of course Greece is entirely in your hands and the ruling people know it, but it does no harm to remind them that you can be nasty if you like." I told Venizelos that I thought our diplomats had not rubbed into the Bulgars sufficiently the fact that we could prevent them from having Macedonia except on our terms, and when we bombarded Dedeagatch the other day they were speechless with indignation, and probably now considered it treachery that we were opposing them in Macedonia. I went on to discuss the present situation, whether the change of Government affected us militarily or not. Venizelos said the situation was no worse. I then said I thought it was thoroughly unsatisfactory and somewhat dangerous if we could not have the Greeks as allies, as they might, without opposing us openly, (which he said was out of the question), give free passage to the enemy to come down and attack us in Greek territory. Venizelos did not think that was possible, but would guarantee nothing. I then sounded him as to what he thought of our clearing out of Macedonia altogether. I said we had already lost our prestige in the Balkans, the proof being that Greece and Roumania had not come in. But in reality we were in a very strong position in Europe, and Germany was already beaten. We could afford to let this theatre of war go if we could act with more effect elsewhere. In fact I hinted we might leave Greece to stew in her own juice. That of course did not at all appeal to Venizelos. He said the Germans would gain immense resources in copper and other supplies if we abandoned the Balkans and Turkey. I had not included Turkey, I told him, in my suggestion. But anyhow, he was very keen that we should continue to pour troops into Salonika even if we were obliged temporarily to abandon the offensive in the West, and eventually perhaps attack the Austrians across the Danube with the help of Greeks and Roumanians. I asked him if he could raise a revolution here, as the King was so thoroughly bound to Germany; or must we continue to base our hopes on the King and Government? Venizelos said he had not thought of that. Perhaps he could. But in a time of grave national crisis, it might be an unpatriotic thing to do. That would depend on circumstances. If he thought the safety of his country depended on it he would not shrink. But if we brought an overwhelming force to Salonika the people would force the King to join us.

About this time there was a parade of the Infantry Division here. I saw three regiments of three battalions each march past without packs. The men looked of very good physique. They marched well. Companies were divided into three platoons in open column and the strength of a company did not exceed 180 men. I lunched at the Russian Legation where there was great excitement because it had been ascertained that of all the foreign Military Attachés only the German and Austrian had been invited and were present at the parade in uniform. The Russian Minister, Prince Demidoff, was furious and said he would demand an explanation. I, not being a properly accredited Military Attaché to the Court at Athens, had not expected an invitation, and was too far from the saluting base, being in plain clothes, to see if any Foreign Attachés were present. It afterwards transpired, or was explained, that the German and Austrian Military Attachés had gone to the Palace on that day in uniform to write their names, as it was the anniversary of the capture of Salonika from the Turks, and presumably had attended the parade afterwards by way of compliment.

Chapter Fourteen.

NEW PREMIER, M. SKOULOUDIS, WARNS FRENCH MINISTER THAT HE WILL INTERN ENTENTE TROOPS IF DRIVEN OVER GREEK FRONTIER — SUGGESTION OF ULTIMATUM TO GREECE AND THREAT OF BOMBARDMENT—ADMIRAL DE ROBECK APPROVES OF TAKING FLEET TO PIRAEUS—SIR FRANCIS ELLIOT VISITS LORD KITCHENER AT MUDROS—I ACCOMPANY HIM—COUNCIL MEETING ON BOARD—LORD KITCHENER'S VIEWS — LORD KITCHENER VISITS KING OF GREECE—COLONEL BUCKLEY SUGGESTS MY RETURNING TO ROUMANIA—ORDERED HOME—CAPTURED BY SUBMARINE—EXPERIENCES ON SUBMARINE VOYAGE TO CASTEL NUOVO—JOURNEY TO VIENNA—PRISONER OF WAR CAMP AT SALZERBAD—EXCHANGED—APPOINTED BRITISH MILITARY REPRESENTATIVE AT SOFIA—DEMOBILIZED.

On November 10th the French Assistant Military Attaché happened to be sitting next to me in the train going down to the Piraeus. He told me the startling news that on the preceding evening the new Greek Premier, M. Scouloudis, had had the impertinence to tell the French Minister that in case the Serbian or our troops were driven across the frontier, the Greek Government would be obliged to intern them. The situation of the French at Krivolak was very serious, and it was possible such a thing might happen. Therefore it was absolutely necessary for us to threaten Athens by bringing warships to the Piraeus. I was very surprised at his news, as Sir Francis Elliot had said nothing about it in the Chancery that morning. The Frenchman said that his Minister would probably inform Sir Francis at their daily conference that evening; so I went to the Legation late. Sure enough the Minister was very perturbed, although outwardly he always took everything very quietly, and even consulted us—Erskine, Sells, and myself—for a few moments. Sells came to dinner with me, and we returned to the Legation at 10 p.m. Sir Francis had written out his telegram, but there were several points that we did not like. One was that while advising our Government to give Greece an ultimatum, he put in brackets that he was sure the King would not accept it. Another point was that he advised the alternative of Greece demobilizing. A third point which I myself had suggested, but had thought better of, was that the French troops and our own should be withdrawn at once to Salonika. I told Sir Francis that I would draft another telegram looking at the question from a military point of view, but it was then too late to cypher it and his telegram was sent. On the following morning I gave him my version suggesting a twenty-four hours' ultimatum to Greece to declare herself for or against the Entente, allowing Greece to keep her agreement with us secret for the present, but compelling her to declare openly to Germans and Bulgars that they would not intern our troops, but would resist the invasion of Greek territory by Germans or Bulgars by force. That we could not ask them to demobilize, but would bombard Athens and the Piraeus if our troops were molested. I also advised that our troops should remain where they they were, if they could avoid a defeat; that was to say, that they should not retire because of the Greek menace. Sir Francis Elliot was very nice about this telegram and said that I had put what he had said in a clearer form, all except the question of demobilizing, and he added to my telegram a remark that he would not place himself in opposition to military opinion on that question, and the telegram was despatched. I told Samson, who was in direct communication with the War Office, and who sent a telegram to the Director of Military Operations to call attention to mine to the Foreign Office. I wondered what would be the result, but hearing that our Government had sent the Greek Consul in London out here unofficially, with orders to ascertain whether it would be of any use our threatening the Greek Government and even ascertain it from Venizelos and the Prime Minister, it made me almost despair

CHAPTER FOURTEEN.

of the Government ever doing anything right in the way of diplomacy. But I hoped that this report might not be true. Some five or six days previously I had sent a telegram to the Director of Military Operations warning our Government that our troops might be largely outnumbered by the Bulgars who could bring against them three well-equipped divisions well acquainted with the country. It had been a question whether it would not be better to withdraw and hold fast to Salonika, but since that time, having heard that two more British Divisions had arrived at Salonika, this anxiety had been removed.

On November 12th, a telegram arrived from Admiral de Robeck to say he approved of moving the fleet here and had asked permission of the First Lord. He asked us to do our best to locate the enemy's submarines. We had had a meeting of Military Attachés previously and they seemed to think that our fleet would come here simply to make a demonstration and not to cut the Gordian knot. I hoped that would not prove to be true. The Chamber had been dissolved the day before, which was a bad sign, and there was a report that some 8 or 9 classes of reservists were being demobilized, presumably for the elections, but possibly because the Greek Consul above mentioned might have suggested the alternative of demobilization. The Greeks would probably jump at that if they had a secret understanding with Germany and Bulgaria, and did not fear a raid on Salonika, which would be the most unfavourable state of affairs for us. If, on the other hand, they had no secret understanding, then we would be disarming them against our own interests. I reckoned that they had three army corps round Salonika and were preparing to send the 1st and 2nd army corps towards Monastir.

On the 15th November, having heard that Lord Kitchener was at Mudros, Sir Francis Elliot decided to go and see him. I suggested accompanying him and we started at 11 o'clock that day in the "Imogen," a small despatch boat belonging to the

Royal Navy, but only steaming 11 knots, and therefore at the mercy of any submarine that thought us worth a torpedo. From this boat we were transferred in mid-ocean to a British destroyer, and reached Mudros after a very unhappy time in a rough sea. Unfortunately the rest of my diary from which these notes have been taken almost word for word was sunk by me a few weeks later, just before I was captured by a German submarine, and many interesting facts and conversations have escaped my memory, but our meeting with Lord Kitchener was not to be forgotten. It took place aboard a battleship, I think the "Queen Elizabeth." Lord Kitchener saw Sir Francis Elliot first privately, and then came into the Council meeting where were assembled Admiral de Robeck, Sir John Maxwell, and Sir Henry McMahon, who was then British Agent and Consul General in Egypt, and many other officers. During the conference Lord Kitchener said to me "So you are in favour of giving Greece an ultimatum and of bringing the fleet to Salamis ready to bombard Athens and the Piraeus?" I replied "Yes, sir, but before doing so I think it would be very advantageous if you would see the King of Greece, who, being himself a soldier, would be greatly impressed by talking over matters with our Minister of War." Lord Kitchener did not at all agree to this and said how could he hope to succeed where Venizelos had failed. I then suggested that if he would guarantee to assist Greece by landing a definite number of men, say 300,000, at Salonika, that might influence the King very considerably. To this Lord Kitchener replied that he certainly would not guarantee the King of Greece a fixed number of men nor tell him how many troops he was sending to Salonika. No doubt the Kaiser would be very glad to know, but he would rather do without Greece's help altogether than do so. I suggested that probably the Kaiser anyhow knew the destination of whatever troops left Great Britain. By this time Lord Kitchener was not in the best of tempers and it was useless to

CHAPTER FOURTEEN.

continue the discussion. However, Sir Francis Elliot who had, I believe, previously suggested the same course to Lord Kitchener, subsequently telegraphed to the Foreign Office recommending that Lord Kitchener should see the King. In a few days time we heard, after our return to Athens, that Lord Kitchener was coming to visit the King.

Lord Kitchener duly arrived and the interview took place. I was told afterwards by the King's A.D.C. that the King was delighted with Lord Kitchener and even General Dusmanis was pleased. No wonder, for it appeared that Lord Kitchener had told the King that he was against the Salonika expedition, and he considered that every shot fired at a Bulgar was a shot thrown away, as we wished to kill the Germans, not the Bulgars.

In recommending troops to be landed at Salonika, my original object had been to prevent the Bulgars from going against us, and afterwards there was the moral obligation of endeavouring to save the Serbian army from destruction. Thirdly, the Roumanians were anxious for a diversion to be made against Bulgaria to enable them to come in, and also assist the Serbs from the North. Knowing that we were not properly equipped for mountain warfare and that the terrain was very difficult, I personally had no faith in the Salonika expedition being able to achieve much headway in the direction of Sofia, or to save the Serbs, without the assistance of the Greek army. When Colonel Buckley came as a Staff Officer for Intelligence with Lord Kitchener to Athens, he asked me what I would like to do in future. I said I would prefer active service on the French front, but he suggested that I would be better employed in continuing the work of a Military Attaché, and proposed my going back to Roumania. I replied that I was convinced that Roumania would do nothing for another six months and that I would be of more use in that capacity if I could first see something of what was going on on the French front and after that on the Russian front. Then, with that amount of experience, I thought I might carry more weight in tending my advice than I would at present. Colonel Buckley promised to send me definite instructions later on. About a week later Sir Francis Elliot wished me to go to Salonika in my capacity as temporary Military Attaché for the Legation. I accordingly took my passage on a steamer for Salonika. Unfortunately the steamer was a day late, and meanwhile I received a telegram from the War Office ordering me home. I therefore embarked for Naples on a Greek steamer the following day, and found myself a fellow passenger with Captain Stanley Wilson, M.P., the King's Messenger, who was conveying a number of Foreign Office bags to London. Hitherto Greek vessels had been immune from submarine attack, and no better means of transport was available. I booked my passage in my own name, travelling with an official passport, and paid the Minister of War a farewell visit the night before leaving. I recollect on that occasion the Minister of War jumped up and offered me his office chair, begging me to be seated. Of course I declined the honour and he then said, " But that is what you and your allies are doing in Salonika." We had in fact at that time been insisting on the Greeks removing their troops from Salonika in order to make room for our own men. I compromised matters by promising that I would recommend that we should leave a small number of Greek troops in garrison to maintain the dignity of the Greek flag, but that to avoid congestion I knew that our military authorities insisted on having plenty of room. No slight whatever was intended to Greece, I told him, although as a matter of fact we were none too sure of the behaviours of the Greek army. We parted, as far as I was able to judge, on very good terms.

I am, of course, unable to say whether or no the Greek Government or enemy spies informed the German submarines of the presence of Captain Wilson or myself on the Greek boat by wireless, or whether it was pure chance; but on the 4th December, just as we were emerging from the Gulf of

CHAPTER FOURTEEN.

Corinth into the Ionian Sea on a bright Sunday afternoon, the wicked-looking snout of a submarine suddenly shot out of water a mile or two away and fired across our bows, ordering us to stop. We had passed some Greek submarines on the way but this was evidently an enemy which had been pursuing us. I at once went down to my cabin which was not near Wilson's, in order to destroy what papers I had. Fortunately I had put no letters or despatches into the Foreign Office bag, as I was going home myself, but I had some very secret papers of my own and some official correspondence which I was taking to London on behalf of the Russian Legation at Athens, as well as some letters from a French gentleman in Athens. I sank my own correspondence (easily done, as it was contained in a thin leaved heavily-bound diary), and confided the French and Russian letters to a Spaniard, my cabin companion, who kindly undertook to deliver them. When I came up again on deck I found Wilson pacing up and down the deck in despair. He pointed to something floating like a buoy 100 yards off the ship. This was one of his immense Foreign Office bags which he had thrown into the water according to his instructions, but which had failed to sink, although it had been previously weighted in the Legation. The submarine was now coming up from the other direction and there was just a chance, if we paid no attention to it, that the bag which was floating away to leeward with us between it and the submarine would escape notice, as it was already getting lower in the water. The submarine megaphoned for the Captain to come over with the passenger list. This he did and presently a megaphone message came for me, for Captain Wilson and Captain Finlay, a medical officer returning from Serbia, to go on board the submarine. The Captain's boat returned for us, the Captain himself being detained. On reaching the submarine we were interrogated by its Commander. Finlay, who was wearing the Red Cross badge, was released, and Captain Wilson and I were declared prisoners of war. We were allowed to return to the ship to fetch some clothes, and on rejoining, the submarine quickly submerged. Captain Wilson had handed over his remaining Foreign Office bags, some four or five in number, to the custody of an American lady who was on board the Greek boat and kindly undertook to deliver them either to the War Office or the nearest British Embassy. On being interrogated as to what had happened to his despatches; Wilson's passport shewing that he was a King's Messenger, the latter replied that they were sunk, and we were convinced that the enemy had failed to notice the bag in the water. No examination was made of the Greek vessel, as it was already getting dark and the submarine Commander was impatient to be off. We remained submerged all that night, came to the surface the next morning and had one or two engagements with British ships. Wilson and I were down below and could not see what went on except that the men stood by, close to our bunks, ready to fire a torpedo in case of need. The submarine, however, confined its activities to gunfire. On one occasion we exchanged some ten or twelve shots with a British vessel said by the Captain to be a cruiser, but it was most probably a trawler, as we kept just out of its range. The sensation was most uncomfortable as each moment we thought we might get sent to the bottom by our own warship. The officer commanding the submarine was a German called Captain Ganzer, and all his officers and crew were North Germans. They were, however, flying the Austrian flag and did not acknowledge their nationality until I assured them that I could recognize by their accent that they came from North Germany and not from Austria. They treated us with every courtesy, shared their food with us, and the Captain gave me up his bunk while the First Lieutenant did the same for Wilson. They said they had sunk some 13 vessels, about one a day, since their departure from Hamburg. They had come out via the Straits of Gibraltar without having had to replenish their supply of petrol. There was one Indian

Lascar on board, a survivor from one of the vessels that had been sunk. In the Captain's cabin there hung two scrolls; on one was inscribed in large lettering, the Kaiser's declaration that he would continue the war to the last breath of man and horse, and on the other was a sentence to the effect that as long as an officer did his duty and obeyed his orders, he was not responsible for anything that might happen. Captain Ganzer gave me the impression of being a gallant and capable seaman and naturally a humane person. After the second night of being submerged, during which we passed under a cordon of patrol boats, we came to the surface on a bright sunny morning, and when we were within a mile or two of the harbour of Castel-Nuovo, three Austrian cruisers came to meet us and escort us in triumph into the harbour. But before we proceeded very far, there was a shout that an enemy submarine was near, and almost immediately a torpedo passed just behind the last cruiser and in front of our bows. As we had been considered to be out of the danger zone, Wilson and I had been allowed on deck, and the sight was most thrilling. The cruisers began firing at a range of a few hundred yards and dashed out here and there. Our Captain was dancing about on the bridge, but fortunately they failed to bag the French submarine which had been lying in wait for us off the mouth of the harbour. When we arrived at Castel-Nuovo after a slight interrogation by an officer of the General Staff, who brought us before the General commanding the garrison, we were conducted to an old Turkish fort occupying a very picturesque position over the town. There we met two French submarine officers who had just been captured after a gallant resistance, from another submarine which had run aground on a sandbank; they had succeeded in landing on an island and carrying on a desultory fight for a couple of hours before they gave themselves up with their crew, after having destroyed their own submarine. These poor officers were as much in despair as we ourselves. We were all treated with great consideration for the few days that we remained together in that fortress. Two of the French bluejackets who had been killed during the engagement were accorded a funeral with military honours, which we could see taking place in the town far below. On being landed, Captain Wilson and I applied to be treated as Austrian prisoners as we had been captured under the Austrian Flag. However, Captain Ganzer considered us as his lawful spoil, and detailed his First Lieutenant and a couple of his blue-jackets to escort us to Berlin by rail. It was not until we reached Vienna that we were taken out of the train and put into an Austrian prison in Vienna for some three or four days, pending a decision as to our destination. We were finally transferred to Salzerbad, a little disused watering place some 30 miles West of Vienna, situated on the lower spurs of the great Alpine range. Here we were incarcerated in a prison camp with some 300 Russian officers, but no other Britishers, and with hardly a soul who could speak a word of English. We were allowed to read all German and Austrian newspapers but none of the Entente or of neutral countries. A room was set apart for a library where the Russian officers had put up maps of every theatre of war, and the movements of troops were accurately marked by flags. Our information was good, as the Germans always published the enemy communiqués as well as their own. A report appeared of the Germans having captured a Foreign Office bag at the same time as we were made prisoners. We did not believe this to be true, until letters were published from members of our Legation at Athens which were evidently genuine, as we thought it had not been picked up. Long after, Captain Wilson heard from the First Lieutenant, who in turn had been made a prisoner by our Navy, that they had fished up the bag when we were below, and had not told us. After some weeks we were joined by our two French submarine fellow-prisoners who had meanwhile been detained for a month at a special kind of punitive camp, under orders from the Austrian Admiralty. Their numbers were subsequently augmented by

CHAPTER FOURTEEN.

some 10 or 12 more French Naval officers and Flying officers. Also, later, came officers of our own mercantile marine, some 20 in number, who had been taken from vessels torpedoed in the Mediterranean. We were treated on the whole very well. The food was, of course, very bad and it would have been hard with us if we had not been able, after some two or three months, to obtain a more or less constant supply of food parcels from home. A large proportion of these were pilfered en route, but nevertheless we were able to form a reserve store which tided us over all difficulties. The Russian officers were not so fortunate. We did what we could to help them but many of them never got any parcels at all. The very few who could afford to buy such luxuries were able to supplement their rations by paying the Austrian caterer who supplied us with food. Captain Wilson and I did not do this, preferring to take the ordinary prisoner's ration, calculated at the price of 3 kronen a day, at that time representing about half-a-crown. For this sum we got coffee and bread for breakfast, soup and milk pudding for dinner, the milk pudding being a special diet in lieu of meat and sanctioned by the doctor on plea of health. In the evening we again got tea or coffee with cold sausage or sometimes preserved eggs or cheese and brown bread. Later on eggs and milk were unprocurable, and our bread got steadily worse. The Austrians themselves after our first year of imprisonment were very hard put to it for food, and we frequently gave our ration of bread to the famished sentries outside the wire enclosure after dark. Whenever caught, the sentries were put in the guard-room, but I do not recollect the case of an officer having been punished for giving food to a sentry. The prison camp was situated on the Northern slope of a narrow valley, rising to over 1,000 feet on either side, so that in winter although we could see the sun on the opposite slope of the hill, it only visited our camp in the extreme corner over a few feet of ground for a brief space of time. We were lodged in one large building containing bedrooms and public dining-rooms which had been formerly used as a kind of store room on the ground floor. There were also three or four small villas with 2, 3 and 4 officers in a room together. The enclosure was about 300 yards long by 50 or 60 yards broad, and was surrounded by a high wire fence with sentries, and bright lights at night, every thirty or forty yards. Within the enclosure we were unmolested, and so long as we did not approach close to the wire fence we were able to walk about at any hour of the day or night. Consequently many of the Russian officers who preferred to turn night into day, used frequently to stroll about singing at 3 a.m., to the great annoyance of others who wished to sleep. Although some of the Russian officers frequently drank too much and occasionally went stark mad, they were very clever musicians and actors, and in the early part of our imprisonment used to provide us with musical plays and concerts. They had one or two bands and procured instruments such as violins, violincellos and balaleikas, (a Russian stringed instrument, something like a mandolin) and they hired theatrical costumes from Vienna. Many of the Russian officers were good dancers of the various Russion national dances, and at least one officer was a professional and very talented comic actor! So that once or twice a month we had some very amusing evenings, on which occasions the Austrian Commandant and his family and Staff used to be invited and enjoyed the performances. Unfortunately the camp was too restricted in the matter of space to admit of any games other than badminton. Wilson and I each procured a set of badminton requisites, and we played daily with the French officers. For about one year, owing to an attempt to escape on the part of a few Russian officers, we were prohibited from taking walks outside the camp. Before that, we had been in the habit of walking along the roads and even climbing the mountain sides accompanied by an escort of some twenty or thirty men armed with rifles and bayonet. The attempt to escape was unsuccessful, and as a punitive measure our walks were forbidden, although it did not occur during a walk. A year later, Russian officers were allowed out on parole every day, and this privilege was subsequently extended to the British once a week. Towards the end of my imprisonment I arranged to hire a piece of ground outside the camp, and procured some hockey sticks from Vienna for our merchant captains. We enjoyed a few games of hockey before I fell ill and was eventually exchanged against two young Austrian lieutenants. During the whole period of my imprisonment, only one officer, a Russian, succeeded in making good his escape. This he did disguised as a Russian private soldier in a fatigue party for cutting wood, and after about six months wanderings, eventually succeeded in reaching the Russian frontier.

Situated as we were, in a lonely spot among the mountains, nearly a months' journey on foot from any frontier, escape was a matter of great difficulty. The railways were very carefully guarded and to reach the Swiss frontier one had to pass through successive zones in which special passports were essential. The camp was so small and sentries so closely posted that one could be seen by at least two if not three sentries in making an attempt to get out of the wire enclosure. At night there were also frequent patrols with wolf hounds. Being only two British officers also increased our difficulties, as one's absence would have been so quickly noticed. Some four months before I was exchanged, the Austrian Government released Captain Wilson for some unknown reason, but possibly recognizing that as an M.P., and not a regular officer, his liberty might be more advantageous to the Austrian Government than if they continued to hold him prisoner. It is probable that they were hoping to secure an honourable peace, and thought that by earning the gratitude of a British M.P., they might secure an influential vote in their favour at a critical time.

When I was eventually exchanged through the help of Slatin Pasha, it was hinted to me that Austria would be glad to send a secret representative to

Switzerland, and that the Emperor would use his best endeavours to induce the German Kaiser to forego the Provinces of Alsace and Lorraine, in order to obtain peace.

On my arrival home I duly acquainted the Foreign office with this suggestion and also that Slatin Pasha was ready to proceed to Switzerland as the Austrian representative in case our Government thought fit to negotiate. Slatin being the head of the Red Cross in Austria and enjoying, as I believed, the confidence of the Emperor would have been a suitable person. His presence in Switzerland would have attracted no special notice as he had already been there on more than one occasion on Red Cross work. The Foreign Office, however, had someone else in view, but in any case the negotiations had no result.

Shortly after my arrival in England, I was obliged to undergo an operation which was partially the result of my long imprisonment, and it was nearly a year before I entirely recovered my health. During this period I was employed for some months in the Censor's department of the War Office, and just before the armistice was signed I was sent out to Bulgaria once again, this time in the capacity of British Military Representative. I arrived towards the end of November, 1918, and took up my quarters at the British Legation at Sofia, where I remained for five months before being demobilized and again reverting to retirement.

The new King, Boris III., who had ascended the Bulgarian throne on the abdication of his father, was behaving with great tact and judgment under extraordinary difficulties. In addition to his charming personality and frank simplicity of behaviour, he possessed the advantage of having been born a Prince of Bulgaria and of belonging to the orthodox Church. He was in consequence extremely popular. The Government at this time represented a coalition of the various Parties, Nationalist, Democrat, Radical, Progressive Liberal, Socialist and Agrarian. Bolshevism had raised its head in certain quarters of the city and at the coal mines.

Military Attaché R.

CHAPTER FOURTEEN.

Stambolisky was still a fugitive, but the Agrarian Party was becoming more powerful, and there was a question of admitting him to the Cabinet, a proceeding not exactly relished by the Premier, M. Theodoroff.

Meanwhile the Government had its hands full in dealing with foreign affairs. During this period I found myself in hearty agreement with the other foreign representatives, notably the French, General Chrétien, the Italian General, Freri, and also his successor, General Count Mombelli, the Italian Minister, Baron Aliotti, who was afterwards accredited to the Bulgarian Government, and the American Chargé d'Affaires, Mr. Wilson. We, however, were not in accord with the general policy that was being pursued by the Entente through the medium of General Franchet d'Esperey. The latter had negotiated the terms of the armistice in which Bulgaria had surrendered to the Entente. Certain promises and hopes were held out to the Bulgars at that time which little by little were gradually whittled away, thereby damaging the reputation of the Entente for honest dealing. I incurred the criticism of my military superiors in the War Office for unduly favouring Bulgarian pretensions and "endeavouring to soften the blow" that was eventually to fall upon them. In spite of this I continued to protest against the imposition of certain fines and other illtreatment of Bulgaria at the hands of some of our allies, as I thought it my duty to do, and I deplored the policy of cutting Bulgaria off from the Mediterranean and of depriving her of her Thracian Provinces in favour of Greece. For these reasons I was replaced by another officer, Brigadier-General Baird, possibly some months earlier than would otherwise have been the case. I fully recognised that in the interest of maintaining the Entente Cordiale with France, our Government was not infrequently obliged to act differently from what it might have done in other circumstances, so I made no complaint. Personally, I was glad at not having been obliged to be present at the final undoing of a gallant little nation that had involuntarily been driven by her King and through the force of circumstances into the opposite camp.

So strongly, however, did I feel that we were pursuing a wrong policy with regard to the Near East, that in passing through Rome, I went to see Sir Rennell Rodd, and after some conversation asked him if he could arrange for me to see someone in Paris, preferably Mr. Balfour, on my way through. He very kindly consented to send a telegram to say that I was passing through Paris, and on my arrival there I at once went to call at No. 23, Rue Nirot, where Mr. Lloyd George and Mr. Balfour were staying. I was received by Mr. Philip Kerr, who was glad to hear my views although he did not share my opinion regarding the advantage of keeping an outlet for Bulgaria on the Aegean Sea, in fact of not depriving her of the coast-line which she then possessed. To my remonstrances at the pro-Greek policy which was then beginning to make itself felt, Mr. Kerr replied that Mr. Venizelos had done more than any single person to further the Entente action in the Near East during the war, and intimated that whatever he asked for must be granted. I was then passed on to Mr. Balfour's private secretary, and after a few minutes conversation, had the good fortune to be received by Mr. Balfour himself. I protested against the idea of basing a policy on the merits of one man, and opined that if one took away Mr. Venizelos there would be nothing left. I emphasised the advantage of keeping an outlet for Bulgaria on the Aegean, which would render her in future more susceptible to our influence, and not throw her back upon the Danube, Central Europe and the Black Sea. I received a most sympathetic hearing from Mr. Balfour, and although I was afterwards very disgusted at finding that Greece had not only been awarded the whole of the littoral, but also Eastern Thrace, I consoled myself with the idea that perhaps I had at least been instrumental in securing to Bulgaria one port on the Aegean.*

The above interview occurred on the 16th March, 1919, but unfortunately even this modest programme

---
* Vide Letter from Mr. Balfour's Private Secretary.

has not yet, in September, 1923, been realised, and a reference to Appendix B shows that it contains the germ of future trouble. I think I may also claim that time has already shown the correctness of my views. No one now remains to defend Mr. Lloyd George's Grecian policy. But I maintain that had it been found possible to treat Bulgaria with greater generosity, the situation of the Near East would have been far better to-day. It was a thousand pities that, owing to our short-sighted policy in the years 1913—15 we were unable to secure a firm ally in this most important strategical position. It is almost as tragic now to think that, unable to profit by our sad experience, we should have backed the wrong horse and attempted to use Greece instead of Bulgaria as Europe's bulwark against Turkish aggression. The result is now apparent in the retrocession of Eastern Thrace to Turkey, and the consequent enforced abandonment of our position dominating the Straits which cost us so much blood and treasure to acquire, and of which it is so important for the League of Nations to retain the control.

The evil genius that watched over the Treaties of Versailles and of Neuilly, but was not able to stifle the birth of that promising infant, the League of Nations, must have smiled sardonically over the result of the Conference of Lausanne, bequeathing as it does a crop of fresh difficulties to the tender care of the League. It was not enough to have bound Bulgaria hand and foot by reducing her total military forces to 20,000 men in face of the hostile armies of Roumania, Yugo-Slavia and Greece, the two former being each capable of raising over a million armed men, and possessing a peace strength of 250,000 and 150,000 respectively. Now Turkey is firmly and legally re-established in Europe, and has even been granted a bridge-head opposite Adrianople enabling her to debouch with ease across the Maritza—a mere detail in comparison with her other gains.

It is instructive in this respect to look back over the map of Europe and note how history is apt to repeat itself. Three hundred years ago the Turkish

Empire profiting by the dissensions of the German States had succeeded in extending her European frontiers up to the walls of Vienna, had swallowed up nearly the whole of Hungary, possessed a common frontier with Poland and had absorbed the Northern shores of the Black Sea including the Crimea. And France, allied with Turkey against Charles V., Emperor of Germany, pushed her frontier nearer to the Rhine.

The latest information shows that Turkey is now still further increasing her military forces in Europe, and Bulgaria has appealed to the League of Nations for protection against Yugo-Slavia. Yugo-Slavia, uneasy at the incursion of Macedonian Bands is threatening to occupy Bulgaria, not questioning her good faith, but her ability to prevent such incursions.

"Surely it is high time that European diplomacy should devote itself to procuring the inclusion of Bulgaria among the Christian States of the Little Entente and that she should be permitted to maintain a force more commensurate with her population and environment. Were a general disarmament in sight, there would be no such need. But with Turkey, outside the League of Nations, restored and confident with an army on the increase, it is impossible to reduce the forces of Roumania and Yugo-Slavia. Now that Germany is in the melting pot, and Russia in the hands of Bolshevik adventurers, the Little Entente is the guardian of the safety of Europe."

In round numbers* the various populations of these countries may now be put at:

Roumania	17,000,000
Yugo-Slavia	11,000,000
Greece	5,000,000
Bulgaria	5,000,000
Turkey	9,000,000

How important is it therefore that Bulgaria should be preserved from again falling into the Turkish orbit!

---

* Footnote.—For more detailed information vide "The Statesman's Year Book."

Appendices.

In Chapter XII of the foregoing diary, mention was made of the Agrarian Leader, Stambolisky, and his outspoken behaviour before the King on the occasion of the latter's audience to the Leaders of the various Opposition parties. Stambolisky did, in fact, threaten him with the loss of his crown in the event of another catastrophe similar to that of 1913 befalling Bulgaria, in consequence of His Majesty having adopted a wrong course. For this Stambolisky was promptly imprisoned by the King, and kept confined until the commencement of the Bulgarian collapse, more than two years later, and the approach of a revolutionary force towards the capital, when he was pardoned and released. Stambolisky, thereupon, went off to Radomir to meet the malcontents, flocking back to Sofia from the front, and issued a proclamation declaring Bulgaria a republic and himself President, with his friend Dashkaloff (now a Cabinet minister) Commander-in-Chief. A battle ensued with the loyalist troops; the rebels, thanks to the intervention of some of Mackensen's troops, were beaten, and Stambolisky, became a fugitive. Nevertheless the King abdicated, as it was clear that the country would no longer support him, and his son Prince Boris was proclaimed King by the Coalition Government then in force.

Stambolisky was amnestied early in 1919, and was shortly after somewhat reluctantly received by M. Theodoroff into the Cabinet. No long interval (August, 1920), elapsed, however, before he became President of an Agrarian Government, pledged, amongst other reforms, to bring to book the leading members of King Ferdinand's Government of 1915, on the charge of High Treason to the State.

This Trial did not commence until the year 1921, and the following items in Appendix A are extracted from the proceedings as recorded in the "Echo de Bulgarie." It is hoped that the reader will find it of interest to compare these revelations with the views and conjectures as recorded from day to day in the foregoing pages by the Military Attaché.

As regards Appendix B, I have translated some extracts from the "Echo de Bulgarie" of the 9th January, 1922, in order to show the opinions of eminent Bulgarians on the question of the award of Thrace to Greece, and the consequent deprivation to Bulgaria of access to the Aegean Sea.

Stambolisky continued in office as Prime Minister until June, 1923. His foreign policy gradually gained for Bulgaria

APPENDIX. 247

sympathy abroad and the Bulgarian indemnity was largely reduced owing to his efforts. He also lost no opportunity of endeavouring to win the approval of the Little Entente, and especially of Yugo-Slavia to Bulgaria's aims, and thereby incurred the hostility of the influential Macedonian party in Bulgaria. This he might have survived, but, unfortunately, M. Stambolisky, although admirable in Foreign Affairs—a sufficiently remarkable fact in a man with little education, who, as a shepherd boy, had belonged to the lowest class of Bulgarian peasantry—was unable to withstand the strong wine of unlimited power, and became a tyrant in Home Affairs. Besides the Ministers whose arraignment for High Treason forms the subject of Appendix A, most of whom were sentenced to varying terms of imprisonment, he also imprisoned in the autumn of 1922 certain Ministers of former Governments, whose chief crime was that they were opposed to the tyrannical Agrarian Party, of which M. Stambolisky was the head.

A sudden revolution* carefully organised for months by retired army officers and others, led to his sudden overthrow on the 9th June, and his subsequent capture and his presumed death near his native village. The fact of his body not having been recovered has given rise to various accounts of his last moments, but the general conclusion is that he was shot by the troops when endeavouring to escape with the help of a band of sympathising peasants. He was, undoubtedly, a great man, and did much for his country.

The revolution, which partook of the nature of a Faschisti movement, seems to have been carried out with a minimum of disturbance and bloodshed.

It is a remarkable fact that the new Government are now using, and intend to continue to use for the current year, 1923, stamps, bearing the head of Mr. Bourchier, the late much-lamented " Times " Correspondent of the Balkans, who was so highly esteemed by the entire Bulgarian nation, that on his death a year or so ago, they accorded him a public burial in the Rilo Monastery, the most romantic spot in the Rhodope Mountains, south of Sofia.*§ These stamps were issued to commemorate the event and were to be used once a year, on the anniversary of his death.

Appendix C contains *inter alia* some letters of mine to the Press on Balkan affairs during 1922-23, and, arising out of them, a short correspondence with M. Stambolisky.

---

* *Vide* Manifesto reproduced from the " Echo de Bulgarie," page 250
§ *Vide* illustration opposite page 264.

Appendix A.
Trial at Sofia.

On the 21st November, 1921, M. Tontcheff, late Minister of Finance, was examined by the High Court on the charge of High Treason. M. Tontcheff, having given certain explanations regarding the dissolution of the Chamber at the end of 1914 and the negotiations with the Powers said: " By the terms of the Constitution the declaration of war is the prerogative of the King who can declare it without consulting the Chamber. Nevertheless the Chamber was consulted on several projects in 1914, concerning the loan of fifty million, another of one hundred and fifty million for the equipment of the army, the laws regarding a state of siege (martial law), the increase of soldier's pay in war time, etc. The opposition declared these credits to be necessary, but premature. Everything pointed to the approach of war. The military convention concluded by Colonel Gantcheff, at Pless, was not a political act. It was in conformity with the spirit of the political treaty. Whilst we were examining the proposals of the Powers, we took into consideration whether they were advantageous, risky, reliable, etc. The British Minister told us that if we did not accept the proposals of the Entente, he would advise Serbia to declare war on us.

A Member of the Court:—

" What was your criterion for judging of these proposals?"

The Accused: " Everybody was certain that the Central Powers would be victorious."

The Advocate General: What was General Fitcheff's opinion?

The Accused: Sometimes he said the Entente would be victorious, sometimes the Central Powers. One day he presented us with a report concluding with the fall of the Dardanelles. The following day he assured us that they would not fall.

The Advocate-General: Do you call it consulting the Chamber to demand loans, and to declare, as in March, 1915, by the mouth of the President, that Bulgaria would remain neutral?

The Accused: *Si vis pacem para bellum;* it was necessary to speak of neutrality. One could not do otherwise. At the private meeting of the majority of the legislature, M. Radoslavoff declared that circumstances demanded, at the instigation of Switzerland, that Bulgaria should proclaim an armed neutrality and he asked for the support of his

Sofia, le 9 Juin 1923.   Prix 1 leva   NUMERO SPECIAL

L'ECHO DE BULGARIE
JOURNAL QUOTIDIEN

Coup d'Etat dans le calme.
Arrestation des ministres agrariens.

L'opération s'éxécute sans incidents selon le programme minutieusement réglé.

Le nouveau gouvernement est une coalition d'indépendants et d'hommes de divers partis.

Les officiers d'active et de réserve et l'armée ont assuré la réussite.

Le programme intérieur est de paix, de concorde et d'union pour la liberté civique et pour un régime fiscal et économique libéral.

La vie des agrariens est sauve est sera respectée.

L'adhésion de la province et complète.

Le coup d'Etat. Cette nuit, vers 4 heures, un coup d'Etat a eu lieu dans le plus grand calme pour renverser le gouvernement agrarien. L'opération qui avait été minutieusement préparée, a réussi sans aucune difficulté. Elle était montée par une coalition sans distinction de parti et avec l'aide des officiers de l'active et de réserve — Les ministres de l'ancien gouvernement sont tous arrêtés.

Composition du gouvernement. Le nouveau gouvernement est ainsi composé:

Président du Conseil, guerre et Affaires Etrangères: Mr. **Alexandre Tsankof**, professeur, sans parti.

Intérieur: M. Général Roussef, sans parti.

Finances: M. Peter Todoroff, radical.

Communications: M. Dimo Kazassof, socialiste.

Justice: M. Boyan Smiloff, national-libéral.

Commerce, Industrie et Travail: M. Zvetko Bobochevski, obédéniste.

Agriculture, Instruction publique: M. Evstati Mollof, professeur, sans parti.

Travaux Publics: M. Tsanko Stoïntchoff, démocrat.

LE CALME. L'arrestation des ministres et le désarmement des quelques unités agrariennes de gendarmerie se sont opérés sans incident.

LE SORT DESAGRARIENS. Vis à vis du gouvernement agrarien qui vient de tomber, les intentions du nouveau gouvernement sont de le protéger, sans aucun esprit de vengeance, et la question de mort ne se pose même pas.

LE PROGRAMME INTÉRIEUR. Le programme de Politique interieure est le régime démocratique moderne de paix avec le rétablissement des libertés civiques et l'établissment d'un régime économique, financier et fiscal entièrement liberal. — Les anciens ministres internés à Choumen sont libérés.

SUCCES EN PROVINCE. Avec la province, les relations télégraphiques sont normales, et les nouvelles sont que partout dans les grandes villes le mouvement a eu lieu de la même manière et dans le même calme qu'à Philippopli, Varna, Choumen, partout officiellement. Toutes les garnisons provinciales avaient adhéré au mouvement.

Les gardes agrariennes ne manifestent aucune activité.

LE PROGRAMME EXTÉRIEUR. Le programme de politique exterieure du nouveau gouvernement est la continuation des principes du gouvernement agrarien. — On veut avant tout la paix, l'exécution des traités, le rapprochement politique et économique avec les voisins et avec les grandes puissances.

Les trains internationaux et les trains bulgares express circulent librement.

APPEL
aux habitants de Sofia.

Habitants de la Capitale!

La liberté de la Bulgarie s'est levée à nouveau. Le régime d'imposture, de mensonge, de violence et de meurtres s'est écroulé sous le poids de ses propres crimes. La poignée d'aventuriers qui n'ont épargné aucun coin de l'âme populaire, qui ont poussé des Bulgares contre des Bulgares, le frère contre le frère, le père contre le fils uniquement pour satisfaire leur manie de grandeur et leur avidité du pouvoir, sont désarmés.

L'ordre, la légalité, la concorde, la paix ont triomphé. Des jours illustres de progrès commencent pour la Bulgarie, car ses destinées se trouvent entre des mains pures, celles de tout Bulgare consciencieux des villes et de la campagne.

Sofiotes,

Défendons le nouveau gouvernement, celui de la loi et de la Constitution. Défendons notre sécurité, l'honneur et l'avenir de la Bulgarie.

Dans un esprit de courage civique, de discipline et de vaillance, montrons nous des citoyens dignes de la Bulgarie démocratique!

Vive Sofia, Vive la Bulgarie!

Le Conseil des Ministres.

ECHO... DE LA NUIT

Il ne faut pas s'en faire.

Ce matin un troupeau de gens divers conduits par des soldats vers de nouvelles destinées — et cette nuit quelques coups de feu; il y a du nouveau, un gouvernement est arrêté, un nouveau a pris le pouvoir.

Tout est en ordre, la machine administrative fonctionne et les amateurs de sensations fortes sont déçus, les trains fonctionnent.

Dans la matinée les rues étaient tranquilles, il est vrai que les magasins étaient fermés et que des postes de soldats jalonnaient les coins de rues.

Mais dès onze heures, et surtout après midi, la foule devient nombreuse, le soleil se met de la partie et des manifestations consacrent le nouvel état de choses.

De joyeuses automobiles sillonnent les artères de la capitale; ainsi se lève une nouvelle aurore, pleine, forte irrésistible et joyeuse.

MANIFESTE
AUX CITOYENS BULGARES

L'effondrement si souhaité et si longtemps attendu du gouvernement de violence et de corruption qu'était celui de M. Alexandre Stamboliisky est enfin un fait accompli.

Un pouvoir qui a élevé la violence à la haüteur d'un principe de gouvernement et la matraque comme moyen d'éducation politique des citoyens, qui pendant des années a foulé aux pieds les droits et les libertés du peuple sans aucun égard, qui au lieu d'unir le peuple semait la haine des classes — un tel pouvoir ne pouvait plus être toléré. Le systéme des asasassins politiques, la terreur sur les masses populaires, le gaspillage inouï des deniers publics, la corruption systématiquement répandue par un groupe d'éléments corrompus des villes et des campagnes, qui par des violences électorales sans précédent dans l'histoire politique de la Bulgarie, avait à deux reprises mis la main sur le pouvoir, — compromettaient la dignité de la Bulgarie dans le Pays et à l'Etranger. Le gouvernement de M. Stamboliisky est allé jusqu'à menacer de réduire en cendres plusieurs départements de la Bulgarie.

La politique de désagrégation de la vie économique du pays, la grande misère résultant de la politique économique et financière d'hommes d'Etat aux instincts feroces, acculaient le pays à une grande catastrophe économique.

L'indignation populaire s'est exprimée par l'audace et la résolution de toutes le forces publiques du Pays, et a forcé le cabinet de Stamboliisky à quitter le pouvoir. En assumant la lourde responsabilité de gouverner le pays, le nouveau cabinet estime qu'il est de son devoir impérieux de faire ses déclarations et d'inviter tous les Bulgares au calme, á la cohésion, a l'union.

Le premier devoir du nouveau gouvernement, c'est d'assurer la Paix et la tranquillité des citoyens, de rétablir les libertés civiques foulées au pied, en élevant le prestige du pouvoir.

Le gouvernement déclare que l'ordre et la tranquillité interieure du Pays seront sauvegardés à **tout prix**. Toute tentative de troubles, toute instigation contre l'Etat et le Gouvernement, toute atteinte aux droits, aux biens et à l'honneur des citoyens seront réprimées sans merci. L'armée, la gendarmerie et la milice policière ont reçu l'ordre d'étouffer, rapidement, résolument, sans pitié et par tous les moyens, toute tentative de compromettre l'ordre du Pays, et de punir toute résistance aux agents du Pouvoir.

Le gouvernement déclare qu'il tient compte de la Paix générale en Europe, respecte la dignité des grandes Puissances et des voisins de la Bulgarie; il déclare aussi qu'il exécutera loyalement le traité de paix et que la Bulgarie est opposée à **toute espèce d'aventures militaires**.

Issu du peuple et représentant une coalition de force, d'ordre et de progrès social, le gouvernement en appèlle à l'appui de tous. En soutenant le gouvernement, les citoyens soutiendront la Bulgarie.

Vive la Bulgarie

(Suivent les signatures des ministres)

APPENDIX A. 251

partisans. He was also in contact with the other parties. On the 7th and 8th of September the members of Parliament were at Sofia and if the Chamber was not summoned it was because the need for it was not felt . . . . .

A Councillor of the Court: Why did you ask for a report on the Dardanelles from General Fitcheff?

The Accused: That interested us. We did not consult the Staff as to the result of the European War. There was not a single soldier who was not convinced of the victory of the Central Powers.

The same Councillor: You say that according to your information the Serbs were preparing to attack us. But M. Tchaprashikoff, Bulgarian Minister at Nisch, in his report of the 17th September (1915) informed the Government that Bulgaria's neutrality was not menaced and that it would be better to keep quiet. Whence then came the opposite information to the Government?

The Accused: I noted several passages in M. Tchaprashikoff's reports, but I do not remember anything at this moment."

Did M. Radoslavoff communicate everything to the members of his Cabinet?

Sometimes he had a mysterious air, but I myself was always informed.

M. Toshkoff, defender of General Jekoff: Was there a connection between the Treaty of the 6th August, 1914, with Turkey and the pourparlers conducted in 1915 by Messrs. Koloucheff and Jekoff?

The Accused: No.

What where the bases of the pourparlers of 1915?

The base of neutrality.

In what capacity was General Jekoff sent to Constantinople?

As a simple delegate of the Government, provided with instructions from the Minister of Foreign Affairs. The question of the Maritza was more a military one, as it concerned the defence of our State. Consequently he was there as an expert. I do not know if General Jekoff was charged with the conduct of political pourparlers. I rather think that he discussed purely military questions. Military delegates were charged with military professional questions and did not mix with politics.

Who gave the order for concluding the military Convention at Pless?

I do not know exactly, but I think it was the King. General Boyadjieff did not approve of it. The King had this right in his capacity of Generalissimo, and he sent a man in whom he had confidence.

The Advocate-General: Are not military Conventions concluded on the basis of political Treaties?

The Accused: Colonel Gantcheff knew the political Treaties.

APPENDIX A.

Advocate Tochkoff: What directions were given to Colonel Gantcheff on the 6th (19th?) August, 1915, when he left for the second time for Germany, when General Fitcheff was Minister of War?

The Accused: I do not remember . . . .

Interrogation of M. Popoff.

The Minister of Justice in the Radoslavoff Cabinet was then interrogated. "The loan of 500 millions placed in Germany did not imply political engagements. We marched with Germany against Russia because the events of 1913 showed for the last time that the latter was against the liberation and its union with Bulgaria. The war was imposed upon us by Serbia. If the Serbs had not attacked us, the armed neutrality might have continued a long time.

The Advocate General: At what date and from whom did the accused receive the order to issue the declaration of war. In the second place if the delay of 35 days fixed by the Germans for M. Radoslavoff to declare war had lapsed without it occurring, what would the Cabinet have done?

The accused: Here there is an error of memory on the part of M. Pecheff. I do not remember having published the Manifesto on my own initiative or upon anybody else's. As for the delay of thirty-five days this is the first time I have heard of it. . . .

A Councillor: Who gave the principal direction to our diplomats abroad? Was it the Ministry of Foreign Affairs or the Council of Ministers?

The accused: I repeat that we were disciples of Montesquieu. We did not meddle with the affairs of the Department of our colleagues. Consequently it was M. Radoslavoff as Minister of Foreign Affaris who generally gave instructions. Nevertheless the reports of our Missions were sometimes read to the Council of Ministers who challenged his point of view during the meeting.

Why did Bulgaria range herself on the side of the double Alliance? What events imposed upon her this choice?

We wanted Macedonia, our ideal since the existence of Bulgaria. The double Alliance was at war with Serbia, who was in occupation of this unfortunate province. As the Serbs would not give it to us or rather as they were, in appearance only, ready to cede us but a portion of it, there was only one thing to be done and that was to march with those who were fighting against them.

The Advocate General: Did the accused know the secret Conventions? Had they been concluded by M. Radoslavoff unknown to his Ministers or with their approbation?

The Accused: Only up to a certain point. For instance, I know that Macedonia was promised to us in exchange for our neutrality.

By whom?

APPENDIX A.

By Germany of course. Turkey also ceded us the valley of the Maritza in exchange for our neutrality.

Did we not foresee the intervention of America?

No one foresaw it. I read the papers of the whole world. No one up to the end of 1917 had said that the Central Powers would be beaten. At Manchester the Professors said, " we shall be beaten." At this time everything was in our favour. We were fighting and we remained three years in Macedonia.

What was the basis of the negotiations of 1914?

The Treaty remained as a project only. The Turks wanted Roumania to enter into the alliance. But the Roumanians wished to be allies of Germany and friends of Russia.

Who sent Colonel Gantcheff to Pless?

I do not know.

Why did M. Tontcheff interest himself especially in Treaties?

Because they were bound up with financial questions.

* * * *

Interrogation of General Jekoff, 22nd November.

The General did not confess to having been guilty of any crime and still less of High Treason. He had always endeavoured to serve his country and denied formally the rumour of his pretended flight, which had weighed upon him even more than his sad fate. He had been sent to Sofia toward the middle of the month of June, 1915, under General Fitcheff, then Minister of War. From there he was sent by M. Radoslavoff, together with M. Koloucheff to open up negotiations with Turkey in order to obtain territorial concessions in exchange for the neutrality of Bulgaria. On his return from Turkey the King sent for him on the 2nd August and told him to go and see M. Radoslavoff, who, thereupon, offered him the post of Minister of War, which he accepted. General Fitcheff resigned on the 4th, after having been informed of his nomination. He entered the Cabinet as a soldier determined to avoid politics. The army belongs to the nation and not to the Government. Thus he had no political convictions. Towards the middle of August, M. Radoslavoff invited him one evening, in the presence of M. Tontcheff, to examine the project of a military convention prepared by the Germans and transmitted to Sofia by Colonel Gantcheff. At the same time Radoslavoff told him that they were about to conclude a treaty of alliance with Germany and Austria, and that the convention was but the result of this treaty. The Germans wished Bulgaria to send six divisions against Serbia, to which he objected, in order not to denude the other frontiers of troops, on account of Bulgaria's special situation. On the other hand, the Serbs had four divisions on the Bulgarian frontier. Thus the Bulgars could not send less than four divisions. The other question about which General Jekoff was most concerned was the appointment of General Mackensen to the chief command. A telegram was sent to General Gantcheff through the palace to the effect that it was preferable that Bulgarian troops should be commanded by a Bulgarian officer. The reply was that the question of the chief command was purely a matter of military concern, and by way of an example the fact was recalled that French troops at the beginning of the war had been placed under a British commander. Thus the appointment of General Mackensen was painful, but unavoidable. The convention was concluded in haste without regard to Jekoff's objection. Nevertheless, on the Serbian front the Bulgarian armies operated on a plan prepared by the Bulgarian General Staff, and their armies in Macedonia had complete liberty of action.

Negotiations with a view to the dispatch of a brigade to Burgas and Varna with the object of opposing an eventual landing did not take place. M. Radoslavoff was opposed to it. No one, in principle at any rate, was opposed to Turkish support, although later on it was one of the causes of the demoralization of the army. General Jekoff's conscience revolted at the idea of a subsidy of 200 million levas having been provided for in the convention. He declared that Bulgars were not mercenaries who would sell their arms, even if they were offered milliards. If Germany was imbued with the desire of helping Bulgaria she had only to assume all the expenses of the war valued at several millions. He was, therefore, of opinion that the financial question should be eliminated from the convention. The responsibility for this was his, but he did not wish Bulgaria to be humiliated by gifts. General Jekoff then gave details about a number of clauses, saying that he had only to do with the military side, the political side being the affair of the Government.

"By this convention," said he, "Germany engaged to guarantee us the neutrality of Roumania and of Greece. I also protested at the moment when Roumania declared her mobilization. That cost me a bad report from M. Radoslavoff to the King. I considered the convention as an annexe to the treaty of alliance concerning which I knew that negotiations were going on without knowing the contents, that is the extent of my participation in the policy of the Cabinet. I was already in the presence of a fait accompli: the way had been already chosen, and in my capacity as a soldier I had only to devote my efforts to making it a success." The replacement of General Fitcheff had been necessitated by purely military considerations, for Jekoff was considered a man who would maintain the point of view that Bulgaria must achieve its union by force of arms, whichever way was selected.

The Advocate General: When the accused became Minister did he express a wish to be informed as to the policy of the Government?

APPENDIX A. 255

The Accused: No; I did not consider my business to be political. The army has been prepared to enter into action and to be ready for every eventuality. The War Minister interests himself solely in the material and moral preparation of the army. At the moment when I occupied the post of Minister of War the question of intervention had been started, and events alone could have stopped it. If the Austrian and German armies had not succeeded in crossing the Danube the convention would have fallen to the ground and we would have observed an armed neutrality, because the situation of Bulgaria would have become dangerous. The concentration of the army on the Serbian frontier took place in accord with the convention, but after the plan which had been prepared long before by the General Staff of the army. I deny categorically that German and Austrian officers had been admitted into the Bulgarian army.

The Advocate General: The Entente Powers had approached the Bulgarian Government, who replied that they had mobilized in order to observe an armed neutrality. Did you not demand explanations?

The Accused: It is the duty of politcians to have recourse to the measures considered necessary. A gesture on their part would have stopped mobilization. Everything depended on the Government. It was only later that I had knowledge of Colonel Gantcheff's mission, and I do not remember who told me of it.

The Advocate General: For how long was the war expected to last?

The Accused: Duty knows no limits. The army had to be ready to fulfil its duty to the very end.

General Jekoff later on explained that the landing of the Entente armies at Salonika was a surprise for Bulgaria. These armies were intended to succour Serbia. Subsequently he took steps to obtain permission for his armies to cross the Greek Frontier in order to reach Salonika, but in the month of November (1915) he was told to stop at the frontier line, without any explanation as to whether Greece was to be treated as an enemy.

The Advocate General: Why had Turkish support been foreseen in the case of a landing at Dedeagatch?

The Accused: Because a landing in this neighbourhood would have been directed against Turkey and not against Bulgaria. . . .

The Advocate General: What do you know about the Serbian frontier incidents?

The Accused: I was Commander-in-Chief and our armies had not yet been concentrated. On the 26th or 27th September (new style 9th or 10th October), 1915, I told M. Radoslavoff that we ought to put off the military operations to a later date than the 28th September (11th October) in order to see the results of the Austro-German operations on the Danube, and I informed General Boyadjieff (Chief of the Staff)

APPENDIX A.

accordingly. On the 27th or 28th September (10th or 11th October) our troops advanced in our own territory in order to occupy points of departure. The Serbs considered this act as a provocation, opened fire, and hostilities commenced. That was the beginning of the war.

The Advocate General: At what date did you read to the Council of Ministers the general order to the army concerning the commencement of hostilities?

The Accused: The 30th September (13th October).
Did you demand explanations about the incident?
No; I thought it was going to be localised as we were not ready.

Examination of M. Pecheff on 28th November, 1921.

The Advocate General: Do you know that in the month of September, 1915, the leaders of the Opposition presented themselves before the King, in order to protest against a new orientation of Bulgarian politics?

The Accused: On the morning of this day the King sent for M. Radoslavoff and told him that he had decided to abdicate in consequence of the attitude of the leaders of the Opposition. That is all that I know.

Why did you write nothing in your journal about the desire of Ferdinand to abdicate?

I do not guarantee that all the pages of my journal have been preserved after having passed through so many hands before reaching the High Court. The King had taken the decision to abdicate on many other occasions also. For example, in 1914, but knowing him well we did not attach importance to this threat. If he had wished to abdicate for good and all, what could we have done?

On being interrogated regarding the direction of the war, M. Pecheff declared he was not guilty. The command, the equipment of the army, etc., were military matters and he was a civilian. He only learnt of the excesses in the region of the Morava after the war.

The Government did its best to assure food, both to the army and to the populace. I did my best against corruption and demoralization. My colleagues did not steal. Who did not speculate? I demand that an end be put to these insinuations that sand was sent to the front instead of flour. It was my duty to note facts and that was all. Regarding relations with the King, everyone had to defend his dignity as he could. When the King insulted us he also ended by excusing himself. As for me I never permitted either the King or M. Radoslavoff to insult me. With regard to the insult which the King inflicted when there was a question of requisitioning the Russian Legation,* I say that the King did what seemed good to him. We could not change it
. . . . .

---

* King Ferdinand prevented the requisitioning both of the Russian and the British Legations during the war.—H.D.N.

APPENDIX A.

Did you discuss at the Council of Ministers the proposal of the Opposition leaders not to declare war on Roumania?

I do not know anything more than what I have noted in my journal. We did not consider any measure for compelling the allies to fulfil the military conventions. We did not discuss the stopping of Bulgarian troops at the Greek frontier. I do not know if there exists a despatch of the President on this subject. We sent grain to Greece with the consent of the Commander-in-Chief. That is all that I know. I do not know exactly if our army was badly clothed. My impression was, as I have noted in my journal that the Generalissimo sent some incriminating letters on the want of food in the army.

Continuation of the examination of M. Tontcheff on 23rd November.

M. Tontcheff was interrogated under four headings, constituting acts in violation of the Constitution, namely, the exportation to Turkey of six waggon loads of cloth in exchange for 80,000 kilograms of wool, which was not imported. Also the exportation of cloth to Roumania and to Turkey in exchange for wool. The accused declared himself not guilty because the exportation of these things, although they were military equipments still constituted an act of friendliness necessary for the negotiations which were being carried on with regard to the cession of territory on the Maritza in favour of Bulgaria.

On the 27th January, 1922, M. Liaptcheff, a former Minister, was examined by the High Court. In reply to a question as to whether he knew anything about the loan of 500 million levas, he replied that in 1913, when M. Tontcheff was at Paris, M. Malinoff was sounded by the Russian Legation on the subject of a loan to Bulgaria. M. Malinoff asked his (Liaptcheff's) advice. He was of the opinion that the loan should be agreed to, but M. Toderoff had insisted on a refusal. The rumour went that it was a firm proposition but such was not the case, although M. Malinoff considered it as such and had a conversation with M. Radoslavoff on the subject. M. Liaptcheff considered that the meeting between the Austrian Heir-Apparent and the Emperor of Germany at Konopitz in 1914 was of great importance. Both at Paris and at Berlin they were inclined to give Bulgaria a loan, but the sacrifices demanded were great. The Government was against it, as they considered it bad for Bulgaria. . . . .

After further questioning on matters of detail, M. Liaptcheff affirmed that in his opinion, if there had been no Des Closières* affair, if the Entente had made serious and suitable proposals to Bulgaria, Radoslavoff's Govern-

---

* The Entente in the summer of 1915 spent a large sum of money in buying up grain in Bulgaria with the object of gaining the sympathies of the peasants, and preventing export to the Central Powers.—H.D.N.

Military Attaché S.

ment would have had much trouble in maintaining itself in power in March or April, 1915.

On the 28th January, the High Court examined the Journalist, P. N. Dashkoloff, as a witness. He expressed himself as follows:—" I am acquainted with the difficulties through which the negotiations were carried out concerning the loan of 500 millions. The conditions offered by the Bank Perrier (of Paris) were inadmisable, even for an Ententeophil Government. This latter Bank demanded a political safeguard to be furnished by Russia. It was not an easy matter to conclude a loan with Germany. Nevertheless, we were able to obtain the loan without political engagements. It was a financial loan and the Bank of Berlin demanded as a guarantee the monopoly of the tobacco export. I do not see any objections in the difficult times through which the country was passing in leaving the Pernik and other mines in German hands."

The President: The witness is invited only to speak about facts. . . .

On the question being put as to what the witness meant by saying that the Perrier Bank had demanded a political guarantee from Russia, the witness replied, " That is quite clear. Russia was to hold in her hand our whole foreign policy. . . . "

On a further question as to how he had learnt of the proposals which had been made by the Perrier Bank and by the Disconto Gesellshaft, the witness replied that he had learnt them from the Minister of Finance. . . .

Examination of M. Malinoff, former President and Minister of Foreign Affairs on the 31st January, 1922.

During the summer of 1915 the Opposition commenced to meet frequently, and M. Malinoff was authorized to speak in its name. On the 4th September, 1915, a Crown Council was assembled at the Palace at which Messrs. Malinoff, Gueschoff, Daneff, Tsanoff and Stambolisky were present. M. Malinoff laid down the unanimous opinion of the Opposition that Bulgaria should maintain neutrality. M. Tsanoff, the head of the Radical Party, read a paper saying that Bulgaria could not march with the Central Powers, but should place itself by the side of the Entente. M. Stambolisky also expressed his views, but did not say anything more than the preceeding speakers. He was correct and loyal. If he did say anything more as he asserts in his brochure, he must have said it after the close of the sitting of the Crown Council.

In 1918 M. Malinoff received a mandate from the Opposition to form a Cabinet, the then possible Cabinet, for there was friction between the parties. The question was raised as to the policy to be followed during the negotiations for the " Bloc." The programme drawn up contained various points; the assurance of the feeding and equipment of the army, the establishment with the Allies of relations in

APPENDIX A.

accordance with the Treaty, and a general tendency towards peace. There was complete agreement on these points. On the 21st June, 1918, the day of the formation of the Cabinet, M. Malinoff went to see M. Radoslavoff, who told him nothing special.

He endeavoured to get his bearings, but it was not until July, 1918, that he saw for the first time the Treaties of Alliance. As he was striving with these difficulties at the hands of the Representatives of the Allies, he demanded, by circular, to be informed of all the agreements and secret conventions passed by them.

The Bulgarian Government had promised to do everything for the army, because at a meeting of the Council of Ministers it was recognised that the situation was deplorable. In certain companies the soldiers were in want of footgear, in others of trousers, etc.

In a note of the 12th August, 1918, M. Malinoff demanded that the Allies should carry out their engagements. He received the reply, very late, that help was on the way.

The result of this was that relations became strained. It was only after the close of hostilities that we were told that the allies had engaged to send us twelve divisions, only in order to beat Serbia.

On the 30th September, M. Malinoff received a letter in which General Savoff offered his services to re-organise the army. It is known by the German papers that General Savoff arrived at Sofia on the 29th September, in order to place himself at the disposal of de Massow (German Military Attaché) with the object of overthrowing Malinoff's Cabinet. At this moment German detachments arrived at Sofia, and took up positions at and around Sofia.

* * * *

Later, on the same day, M. Malinoff continued his defence before the High Court as follows:—

"When I met General Jekoff in September, 1915, the latter did not plead the cause of the Liberals (Radoslavoff). The General did not occupy himself with politics, nor with party affairs. He was said to be a Democrat, but I do not know to this day if he belongs to my party.

"It is said that England advised us not to attach importance to the proposals of her allies (remark attributed to the British Minister, M. Ironside), but I never heard such a thing, and the documents which I have studied do not permit me to believe it. However, nobody can deny that there was a divergence of view between England and Russia.

"I know M. Fitzmaurice who often came to see me. He was an able man who had not come to make politics, but to see how they were made. He observed and tried to gain the sympathies of our country for his own country."

Dr. Ghenadieff, former Minister for Foreign Affairs, on being examined said: "At the end of 1913 I was charged with the task of sounding the "terrain" at Paris for a

APPENDIX A.

loan. The first condition that France laid down was the assurance that we were not bound to Germany and Austria. I told M. Poincaré that if that were so, we would not have come to Paris. He promised me the loan, not at the moment, but later on, in view of the fact that France was herself in want of money, and that others had asked for loans before us. I accordingly left, convinced that we would get the loan. Afterwards—I had already left the Ministry for Foreign Affairs—I was told at the (Bulgarian) Council of Ministers that France had laid down the condition that we should obtain the political guarantee of Russia. Up till this moment the Council of Ministers had firmly decided to conclude the loan in France. This condition was laid down at the instance of Russia, and many speakers in Parliament blamed the French Government for having agreed to Russia's condition. After this we looked elsewhere for a loan. At Berlin they asked for the tobacco monopoly, which was rejected. In my opinion the loan which was eventually concluded, had not a political character, for even after it, the Entente continued to make proposals to us to march with them, which showed they did not believe we were politically bound by the loan."

On the 2nd February, Dr. Ghenadieff, continuing his evidence, said that after his return from Rome, Paris and Vienna, he presented his Government with a report that Germany and Austria would be beaten, and that Bulgaria should march with the Entente. He knew that the King was not satisfied with his report. He learnt, finally, that the alliance with the Powers had been concluded, and that Roumania and Greece would not intervene against Bulgaria. During 1916 the King tried to put an end to him, but in spite of that he refused to seek refuge abroad. He likewise recalled the fact that at Rome the Austrian Prince Kevenhuller, charged with a mission, did not disguise his apprehensions as to the result of the war, which he hoped would soon be over in order that the conditions of peace might be less severe. He considered that Bulgaria ought to profit by the occasion to occupy Eastern Thrace, because after the fall of Constantinople, Russia would take possession of it.

On the 3rd February, the Engineer, M. Morphoff, former Director General of Railways, on being examined as a witness, said that both before and after the intervention of Turkey, waggons, loaded with munitions, arms and food, traversed Bulgarian territory with the authority and by order of M. Radoslavoff. He, the witness, and M. Apostoloff, the Minister of Railways, often stopped these trains, but after the orders given by M. Radoslavoff they were allowed to pass.

Another witness, M. Tocheff, former Bulgarian Minister at Vienna and Constantinople, said that, when he was at

Vienna, he knew nothing about the loan. He had always advocated a policy of neutrality to his Government. . . . The news given in August, 1915, by the German Minister at Athens to M. Venizelos that the witness and M. Ghenadieff, who was at that moment at Constantinople had concluded an alliance between Bulgaria and Turkey, was nothing but a German intrigue. When he was transferred to Vienna, he drew the attention of his Government for the last time in a report of the 5th August, 1915, to the effect that Bulgaria should remain neutral. In 1916 the King said to him, "We shall lose the war. But it is too late to repair the error. I cannot betray my allies." This, he repeated, in reply to the witness, who opined that it was not too late to repair the error. The King said that peace could only be made in common with all the allies.

On the 6th February M. Madjaroff appeared as a witness. As former Bulgarian Minister in London, although without instructions, he had assured Government circles that Bulgaria would maintain neutrality, and that as compensation it would be necessary to cede her the uncontested zone in accordance with the Bulgaro-Serb alliance of 1912, also the line Kavala-Seres and the Dobrudja up to the 1913 line, and the line Enos-Media. He was told that the first three points would be taken into consideration, but that England could not give complete assurances as to the fourth. England looked with mistrust on the neutrality of Bulgaria. Then he was transferred to Petrograd, where he met the same mistrust, although he gave assurances that if Bulgaria intervened, it would be on the side of the Entente. France promised Kavala. But the ex-King Ferdinand was firmly decided to fight on the side of the Central Powers. Nevertheless, until the last moment the witness did not believe it. He contradicted the assertion of the accused that Russia did not formulate any concrete proposals.

M. Tontcheff, one of the accused: Does the witness know that Izvolsky said that the Entente was not interested in Bulgaria?

The Witness: I know nothing about that.

Hereupon, M. Tontcheff accused the witness of partiality as having signed the order for his arrest in 1919, but the objection was over-ruled.

M. Tchaprashikoff, former Bulgarian Minister at Belgrade and Nisch, a further witness, said that the only instructions which he received from M. Radoslavoff were that we should maintain a strict neutrality. In December 1914, M. Pashitch demanded an interview with M. Radoslavoff, but the latter refused. The same year Prince Trubetzkoi arrived in Serbia, as Russian Minister, with instructions to form an entente between Bulgaria and Serbia. He told the witness that for active intervention of Bulgaria on the Entente side, she would receive the uncontested territories of Macedonia. His mission was a failure. The Serbs were not disposed to make concessions in exchange for Bulgarian neutrality. During an interview, M. Pashitch promised him the territory up to the Vardar, if Bulgaria joined against the Central Powers. In May, 1915, the Entente proposed to Serbia to cede to Bulgaria all the uncontested zone in case of the intervention of Bulgaria and not only up to the Vardar. On the 22nd July, 1915, the Entente repeated the demand in a threatening way. The Serbs replied in an unsatisfactory manner on the 20th August. For example, they would not cede Prilep and Okhrida, but consented as to Bitolia (Monastir). He knew for certain that the Entente was then preparing to bring great pressure on Serbia in induce her to cede all the uncontested zone, but then Bulgaria mobilized and the negotiations fell through.

It was true to say that the military party—the Black Hand—wanted war against Bulgaria.

On the 9th February, M. Dragueff, former leader of the Union of Peasants, appeared as a witness, and said that the parliamentary groups were divided as follows: the three Liberal factions were for the Central Powers, whilst the Populists, Progressives, Democrats and Radicals were for the Entente. The Union of Peasants and the Broad Socialists and the Communists were for neutrality. The witness insisted several times, before M Radoslavoff, on the formation of a Coalition Cabinet, in order to prevent Bulgaria's entry into the war, on either side. All the Opposition was in favour of neutrality.

On the 28th August, 1915, the witness was summoned by M. Radoslavoff, who said amongst other things that the war was nearing its close, and that Bulgaria was placing herself on the side of the Central Powers. M. Radoslavoff then demanded the support of the Union of Peasants. The witness expressed the opinion that if Bulgaria entered the war, she would expose herself to a worse catastrophe than in 1913. If we desired territorial acquisitions, they must be the price of neutrality. On the following day the Opposition demanded an audience of the King, to examine the situation.

On the 10th February, M. Tcholakoff, former Governor of the National Bank of Bulgaria, was examined as a witness. He had not taken part in the negotiation for the 500,000,000 loan, but he had spoken for a long time against granting the Pernik mine as a guarantee, which was contrary to article 60 of the law of mines. The secret clauses of the loan were unknown to him.

Another witness, M. Kolutcheff, Bulgarian Minister at Constantinople, said that before rejoining his post in December, 1914, he saw M. Radoslavoff, who told him that Bulgaria was closely following events and would intervene if a favourable occasion presented itself. When the European squadrons began to force the Dardanelles, the Turks became seriously alarmed as to Bulgaria's attitude. The Turks

APPENDIX A. 263

consented to a rectification of the frontier in order to arrive at a defensive alliance with Bulgaria. But the pourparlers carried on with himself and General Jekoff led to nothing, because the Turks would not cede Kirk Kilisse. The negotiations were brought to a conclusion at Sofia. The witness learned from the German ambassador that there was a dispute on the question of restoring to Turkey territory ceded to Bulgaria. M. Kolutcheff reported to his Government that a German submarine, which was operating in Greek waters, was being victualled by the Royal Palace at Athens. He asked that M. Bourchier, Correspondent of the Times, should be informed. But although Bulgaria was then neutral, the request was branded by the King and M. Radoslavoff as an act of treason.

M. Hadji Misheff, Bulgarian Minister at London, the Hague and Rome, on being called as a witness said, that on leaving to take up his post in October, 1914, he received instructions that Bulgaria would observe a strict and loyal neutrality. Nevertheless in England they believed that the question of the intervention of Bulgaria was decided at Sofia, and that her relations with the Central Powers had been fixed since 1913. The witness reported this distrust to his Government. He was not kept informed as to the pourparlers with the Central Powers.

At the examination of witnesses on the 8th February, M. G. Youtoff said that the impression obtained by the delegation sent by the Ghenadieff group in September 1915 to M. Radoslavoff was that Bulgaria was engaged to the Central Powers. M. Apostoloff, the accused, remained in the Cabinet in order to prevent Bulgaria from entering the war.

M. Dotcheff, Colonel of Reserve and former Military Attaché at Berlin, explained that from the time of his arrival in Berlin he was besieged by contractors for boots, equipment, etc. He was able to establish the fact that the supply of boots arranged by Guermanoff in accord with Colonel Gantcheff was fixed at the price of 40 marks the pair, whilst the offers made were for prices between 14.50 and 17.50 marks. He made a report on the matter, but M. Radoslavoff, as well as the Minister of War, General Naidenoff, replied that they could do nothing because Colonel Gantcheff was strongly supported by the Palace, and that he could not be recalled without the consent of the King. Colonel Gantcheff as delegate to the Grand Quarter-Master Generals' Department, also occupied himself with the sale of decorations to the Germans, who fixed the price. He had only to present a list of people to be decorated, to be sent immediately the decorations to " those who had deserved well of Bulgaria."

On the 11th February, two journalists were examined as witnesses. M. Ikonomoff explained that during a visit to

Bukarest he visited the German Legation, where he was offered a large sum in return for pushing German propaganda by means of the Press, but he declined the offer. The witness said that he did not remember the names of journalists who had been won over by this method.

M. Changoff also declared before the Court that he had been offered a sum of 100,000 leva (francs) to win him over to the German propaganda, but he had refused it.

Finally a merchant, B. Moskovitch, furnished certain details regarding the organization of the German propaganda in the Balkans, and the means they employed to gain the support of the Press. He confirmed the fact that in 1914 a "consortium" was formed in Berlin for propaganda in the Balkan countries, and that agents belonging to it were directed to bring Bulgaria and Roumania into the war on the side of the Central Powers.

STAMPS ISSUED BY THE BULGARIAN GOVERNMENT
IN COMMEMORATION OF MR. BOURCHIER.

*The centre stamp depicts Mr. Bourchier in the costume of a
Bulgarian peasant.*

Vide page 247.

Appendix B.
The Question of the Access to the Aegean Sea.

From the date of the signature of the Treaty of Neuilly to the present day, this has been a burning question with Bulgaria. In the "Echo de Bulgarie" of the 9th January, 1922, there appear the results of interviews between the Press Association of Sofia with many past and present Ministers of State, including M. Stambolisky, the Prime Minister. From these it is evident that this has become a more urgent matter than even that of Macedonia. M. Stambolisky says :—

"That of all the heavy clauses for Bulgaria in the Treaty of Neuilly the most cruel is that which deprives them of the Thracian littoral and their issue on to the Aegean. He considers it is like a slip knot round the neck, which does not necessarily entail death, but, undoubtedly, will interfere with normal respiration. He understands that Bulgaria should be punished but not that this punishment should last for ever. He cites the heavy storms that have recently taken place on the Black Sea and the freezing up of the Danube as the work of destiny to show the world that they have not got sufficient access to the open sea. He states that when he was in London a very competent person assured him that Great Britain had made a special treaty with Greece which assured Bulgaria, by the signature of M. Venizelos, an exit to the Aegean. To this he replied that it was the work of M. Venizelos and not of the Greek people.

But let that pass. "An important point to remember," Stambolisky continues, "is that the Great Powers guaranteed Bulgaria access to the Aegean, and the signature of M. Venizelos, as well as that of 28 representatives of other States including Great Britain, are attached to the document. The Bulgars argument is that Bulgaria has been placed in an illusory, inefficacious and impossible situation." The opinion of M. Gueschoff, a former President, was also consulted by the Press, and he said that there are no two opinions in Bulgaria with regard to Bulgars interests in the Aegean, which are vital. Venizelos himself declared in 1913 in Parliament that the possession of Thrace would be a source of weakness to Greece. It is true that in May, 1920, he changed his opinion and declared that a strong State could extend with impunity in all directions. But it is a question whether, after the defeats and the exhaustion of last year and after the revision of the Treaty of Sêvres, which is imminent, Greece will be any stronger than she was in 1913.

M. Kostourkoff, a former Radical Minister. said:—
"Whoever knows the East will reply without hesitation in the negative to the question whether the régime established in Thrace to-day can ensure to the Thracians repatriation with their liberty, property, rights, honour and existence. In the past neither Turks nor Bulgars had been able to live within the limits of the Greek Kingdom, and these two races constitute to-day the enormous majority of the population.

"The Treaty of Neuilly confers on Bulgaria access to the Aegean through Greek territory. But this right is impossible of realisation. He who knows the secular relations between Bulgars and Greeks can have no illusions as to the possibilties of Bulgaria profiting by the issue accorded to it. And yet the vital interests of Bulgaria demand that she obtain an exit which is also in the interests of international conduct. The Great Powers should make an autonomous Province of Thrace, placed under their protection or under that of the League of Nations where all people would be treated on a footing of equality. This autonomous State would be a guarantee for the tranquility of the Balkans and for the interests of commerce of Europe towards Asia."

M. Ghenadieff, a former Liberal Minister, said that the Bulgars were a people exclusively agricultural who would have to cultivate and exploit in the future the immense fertile plain of Thrace. The necessity which forced them during the last 30 years to leave the regions comparatively densely populated of Philippopolis and Stara-Zagora to establish themselves in the regions of Burgas, Karnobat, Aitos Kavakli, and to increase their agricultural production, will oblige them one day to establish themselves in Thrace which is to-day placed under the domination of a population more maritime and commercial, and incapable of rivalling the Bulgars in the domain of agriculture. The Bulgarian people also have need of a port on the open sea which was recognised by the authors of the Treaties of peace concluded at Paris in providing for them a commercial opening on the Aegean. But this outlet has not yet been given. The Bulgarian Government should profit by every favourable moment in making a step forward toward the fair adjustment of this question so vital to Bulgaria. Such a moment presents itself to-day when the interminable Turko-Greek war in Asia Minor has imposed a revision of the clauses of the Treaty of Peace of Sêvres by the terms of which Western Thrace was torn from Bulgaria and given to Greece.

Appendix C.

British Delegation,
Paris.
31st March, 1919.

Dear Colonel Napier,

Mr. Balfour asks me now to return to you the original documents which you were good enough to send for his perusal just before you left Paris. He has had copies of these made for his own confidential use, and trusts that you have no objection to this. He has given much thought to the questions which you brought to his notice, and since your departure has seen two or three others who have just returned from Sofia and the Balkans with very interesting information.

Believe me,
Yours sincerely,
IAN MALCOLM.

On the death of Mr. Bourchier in January 1921, the "Times" printed a leading article on their former correspondent. It is from this article that Col. Napier quotes in the following letter :—

To the Editor of the "Times."

SIR,

In my capacity as B.M.A. at different times, since 1908, in Serbia, Bulgaria, Roumania and Greece, I had frequent opportunities of appraising and appreciating the work done and the views expressed by Mr. Bourchier in your columns, with reference to Balkan affairs. Though attracted, as you say, by his classical education and tastes to Greece, and though, as he told me himself, he did contribute largely towards uniting Crete with Greece, it is a remarkable fact that he eventually "identified himself more and more with the Bulgarian cause" and was, I believe, burnt in effigy in the streets of Athens in consequence.

It is no small evidence of the worth of the Bulgarian people that they should have won a devotion so complete of an entirely disinterested and high-souled English gentleman.

H. D. NAPIER.
41, Stanhope Gardens,

January 3rd, 1921. London.

To the Editor of "The Sunday Times."*

SIR,

With reference to Mr. Crawford Price's article in the "Sunday Times" of the 12th inst., on the mistaken policy of Lord Grey in regard to Bulgaria, and the letter by "Eirenophilos" in that paper, I agree with the latter that

---

* The contents of this letter were embodied in Colonel Napier's Preface.

the conclusions of Mr. Crawford Price are not borne out by facts, and that it desirable, in view of the attack on Lord Grey's policy that something should be said on the other side.

It is true that owing to the events of the second Balkan war, and the Treaty of Bukharest, it was a matter of extraordinary difficulty to bring Bulgaria to fight on the same side as Serbia, and all the influence of her neighbours, Greece, Serbia and Roumania, who had profited by the Treaty, and were apprehensive of having to sacrifice some of these gains, was brought into play to prevent us from obtaining her as an ally.

But in spite of the Kaiser's assurance to King Constantine, noted by Mr. Price, Bulgaria was still free to choose her own path until August, 1915, as recently disclosed in the trial of members of the Bulgarian Government of 1914-15 now proceeding at Sofia.

The chief difficulty, however, for the Entente lay in the fact that Russia, greedy for Constantinople and the intervening territories, did not wish to call in the help of the Balkan States, and it was only as the need grew month by month more urgent, that the Entente was finally persuaded of the urgent necessity of Bulgaria's help, owing to her geographical position, and set to work in earnest to win her over.

Even then, as " Eirenophilos " remarks, " France was against Greece making any concession to Bulgaria, and Russia took up the same attitude as regards Serbia." Added to all this, the tide of battle set in steadily against the Entente in 1915. The retreat of Russia and the Dardanelles fiasco were the deciding factors in the mind of King Ferdinand, who, although his sympathies were naturally with those of his own kith and kin, was chiefly interested in preserving his crown and dynasty by not going against the winning side. Nevertheless, the great mass of public opinion in Bulgaria was in favour of the Entente, and might have been utilised as a check on the King, had it not been for Serbia's selfish obstinacy in refusing the necessary concessions in spite of the urgent appeal of the Entente.

Mr. Crawford Price blames Lord Grey for not having accepted Greece's offer of her army and navy to attack the Dardanelles in August, 1914. But at that time it was by no means certain that Turkey would enter the war against us, and it would have been contrary to our high moral code to have initiated an agressive war against Turkey, however profitable it would doubtless have been. Still, had the Gœben and Breslau incident been promptly and firmly tackled diplomatically, there is little doubt that Turkey would have surrendered them and have remained neutral.

Later on, in 1915, when Greece renewed her offer of assistance, it was linked with the proposal to march through Bulgarian territory in company with the Entente troops to the Dardanelles. This would, undoubtedly, have brought the Bulgarian army in full strength—at that time much superior to the Greek army—on the opposite side. It does not need a great strategist to perceive that the prospect of a long land march with a powerful enemy situated on the flank, in its own territory, was hardly a profitable one for the Entente.

Mr. Crawford Price opines that General Sir Arthur Paget was duped by the King. The facts are that at the time of his visit our fleet was sweeping up the Straits. There was a panic at Constantinople, refugees were pouring into Bulgaria, and the Turks had commenced to shift their railway archives. Radoslavoff's Government was hesitating and was within an ace of joining us. But then came the news of the disaster to three of our warships, and the consequent abandonment by the navy of the attempt to force the passage of the Dardanelles. This gave the Bulgars breathing space, and changed the whole aspect of affairs. The situation then gradually grew from bad to worse as has been already stated.

It is true that, after that time, Bulgaria passed war material through to Turkey, as Mr. Price has pointed out. But he omitted to mention, perhaps he was not aware of the fact, that most of this war material had already passed through the territory of our friend and future ally, Roumania. It was, therefore, no proof of Bulgaria's intentions.

Mr. Price's final indictment that Lord Grey did not permit the Serbs to attack Bulgaria, when in the act of mobilizing, has some force. The Serbs would have destroyed one division and have seriously delayed the Bulgarian mobilization, but could not have given them a knock-out blow. On the other hand, the evidence given by the Bulgarian Commander-in-Chief at the trial now proceeding shows that, even at this stage, Bulgaria's assistance to Germany and Austria was not absolutely certain, but was conditional on the German's successful passage of the Danube in the face of the Serbian army. The late and much-lamented Mr. O'Beirne, at that time British Minister at Sofia, and one of the ablest diplomats of the day, held the opinion that even at that late hour Bulgaria might have been kept neutral had not the Russians lost patience and demanded the immediate march of Bulgaria against the Turks in a 48 hours' ultimatum. Mr. O'Beirne may have been right or he may have been wrong, but I have said enough to show that Lord Grey's policy was not entirely misplaced. The Entente doubtless erred in not pushing its policy of bringing in Bulgaria sufficiently early or with sufficient vigour. Had they done so, and found it of no avail, there would still have been time to have had recourse to Greece before that Power became intimidated by the threats of the Kaiser and the continuous successes of the Central Powers. When one thinks of the enormous prestige that Lord Grey enjoyed both in Russia and France, one may regret that he did not over-rule, and no one but he could have done so, the discordant opinions of our allies in time to be of use. Unity of command in the diplomatic field was quite as urgent as in that of the strategical conduct of the war.

Yours faithfully,
H. D. NAPIER,
Lieut.-Colonel, late Military Attaché
in the Balkans.

41, Stanhope Gardens, S.W.7.
February 13th, 1922.
(This letter was not inserted).

M. Venizelos and the Proposed Turkish Frontier.

("Manchester Guardian," 3/5/22).
To the Editor of the "Manchester Guardian."

SIR,

An interesting letter from M. Venizelos to a friend in Athens has recently been published in the Greek Press. M. Venizelos says :—

All our work is shortly to be destroyed Northern Epirus and Asia Minor are already lost. I see by reading the papers that in view of the insistence of France in wishing to give back all Thrace to the Turks England has consented to remove us from the frontier of Tchataldja to the line Rodosto-Midia. This, combined with the revision of the Treaty of Sèvres and the right granted to Turkey to maintain troops in Europe, is virtually equivalent to the complete loss of the whole of Thrace. For our military position in this province between the Bulgarian forces in the north and the Turkish forces to the east and south will be desperate. Thus the change which has occurred has upset the entire plan of the admirable edifice which our participation in the war had permitted us to raise, and this change involves, as I fear, a rapprochement between Serbs and Bulgars, and we shall be thrown back beyond the Alyacmon. . . .

This frank avowal from so distinguished a statesman and strategist as Venizelos is of the utmost importance at the present moment, when there seems to be a possibility of the revision of treaties at Genoa. The Balkan League in London recently submitted to the Government on the eve of the Genoa Conference its opinions regarding the problem of Thrace, and recommended, in view of the fact that article 48 of the Treaty of Neuilly, granting to Bulgaria access to the Ægean Sea, is impossible of fulfilment, that Thrace should be made an autonomous province, either under the Allies or under the League of Nations.

From the letter quoted above it is clear that M. Venizelos does not put much confidence in the will or capacity of the Allies or of the League of Nations to continue to maintain permanently Greece's right to the "admirable edifice" which he himself, by the help of the Allies, was able to erect. If

M. Venizelos is right, it becomes a question whether the Allies or the League of Nations will wish to saddle themselves with the care of an autonomous Thrace. There remain three possibilities : one, to restore Thrace in its entirety to Turkey; another, to revert to Bulgaria's pre-war boundaries, leaving Eastern Thrace to Turkey; and a third, to advance Bulgaria's boundary to the Rodosto-Midia line.

The first or second would be a retrograde step from the point of view of Christianity and of Western civilisation. The consistent massacres of Armenians by the Turks before, during, and after the war should suffice to put them out of court.

The third plan appears to be the only practical and permanent solution, in spite of the natural desire to reward our late allies and punish our late foes. From the point of view of balance of power, now that Roumania and Serbia have both so largely increased their territories and populations, there can be no longer any fear of Bulgaria, the weakest of her neighbours, securing the hegemony of the Balkans. And as regards a possible rapprochement between Serbia and Bulgaria, feared by M. Venizelos, the acquisition by Bulgaria of the Thracian littoral would do away with the chief incentive of the latter Power to ally herself with Jugo-Slavia.

Sooner or later, the inexorable logic of events will result in the acquisition of the littoral by the hinterland, which has need of it, and Bulgaria, which more than any other of the Balkan States, has given proof of her capacity for impartial government of alien races and religious tolerance, combined with an aptitude for carrying out public works, such as roads, railways, and harbours, will reap the reward of her undoubted efficiency.

Yours, etc.,
H. D. NAPIER,
Lieutenant Colonel, late Military
Attaché in the Balkans.

London, May 1st.

To the Editor of " The Times."

SIR,

The Turkish demand for the restoration of Eastern Thrace obviously includes the considerable extent of territory (more than one thousand square miles) which they held, under the Treaty of Constantinople, of September 30 (October 13), 1913, to the west of the Maritza—in short, all their pre-war territory.

Whilst thus reverting to pre-war geographical conditions it would undoubtedly save future Balkan complications if we restored Thrace west of the Maritza to Bulgaria and gave her that access to the Aegean Sea which is so important to her commercial development. She won this territory south of the Rhodope mountains (with its seventy miles of coast line) after a most severe and bloody campaign with Turkey,

APPENDIX C.

to which the Turkish advance on Smyrna was but child's play. The pre-war Greek boundary on the east terminated at the Mesta river, opposite the island of Thasos. It might well do so again. The geographical status of the pre-war boundaries in the Balkans was comparatively sound.

Yours truly,
T. H. HOLDICH, Vice-President,
Royal Geographical Society,

Kensington-gore, S.W.7.
October 7th, 1922.

From Lieut-Colonel the Hon. H. D. Napier.
To the Editor of "The Times."

SIR,

Colonel Sir Thomas Holdich's letter in to-day's "Times" will be read with great interest. As Vice-President of the Royal Geographical Society and with his great experience in delimitating boundaries, his words will carry especial weight with those who realise that geographical conditions cannot be ignored with impunity in fixing frontiers. To continue, therefore, to deprive the Bulgarian hinterland of access to the open sea of the Aegean, by a narrow strip of Greek territory that now leads nowhere, is not sound policy or likely to prove a permanent settlement.

In the past M. Venizelos himself realised the necessity of granting Bulgaria free access to the Aegean, and without the prospect of Eastern Thrace and the ultimate goal of Constantinople, would hardly have saddled his country with the passage-way of Western Thrace, which can only be retained owing to the impotence of Bulgaria and the restraining hand of the Little Entente. But these conditions will not last for ever. Already Yugo-Slavia begins to look with regret at the re-occupation of Eastern Thrace, which cost them and the Bulgars so much blood to win from the Mahomedan Turk a year or two before the Great War, and it only needs a rapprochement between the Little Entente and Bulgaria to entirely change the situation.

The voluntary surrender by Greece of a portion of Western Thrace to Bulgaria would go far towards re-cementing the former alliance between the Christian States of the Balkans, which is their's and Europe's best guarantee against a combined Russian Bolshevic and Turkish invasion.

Yours truly,
Lieut.-Colonel, formerly Military Attaché in
Russia and subsequently in the Balkans.

October 9th, 1922.

(Not printed by "Times" in extenso—only first and last paragraphs)

APPENDIX C.

Mr. Lloyd George's Policy in the Near East.
(October 14th, 1922.)
To the Editor of the "Manchester Guardian."

SIR,

In 1919, when British Military Representative in Bulgaria, I was forced to relinquish my post because I was unable to agree to the policy of Great Britain and also at that time of France, of unduly favouring the Greeks at the expense of the Bulgars. I especially deplored the subsequent cutting off of Bulgaria from the Ægean Sea, and the granting of both Western and Eastern Thrace to Greece.

That policy was utterly wrong, and was due to the overwhelming influence of M. Venizelos. Venizelos had deserved well of us, but the Greek nation had not. The Greeks had refused to succour their allies the Serbs, as by treaty bound, in their desperate position of 1915; were guilty of treacherous conduct time and again, and were only compelled to make a tardy entry on our side by their geographical position and the steadfast loyalty and foresight of M. Venizelos.

But the policy of Mr. Lloyd George in the recent crisis of defending the Straits at all costs in spite of the attitude of France and Italy has been right, splendidly right. To have acted otherwise would indeed have led to an overwhelming disaster and it is hard that Mr. Lloyd George should be arraigned for this one courageous and prompt act of statesmanship.

Nevertheless, his former errors have left a crop of troubles in their wake. The refusal to recognise that Bulgaria is not the natural ally of Germany or of Turkey, but was driven into the war against us as much by the combined hostility of the neighbouring Christian States as by the command of their German king—a king who was none of their own choosing—led to the policy which acquiesced in her total disarmament and the deprivation of her southern seaboard.

Thanks to this, Europe has now to bow to the demands of a victorious Turkish army, retrace her steps, and restore the sovereignty of the Turk in Eastern Thrace, the scene of her periodic massacres of Christians for centuries, the scene also of her signal defeat in 1912 at the hands of the allied Bulgarian and Serbian soldiers.

Now rumours are rife of an understanding between the Turks and the Russian Bolsheviks to rid themselves of control of the Straits and to invade Europe. Bulgaria was the key to the former Balkan alliance of 1912, and must always remain so, owing to her central position. The failure of European statesmanship to reconstitute this alliance led to the prolongation of the Great War for at least two years. It should now be the task of European statesmanship to reconstruct that alliance as a defensive one against both Turk and Russian. Doubtless misfortune will have taught Bulgaria to abandon the grasping and arrogant attitude which

Military Attaché T.

estranged her neighbours, but it is essential that she should be treated with some degree of generosity, and that some part at least of the Thracian littoral should be restored to her. Now that Eastern Thrace has gone and with it the dream of a Grecian Constantinople, Western Thrace constitutes for Greece nothing but an *impasse*, and a source of discord and danger in shutting off the hinterland from quicker access to the open sea. Bulgaria must also be granted the means of self-defence against her Turkish border until such time as the League of Nations will have brought about the disarmament of Turk and Russian, and the Great Powers must remain in actual occupation of the Straits pending such millennium.

Yours etc.,
H. D. NAPIER,
Lieutenant Colonel, formerly Military

London, October 12th, 1922.   Attaché in the Balkans.

Délégation Bulgare
    à La
Société des Nations.   Sophia, Oct. 23, 1922.

DEAR COLONEL NAPIER,

I wish to thank you for your very generous support of the Bulgarian cause. I read your letters to the papers with deep interest and warm appreciation.

Believe me, always yours gratefully,

N. STAMBOLISKY,
Bulgarian Prime Minister.

DEAR MR. STAMBOLISKY,

Your kind letter, of the 23rd October, gave me very great pleasure. I have been glad to testify, in my small way, whenever I could to the truth regarding the Balkans in general and Bulgaria in particular, and that my brief letters should have attracted your attention and won your approval, is a source of great satisfaction.

I must confess that, lacking as I am in any political influence, I did not expect my words to carry much weight in the British Press. But I hoped that the " Manchester Guardian," besides informing an important section of our own people, might prove a good vehicle for conveying a message to my friends abroad as to the desirability of a rapprochement between the Christian States of the Balkans, which cannot fail to be to their mutual benefit.

Now, reading your recent exposé of your Foreign policy in the " Echo de Bulgarie," of the 28th October, I am delighted to find that I am in complete accord with it.

I also think that I saw a notice in our Press of a recent visit of yours to Belgrade. I trust this will not have been without good results.

But I am fully aware of the difficulties in your Excellency's path: that it took several hundred years before they (Serbia, Bulgaria, Greece) were able to form the alliance which defeated Turkey, and that then they had the powerful aid of M. Hartwig, the Russian Minister, to help them.

However, it is an object well worth striving for, and I am sure that the great Powers of Europe cannot fail to be impressed with the honesty and sobriety of the Bulgarian nation and of their leaders.

Pray convey my humble respects to His Majesty the King.

Yours sincerely,
H. D. NAPIER, Lt.-Colonel.

41, Stanhope Gardens,
London, S.W.7.
November 5th, 1922.

The Straits and the Black Sea.

To the Editor of the "Manchester Guardian."

SIR,

There appear to be two very important matters still awaiting a favourable solution by the Lausanne Conference. The most important of these, the question of the Straits and the Black Sea, you deal with in your very interesting leading article of to-day's date. As one who has had a long acquaintance with Russia, dating from some 20 years, I venture to point out that it has always been Russia's policy to obtain the free passage of her own warships into the Mediterranean, but to close the entry into the Black Sea to warships of other Great Powers. I believe I am correct in stating that at the time of the Anglo-Russian Agreement, after the close of the Russo-Japanese War, the question of opening the Dardanelles to ships of war was raised by Russia. The British Government would have given their consent on condition of equal treatment—that is to say, that warships of all nations might have free ingress and egress. But that did not suit Russia's book and the matter was dropped. The possession of Constantinople has been, I believe, hitherto, the ambition of every patriotic Russian, whether Imperialist, Republican, or Bolshevik. This is but natural, apart from commercial interests, both for purposes of offence and defence. Similarly it would appear to be to the interest of Great Britain to secure the freedom of the Straits for ships of war, because if Russia is our friend, as in the last war, we wish to bring her assistance in shape of munitions and supplies, which need to be escorted by warships whether great or small. And if she were unfortunately our enemy, as in the Crimean War, the most vulnerable counter-attack against a possible invasion of India would be by way of the Black Sea. I do not think it has ever been realised in England to what an extent we bled and exhausted Russia by the year-long siege of Sebastopol, and what a tremendous moral effect its fall produced on the Tsar of that day.

APPENDIX C.

But you mention in your article that Russia is now "seeking an agreement with the States on her eastern and southern borders for disarmament, and in this connection she has even indicated a willingness, if the Straits were neutralised, to neutralise the Black Sea." If by this is meant that Russia will agree to put down all her warships and submarines in the Black Sea and build no more, it would, of course, greatly simplify the whole question. In that case it might be sufficient to "demilitarise the shores of the Straits, allowing them to remain unfortified and unoccupied." Otherwise, nothing short of actual occupation of both sides of the Straits by an international force would appear to give a real guarantee that in time of trouble the Straits would not be open or closed to vessels, whether war or merchant ships, as might suit the Turks or their allies.

As regards the second question, there seems to be a danger that the refusal of M. Venizelos to agree to the cession of Dedeagatch to Bulgaria will wreck the fair prospects of a new Balkan *bloc*, which is so desirable in the interests of peace and for the defence of Europe against a possible Bolshevik and Turkish onslaught. It was comprehensible, before the mad action of the Greek Government in shooting the members of their late Government, that M. Venizelos realised he would be unable to return to Greece if he made any further concession of territory, however wise and statesmanlike. Now the whole world will realise that the Great Powers need not and should not permit the susceptibilities of such a Goverment to stand in the way of a satsfactory settlement.

It must be borne in mind that Dedeagatch is nothing more than an open roadstead, with no harbour facilities for any vessel larger than a fishing smack. It will require much money, time and labour to build a suitable harbour, and, naturally, the Bulgarians are not willing to undertake this great work except upon Bulgarian or international soil. The importance of bringing Bulgaria into the fold of the Christian nations of the Balkans, and of not repeating the errors of former years, cannot be exaggerated.

Yours. etc.,
H. D. NAPIER,
Lieut.-Colonel, formerly Military Attaché in Russia and in the Balkans.

November 29th.

[If Colonel Napier will refer to Karl Radek's article in yesterday's "Manchester Guardian" he will see that that very able and important member of the Russian Central Committee utterly repudiates any desire on the part of his Government for the possession of Constantinople. We believe also that the Russian Government would make no objection to the closing of the Straits to Russian as to all other warships. It is a changed Russia with which we have to deal.—ED. "GUARD."]

The Foreign Policy of Russia.

II.
Her Interest in the Near East, the Straits, and the Black Sea.

By Karl Radek.

[We print below the second part of an article on Russian Foreign Policy by Karl Radek, the well-known Bolshevist leader and member of the All-Russian Central Executive Committee.]

Moscow, November 2nd.

Russia is not only a European but also an Asiatic country. Your Philistines of civilisation even say that she is a country more Asiatic than European. Let us admit this. But, as an Asiatic country, she cannot be indifferent to what is going on in the Far East, Central Asia, and the Near East. She is a neighbour of the peoples who live in Asia, bound up with their fates, and what happens on the territory of these peoples is, in the deepest sense, not a matter of indifference for Russia. Asiatic questions have been for centuries the source of profound conflicts between England and Russia. We have renounced the Tsarish policy of robbery with regard to the Asiatic peoples, but, naturally, we have not been able to declare that we do not interest ourselves in questions concerning them. Your Government concluded with the Tsar's Goverment a treaty concerning the partition of Persia, whereas we have renounced special rights in Northern Persia. But we cannot be indifferent to the question whether, as a neighbour for Baku, we have a Persian Government or an English occupation disguised with a facade of a Persian Government. It cannot be a matter of indifference to us whether in the neighbourhood of Baku are the troops of Riza Khan or an English Expeditionary Corps, for Persia and Riza Khan will not fight for Baku oil, whereas Royal Dutch and Shell are licking their lips for it. We have renounced, not only outwardly but in the depths of our souls, the shameful treaties concluded by the Tsar's Government with the Allies, treaties which gave it a right to the capital of the Kaliph and to the Straits. But it cannot be a matter of indifference to us whether that capital is in the hands of the Turkish people or within range of the guns of the Iron Duke.

From the moment when we concluded the trade agreement with England, Lord Curzon has showered upon us papers of protest with regard to actions by us alleged to be directed against England over the whole extent of Asia. We have always made the same reply: "Be so good as to tell us in what consist the interests of England in Persia, Afghanistan, and Turkey. Be so good as to come to terms with us as to which of our interests in these countries will be taken into account by England." But to all our demands we have received no answer of any kind. Lord Curzon contented himself with his notes of protest and did not reply, even when we proved to him that his protest was based on false documents, cooked up by the agents of the German Secret Service who were seeking additional earnings in pounds sterling. This policy ended—you know how—in the fall of English prestige in Persia, it ended in the bankruptcy of English policy in the Near East. We observe this without malicious glee, but (I do not hide it) with a joy of which it is possible to speak publicly, since we do not consider that the interests of the English people demanded that its Government should establish a feeling of ceaselessly growing hatred of the name of England (of a country which could contribute so very much to the youthful, developing peoples of the East). English public opinion declares that it is necessary to liquidate the policy of struggle with Turkey, the policy of destroying Turkey.

Relations with Turkey.

We can but rejoice at this, for we know that Turkey needs peace, and we know that renunciation of the policy of enslaving Turkey gets rid of one of the reasons of conflicts between England and Russia. Our relation to the peoples of the East and Turkey is not one of romantic sentimentalists. In the Turkish question we are not pupils of the David Urquhart who, in the words of Marx, if he had not been an Englishman and a Presbyterian, would have wished to be a Turk and a Mohammedan. But we represent a great people of peasants and workers, which is continually threatened by the capitalist world. The capitalist world, at Genoa, put demands before us which amounted to the introduction into Russia of the system of capitulations and of " Dettes publiques russes." How can you be surprised that we consider ourselves at one with those who have suffered for hundreds of years under the régime of capitulations and for tens of years under the régime of the " Dettes publiques ottomanes?" Our relations with the East are based on the fact that the poor and hungry are stronger when they are united, and the peoples of the East and the peoples of Russia are alike poor and hungry. If England, indeed, comes to the policy of compromise with regard to these peoples of the East we shall welcome the fact from the point of view of their interests. But at the very moment when the liquidation of the policy of the partition of Turkey opened perspectives towards the removal of one of the most serious obstacles in the settlement of peaceful relations between England and Soviet Russia, in that very moment the Allies declared to us that they abandoned the policy of Gladstone with regard to Turkey only to take up the policy of Beaconsfield with regard to Russia. Inviting to the conference on Near Eastern affairs even Japan, who, as you know, can hardly be considered one of those most directly interested in the Black Sea, the Allies, on September 23, in their Note to Turkey, excluded Soviet Russia from participation in the Conference. Only after our emphatic protests they persuaded themselves, by looking at the map, that we were a Black Sea power and invited us to Lausanne as unpaid consultants.

It is of no great interest to us to investigate who is telling the truth over this question: the English press, which says that difficulties are raised by France, or the French press, which says that the difficulties are from the English side. With France we have as yet no treaty relations; we do not promise not to struggle against the interests of France in Asia. But we have treaty relations with England, and we have given public undertakings with regard to English interests in the Near East. Wherefore we ask ourselves: " Is England accessory to the attempt to exclude us from the settlement of the vital interests of the Russian people in the Near East?" and to this question we reply: " Not merely is she accessory, she is the instigator of this exclusion, for, as in many other questions, one must ask *Cui prodest?* Since the English Fleet is stronger than the French, it is obvious that the Straits will be in English hands, if they are to be in the hands of the Allies, even if this should be under the flag of the League of Nations. Chile and Argentine, and, if we are not mistaken, even Denmark and Holland, are not going to quarrel with England if she, in the name of the League of Nations, closes and corks the Straits.

THE STRAITS.

We are for the freedom of the Straits. The Straits are the road by which in the future the Black Sea nations are going to export their bread and oil and import European goods. Russia has lost Riga and Reval, and Russia desires to be free to make use of Odessa, Novorossisk and Batum. On the Black Sea there are no considerable forces of war (naval forces), and if the great Western European Powers do not force their way into the Black Sea and light the flames there, the Black Sea will be a corner of the world secure from the conflagrations of war. The Black Sea will be a single great harbour for all the Black Sea peoples. If the English Government demands the insurance of the freedom of the Straits by the handing over of the guarding of the Straits to England and France under cover of the League of Nations, then we say, " The Allies, including England, are destroying the freedom of the Straits as a trade route." But you ask, " Cannot Turkey close the Straits to trade?" We are not making ready to fight with Turkey, and Turkey is not making ready to fight with us. The peasant masses of Turkey are awakened by the war, and they will thank Allah if they can live in peace. The Government of Kemal Pasha performed a miracle in organising the defence of its country after so many years of war, but it could perform this miracle only because it was calling these masses to the defence of their own hearths. We do not threaten these hearths, and never shall threaten them, and, therefore, we not only do not fear the hostility of Turkey, but are convinced that the Turkish popular masses, together with the Russian popular masses, will be the basis of firm friendly relations between the two nations. Regardless of the fact that capitalistic rulers are already dreaming of the possibility of getting up a quarrel between the two peoples, between Russia and Turkey there are no contradictory interests of any kind. Wherefore it is laughable to wish to defend the people of the Black Sea from "Turkish Imperialism," and for this purpose to hand the key of the Black Sea to such innocent lambs as the heads of the French and English Admiralties.

The question of the Straits is a question of the great and vital interests of the Russian people in the near future. We do not merely seek participation in the Peace Conference. We want England and France at this Conference to consider our interests. When they seek a way out by not admitting us to the first part of the Conference at which will be established peace between Turkey and the Allies, as a punishment because we concluded peace earlier, and when they promise to let us in to the second part of the Conference it is a pitiable attempt to wriggle out of the difficulty. The "Manchester Guardian" quite rightly pointed out that having regard to the present state of military technique and to the rôle of aeroplane and submarine boats, whatever might be the decision of the Dardanelles questions, much would depend upon whether or no Turkey is to be forced one-sidedly to agree to a considerable reduction of her forces. That is as much as to say that the decisions of the first part of the Conference may have a decisive significance for the decisions of the special Conference on the Straits, and that, therefore, we ought to take part in the whole Conference. Nor is that all. Who can believe that the Allies will agree to sign a peace treaty with Turkey without deciding the question of the Straits? Accordingly, division of the Conference would mean a piece of play with us, a piece of politeness towards us. But we do not ask courtesies from our opponents, but rather that they should reckon with our interests as we are compelled to reckon with theirs.

SUBMARINES.

We do not seek the honour of sitting at the same table with Lord Curzon, but the opportunity of influencing the decision of the fates of the Straits in the interests of Russia. The "Manchester Guardian" quite rightly insists all the time that the absence of Russia from this decision will destroy the significance of whatever agreement may be reached. We shall not sign a treaty that contradicts the interests of Russia, and anyone who is prepared to decide this question in despite of Russian interests should know that to do this is to prepare a basis for new struggles and further conflicts. We do not flourish our weapons, but we firmly declare to the whole world that September 23, the day when we learnt of the attempt to exclude Russia from the decision of this question so vital to her, merely because at the present moment she is unable to send twenty submarines to the Straits and a squadron of aeroplanes, will be the day of a turning point in Russia's consciousness. If we are forced to it, we shall work, if necessary many years, to make Russia no longer defenceless at sea. We have the more right to say this quietly because everyone knows how badly we want peace. Everyone knows that our offer in Genoa of a reduction of armaments was a sincere offer, based on the interests of the huge masses of peasantry and of the working class. But just as we were forced to take up rifles, so we may be taught to build submarines.

After what I have said above, there is surely no need for me to add much more about the fact that we could not ratify the agreement with Urquhart at the very moment when the English Government said to us, "Your attempts to arrange peaceful relations with England are in vain. You are throwing your concessions and your compromises into empty air. We do not wish to consider the interests of Russia, nor shall we consider them." We should be children if we were to try to believe that is possible to strengthen business relations with England, regardless of the fact that the English Government is in a hostile mood with regard to us. You wrote in your paper that it was only the fault of our Marxism that we considered the English Government bound up with the interests of capitalists. I am ready to admit I was in the wrong, ready to admit that the Government of Mr. Bonar Law has nothing in common with capitalist undertakings, and that English Conservatives express the music of the heavenly spheres, and not the interests of other spheres a little nearer to the earth. But from this there is but one deduction to be made: so much the worse for Mr. Urquhart that he did not take care that the hand of the Admiralty did not take away what was given by the hand of Industry.

"Equal Rights."

But what is the use of all this sociology? The Soviet Government is a Government of peasants and workers to which the policy of nationalism and of prestige is foreign. The policy of nationalism is a policy of demanding privileges. The Government of Russian peasants and workers demands not privileges but equal rights. The policy of prestige is a policy of struggle for shadows, for phantoms, for fetishes, but the demand that the Great Powers should consider the interests of future Russian export and of peace on the Black Sea, that is not a struggle for fetishes, not a struggle for phantoms, but a struggle for the export of bread, for freedom to import agricultural machines, a struggle for assurance against the danger of war on the Black Sea. And the Government which should make concessions, enormous economic concessions, to persons who do not consider such interests of its people, that Government would lose the right to ask from the popular masses of its country that they should consider it a Government defending their interests. There you have the reason why we rejected the treaty with Urquhart. Let these reasons be removed and we shall be the first to rejoice when we can conclude business deals with the English business world.

In the English and foreign press there is much talk of new orientations in Soviet Russia, of a struggle between a Francophil and an Anglophil tendency. I can tell you a secret. There exists with us an old tendency, a Russophil tendency. We can say this quite openly, boldly, and with pride, for we consider that the interests of our country are those of the peace and well-being of the popular masses of all countries. We do not play games in orientation, and our ship follows a single course—the course of a struggle for peace and bread. And on this course we shall meet ships bringing us goods and ships bringing weapons intended for our destruction. We shall open our harbours to the first and struggle with the second. It depends on England what she will bring to Russia—goods from Manchester and Sheffield or armaments from the Clyde. This decision of England will decide our decisions in advance. There is not in Russia a single lunatic who, attracted by the play of diplomatic shadows on the screen of history, would forget the strength of England, would forget what might be given us by the greatest industrial country in Europe. If in Russia there is to be hostility to England, then be assured that it will be the result of a policy of the English Government hostile with regard to the interests of Russia. If there is no such policy, then we, striving towards peace and agreement with all peoples and States, shall have no reasons whatsoever for seeking alliances and agreements directed against England. The English people will soon be electing a new Parliament. I, as you know, am not a great admirer of European democracy, and the recent Eastern crisis has not done much to persuade me that Parliament is capable of directing a country's policy. You know that we are suspicious folk who seek behind the scenes of Parliament other driving forces which do not allow the policy of the country to follow the will of the popular masses. But if these elections should result in an English policy directed towards the creation of firm peaceful relations between Russia and England, this would produce in Russia a feeling of joy and a readiness to make business deals necessary not only for the restoration of the economy of the Russian people, but also for the restoration of English economy.

("The Manchester Guardian," November 30th, 1922).

APPENDIX C.

41, Stanhope Gardens,
S.W.7.
December 1st, 1922.
The Editor, "Manchester Guardian."

SIR,

While thanking you for your courtesy in printing my letter of the 29th ult., and at the same time referring me to Karl Radek's article in your issue of the 30th, I feel bound to mention that I have now read the very able article in question. But far from gaining any comfort through its perusal, the new situation appears to me in some respects more menacing than the old, and in others " plus ça change, plus c'est la même chose." Formerly Russia was bent on the acquisition of Constantinople. Rightly or wrongly, Lord Beaconsfield opposed this. The result was Skobeleff's campaign in Central Asia in the early eighties and the advance to Merv. Skobeleff himself owned that the object of this campaign was not the acquisition of miles of waterless desert, but, by the threat of an invasion of India to force our policy to be more friendly to Russia in Europe, and in fact to acquiesce in Russia's advance on Constantinople. Subsequent advances towards the Indian frontier were carried out with the result that in the course of the next twenty years we were more than once on the brink of war with Russia. Then came the Russo-Japanese war which was followed by an Anglo-Russian agreement. Then after that ensued a period of some ten years of friendship which proved that, given goodwill, the Russian and British Empires had really no conflicting interests. Still the old Russia was bent on the acquisition of Constantinople, and soon after the outbreak of the world war, the Czar had informed us that, apart from the prospect of obtaining Constantinople, Russia had no interest in continuing the war, and we concurred.

The Russia of to-day no longer asks for Constantinople. There is a change. As Karl Radek admits, it is more Asiatic than European. It is also less Christian. The Bolshevik Government has done its best to abolish Christianity in Russia. Gone is the crusading spirit that would drive the Turk out of Europe and restore the Cross to St. Sophia. On the contrary, its Asiatic tendencies and Bolshevik creed incline it to foster friendship with every race which is either hostile to Western Europe or which gives promise of becoming the enemy of Western civilisation. The British Government has ventured, as in the past, to oppose the present autocratic rulers of Russia. Rightly or wrongly, recognising that the Bolshevik Government had not been elected by the people, and in no way represented the masses, we supported the armies of Koltchak, Denikin and Wrangel. But the Russian people proved unable to overthrow the Bolshevik tyranny and we ceased our opposition. Nevertheless the Bolsheviks, not content with the havoc they have wrought in Russia continue their aggressive action in the shape of propaganda unceasingly, and thereby constitute themselves the enemies of all civilised States.

And in order to be able to contiune this same policy with impunity, the Black Sea must be made secure. The astute Bolshevik rulers have discovered that there is no need, even if they were able, to seize Constantinople. Instead, they form an alliance with the Turks. There is a community of interests. Both are poor, both are hungry. But when have the Straits ever been closed to the passage of food or merchandise by the British navy?

The latest reports from Lausanne point to the Powers adopting perforce a scheme of demilitarisation instead of active occupation, owing to the return of the Turks to Eastern Thrace. But only active occupation can render nugatory Karl Radek's threat to increase the number of Russia's submarines and aeroplanes in the Black Sea.

(Not inserted).

To the Editor, "Manchester Guardian."

DEAR SIR,

Thank you for acknowledging the receipt of my letter, of the 2nd inst. I wish you could have printed it, but I suppose that my remarks about the Bolsheviks would not have suited the majority of your readers.

In any case, I could not have received a more striking proof of the truth of my views than the demands put forward by M. Chitcherin on the 4th inst., namely, that the Russians have always wanted and still want to close the Black Sea to all foreign warships, except their own or those of their ally, for which they require free ingress and egress. The only change is that now they reckon on Turkey for an ally. Now that the Turks are back in Eastern Europe, I fear it will be difficult for the League of Nations to retain effective command of the Straits. That is why I always advocated placing the Bulgars up to the Rodosto-Midia line, regardless of whether or no they had deserved it.

Yours, etc.,

December 5th, 1922.   H. D. NAPIER.

41, Stanhope Gardens,
London.
March 14th, 1923.

DEAR MR. STAMBOLISKY,

It was with great distress that I read in the "Times" a day or two ago, that Messrs. Gueschoff, Daneff, and Malinoff are to be brought to judgment as traitors to Bulgaria. I do not make this letter public, because I know that any independent people would resent the interference of a foreigner in such matters. But your kind letter to me of the 23rd October, 1922, saying that you appreciated my

APPENDIX C. 285

notices to the press on Bulgarian affairs, tempts me to write you a few lines on this subject, privately and confidentially.

Since the death of the lamented Mr. Bourchier, there is no one in this country who has had so many opportunities for learning to know your country and your people as I myself have. I first came to Bulgaria in 1908, as Military Attaché to Bulgaria and Serbia. Before that I was in military service in India. I had been a Military Attaché in Persia, and for four years a Military Attaché in Russia. I only mention this to show that I had already had experience of a varied kind. I was in Bulgaria and Serbia for the next three years, and on the outbreak of war I was again sent by my Government to your country, and finally, in 1918-19, I was British Military Representative there. So I have known these three gentlemen for a long time. I have had dealings with them, both officially and privately, and am glad to claim them as friends. I have no doubt they are all three Bulgarian patriots.

I remember Mr. Gueschoff as a very independent Prime Minister to King Ferdinand, devoted to the interests of his country, and although a rich man who need not have worked, always working for those interests. In 1915, I think, he was head of the group of opposition leaders that petitioned King Ferdinand to declare himself in favour of the Entente, at the same time that you yourself told the King that he would lose his crown if he led Bulgaria into the wrong path.

Mr. Daneff was head of the Mission that came to London to discuss the terms of peace with Turkey after the first Balkan war, and if he was a little " intransigeant " in supporting the claims of Bulgaria, it was due to his excessive zeal as a Bulgarian patriot. At another critical time in the history of your country, when General Savoff had transmitted King Ferdinand's orders to attack the Serbs and Greeks, Mr. Daneff was then Prime Minister. It had been done without his knowledge, and he at once gave the order to cease hostilities. Unfortunately, once begun, they could not be stopped.

In 1915 just before we handed in our ultimatum to King Ferdinand, Mr. Malinoff had been pressed by the King to enter Radoslavoff's Cabinet. Mr. Malinoff tried to extract from the King an indication of the policy which he was pursuing, and an assurance that it would not be against the Entente. The King refused to do so, and Mr. Malinoff, at the risk of his own life, told the King that his attitude was that of a sphinx, and declined to enter the Cabinet. Later on, when you were committed to the German side, Mr. Malinoff took office and did his duty by his country. He is now to be judged for not having gone over to the Entente before the final debâcle.

But I have always admired the steadfastness of your people and the way in which, once committed, you stuck to your allies. I do not think that my countrymen would have esteemed you any the more, had you gone over to the winning side before your were obliged to do so, and I am sure that if you sentence these men unjustly, you will lose whatever British sympathy remains. And I assure you that there is a great deal of sympathy with Bulgaria in this country among those who know, and it will go on increasing as your admirable conduct in adversity continues. Personally, I much admire your policy of making friends with Yugo-Slavia and Roumania at whatever sacrifice, and am sure that it is in the interests of Europe and also of Bulgaria that your efforts should be crowned with success. And I much hope that you will obtain the outlet on the Ægean Sea which you desire.

  Believe me, Mr. Stambolisky,
    Yours sincerely,
      H. D. NAPIER.
(Forwarded through the Bulgarian Legation in London under sealed cover. No reply received).

---

* These Statesmen were released by the new Government after M. Stambolisky's death in June, 1923.

"MAP OF THE BALKAN PENINSULA."

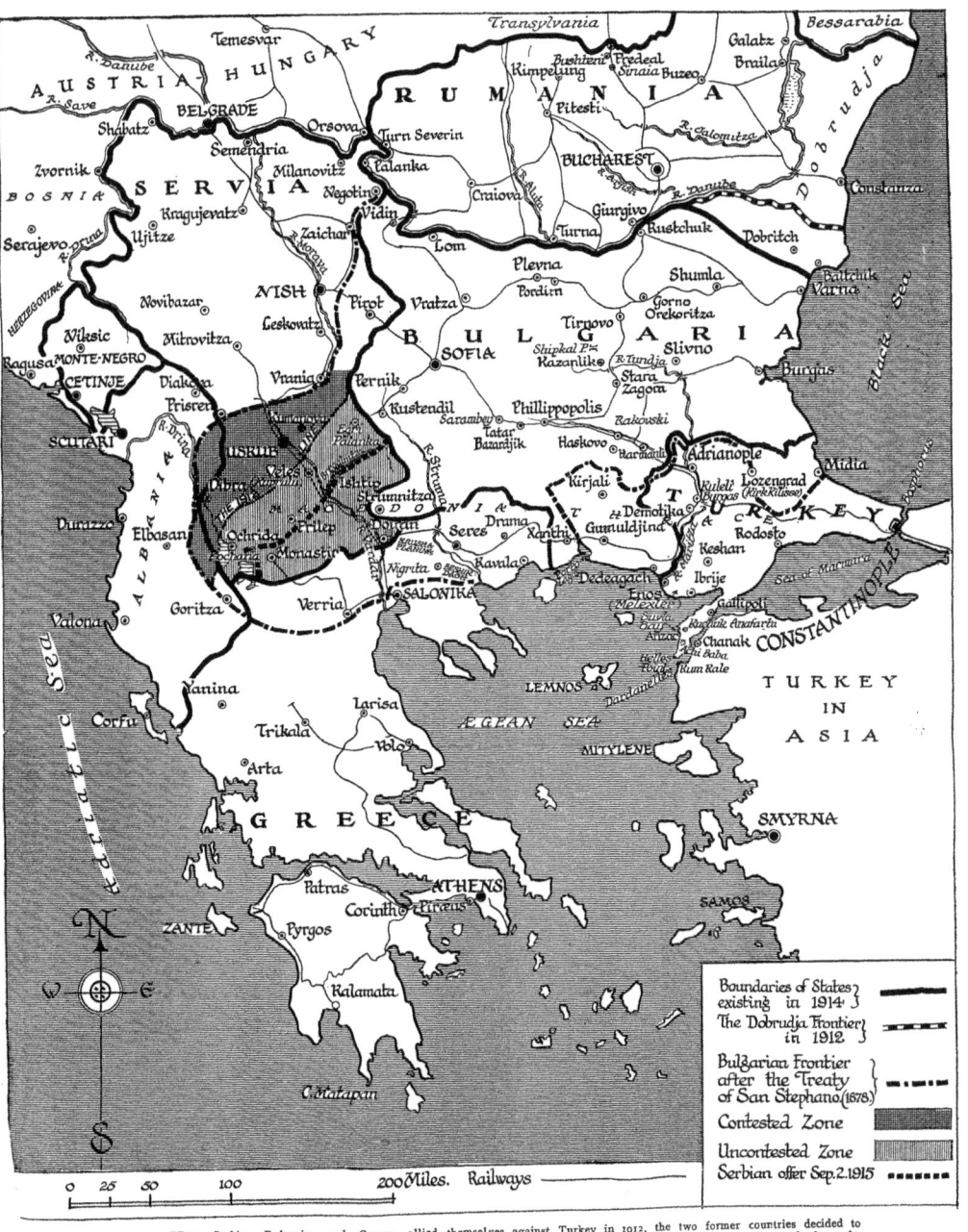

When Serbia, Bulgaria and Greece allied themselves against Turkey in 1912, the two former countries decided to partition Macedonia, then belonging to Turkey, in anticipation of victory. The contested zone, together with the uncontested, shows the amount of territory claimed by Bulgaria and the uncontested that granted by Serbia. In the event of disagreement, the Emperor of Russia was to have been the arbiter, but before that could take place the 2nd Balkan war occurred and caused the frontiers to be fixed, as shown for 1914.

Index.

Akers-Douglas, Hon. A. First Secretary at Bukarest; pages 74, 75.

Alexander, Crown Prince of Serbia (now King of Yugo-Slavia); 58, 112, 113.

Aliotti, Baron, Italian Minister at Sofia; 242.

Amery, Captain, M.P.; 161.

Amir of Afghanistan; 60.

Andonovitch, Colonel, Serbian M.A. at Bukarest; 77, 79.

Antitch, M. Colak, Serbian Minister at Sofia; 35.

Antwerp, Fall of; 46, 49.

Arsenieff, M., Russian First Secretary at Bukarest; 77, 78, 123, 124.

Austrian Army, 97; threatens Roumania; 104, 110, 111, 123, 126.

Baird, Brig.-General; 242.

Balfour, Earl; 243.

Barclay, Sir George, British Minister at Bukarest; 30, 33, 73, 105, 122, 135.

Bax-Ironside, Sir Henry, British Minister at Sofia; 18, 19, 27, 28, 35, 36, 44, 71, 132, 142, 167, 171.

Bax-Ironside, Lady; 111, 112, 145.

Birdwood, General Sir William; 201.

Blakeney, Mr., British Consul at Sofia; 24.

Blondel, M., French Minister at Bukarest; 68, 100.

Boppe, M., French Minister Serbia; 115.

Bourchier, Mr., Times Correspondent in the Balkans; 31, 34, 46, 90, 91, 99, 131, 135, 136, 196.

Boyadjiew, General, Bulgarian Minister of War, later Chief of Staff; 24, 25, 26, 34, 178, 179, 190.

Bosdari, Count, Italian Minister at Athens; 214, 224.

Braithwaite, Major-General, Chief of Staff Dardanelles; 147, 200.

Bratiano, M., Roumanian Prime Minister; 54, 55, 58, 91, 105, 166, 167, 168.

Braquet, Colonel, French M.A. at Athens; 19.

Buchanan, Sir George; p 12-15, 174, 175.

Buckley, Colonel, General Staff; 232.

Bulgar, Character of, 10; Hatred of Serbs, 11; possibility of using against Turks, 11; peasant, 50.

Bulgarian Policy, 78, 102; favourable moment for Entente past, 109; non-committal reply, 167, 170; convention with Germany, 181; negotiations with Turkey, 182; Opposition leaders interview with King, 198, 250, 258.

Bulgarian Army, Strength of 23, 48; training, 109, 110; preparing for war, 116, 138, 155; regains confidence, 156; mobilization preparations, 178; manoeuvres, 191, 192, 193, 194; mobilization, 203.

Buxton, Mr. Charles, 29, 33, 35, 43, 46; wounded, 47; 51, 52, 56, 59.

Buxton, Mr. Noel, M.P.; 29, 33, 35, 43, 46; wounded, 47, 51, 52, 56, 59.

INDEX

Busche, M. von dem, German Minister at Bukarest; 52, 82.
Capitaneanu, Colonel Douglas, Roumanian Army; 105.
Charles, King of Roumania; 32, 47.
Chrétien, General, French Military Representative at Sofia; 242.
Chirol, Sir Valentine; 168, 172, 175, 176, 195.
Churchill, Mr. Winston; 49, 56, 163.
Constantine, King of Greece; 219, 223.
Constantinople, destined for Russia, 141; complicates our task in Balkans, 142, 153.
Contraband; 66, 67, 112, 135, 137, 161, 163, 170.
Crest on book Cover; old family crest, a relic of the Crusades: appears on the seal of the third Napier of Merchiston in 1482.
Crown Prince of Roumania; 129, 130.
Cucchi-Boasso, M., Italian Minister at Sofia; 89.
Cunninghame, Colonel Sir Thomas, M.A. at Athens; 214, 217, 218, 219.
Daneff, M., Bulgarian Statesman; 41, 284, 285.
Danube, River; 78, 131, 216.
Dardanelles; 132, 133, 154, 186, 216; Russian officers report on, 197, 198.
Dedeagatch, suggestion from Athens to land at; 139, 140, 146, 150, 151, 174, 211.
Des Graz, Sir Charles, British British Minister in Serbia; 21, 115, 117.
Demidoff, Prince, Russian Minister at Athens; 227.
Diamandi, M.; 44, 87, 88, 89.
Dimitrieff, General Elias, Chief Intendant, Bulgarian Army, 24; Views on Russian strategy, 94—96.

Dimitrieff, M., Bulgarian Foreign Office; 92.
Djemal Pasha, Commander of Syrian Expedition; 96.
Dobrovitch, M., Private Secretary to King of Bulgaria; 21, 92, 142.
Dobrudja; 54, 55, 58.
Doughty-Wyllie, Colonel; 147.
Dusmanis, General, Chief of Greek General Staff; 220.
Elliot, Sir Francis, British Minister at Athens; 19, 214, 215, 224, 228, 229, 231.
Entente; 158, 196, 210, 211.
Enos-Midia Line; 69, 111.
Erskine, Hon. W., First Secretary at Athens; 224, 228.
Exarch Bulgarian, 124; funeral of, 169, 170.
Falkenhausen, Captain, German M.A. at Athens; 219.
Ferdinand, King of Bulgaria; Rarely seen, 21; depressed, 47; sends mission to Italy, 102; 116; a question of indemnifying, 168; 184, 192, 207, 254, 256.
Ferdinand, King of Roumania; 75—77, 126.
Ferigo, Colonel, Italian M.A. at Bukarest; 101.
Feteh Bey; 182.
Filipescu, M., Roumanian ex-Minister of War; 30, 53, 73, 78, 79, 80, 100, 155.
Fitcheff, General, Bulgarian Minister of War; hostility of Bulgars to Serbs, 34, 90, prophecy of present war, 82; estimate of European Armies, 97; improved relations due to him; territorial wants of Bulgaria, 97; adopts hostile attitude, 107; makes advances to Entente, 119, 132, 144, 145; ready to co-operate, 150, 151; so informs Cabinet, 154; cools off, 157; procrastinates, 158, 159, 162; dismissed, 180, 182; Evidence of indecision, 248, 251, 254.

INDEX. 289

FitzGerald, Colonel; 150.
Fitzmaurice, Mr. Gerald, First Secretary at Sofia; 138, 143, 146—150, 156, 157, 159, 162, 168, 174, 190, 214.
Foreign Office; first offer to Bulgaria, 40; realises importance of, 56; asks Bulgaria for her conditions for joining Entente, 118; asks Fitzmaurice's opinion re 1912 line, 156.
Franchet D'Esperey, Marshal of France; 242.
Fraser, Mr.; 153.
French Army; 120, 228.
Freri, General, Italian Army; 242.
Fyler, Captain R.N.; 147.
Gantcheff, Colonel, Bulgarian Army; 176; military convention with Germany, 248, 251, 252, 255.
Gallipoli Peninsula, Bulgarian Views as to attack of, 98, 148; landing effected on, 152, 166; British Forces on, 202.
Ganzer, Captain, German Submarine Commander; 237.
Garnett, Mr., First Secretary at Sofia; 138.
German Army; 97.
German Loan; 109, 111.
Ghenadieff, M., Bulgarian Statesman, 34; mission to Italy, 102, 196.
Goltz (Pasha), Field-Marshal von der, Turkish Army; 93.
Goltz, Major von der, German M.A., at Sofia; 24.
Goudine-Levkovitch, Colonel Russian M.A. at Athens; 19, 214.
Glyn, Captain, A.D.C. to Gen. Sir A. Paget; 128, 129.
Granet, Colonel, M.A. at Rome; 18.
Greece, Offer of help, 11, 82; refused to allow Entente to land troops, 116; 139, 152, 153, 169; rumoured intention of marching through Bulgaria on Constantinople, 173; 177, 196, 215; General Staff wishes to join Entente, 216; 219, 226; announces intention of interning Entente Troops if driven back, 228; consequences, 229 et seq.
Green, Mr.; 83.
Grey of Falloden, Earl; 12, 37, 71, 85, 86, 109, 136, 143, 174.
Gregory, Mr., British Foreign Office; 172, 176.
Grube, M., Russian Financier; 168, 176.
Grouitch, M., Serbian Diplomat; 21, 112, 113.
Gueschoff, M., Bulgarian Statesman; 111, 198, 284, 285.
Guranesco, M., Roumanian Chargé d'Affaires at Sofia; 35, 43, 44, 88.
Hadji Mischeff, M., Bulgarian Minister in London, 132; pourparlers in London, 136, 142, 143, 144; not kept informed from Sofia, 263.
Hakki Pasha; 177.
Halil Bey; Mission to Germany to prevent Bulgars from attacking Turkey, 152.
Hamilton, General Sir Ian; 136, 149, 150, 201, 202.
Hohenlohe, Prince; 106.
Hunter-Weston, General Sir Aylmer; 147.
Ianopol, M., Greek Inventor; 124, 125.
Iliescu, General, Roumanian War Ministry, 60; declares Roumania ready to march into Transylvania, except for Bulgaria, 61; Roumania has finished with Austria, but hostile to Bulgaria, 71; is obtaining ammunition, guns, etc., from Italy and Germany, 101; suggests Bulgaria be asked to send troops to Bukovina, 104.

Military Attaché U.

INDEX.

Italy, joined Triple Entente, 155; declared war on Austria, May 23rd, 156; idea of expedition to Vallona, 218.

Jekoff, General, Commander-in-Chief, Bulgarian Army, 91; studies German concentration against Roumania, 107; thinks firm offer of 1912 line would bring Bulgaria to side of Entente, 110; estimates German and Austrian forces opposed to Serbia and threatening Roumania, 111; mission to Constantinople, 177; succeeds General Fitcheff, 183—185; reproaches Entente for delay in making offer, 186; sees Col. Thomson, still distrusts Roumania, 187, 188; denies presence of German officers in War Office, 206; trial, 251 et seq.

Justoff, Colonel, Bulgarian Army; 177.

Karageorgevitch, Prince Alexis; 20.

Karageorgevitch, Prince Paul; 21.

Katsikoani, Colonel, Greek M.A. at Sofia; 196.

Kaufmann, M., German Agent at Sofia, 24.

Kerr, Mr. Philip; 243.

Keyes, Admiral Sir Roger; 148.

Kingham, Mr.; 161, 162.

Kitchener of Khartoum, Field-Marshal Earl; 45, 230, 231.

Kolev, General, Bulgarian Army; 204.

Kouchakovitch, Colonel, Serbian M.A. at Sofia; 23, 38, 40, 108.

Kutso-Vlachs, The; 158.

Lachsa, Colonel, Austrian M.A. at Sofia, 24, 90.

Lemnos, Troops landed; 133, 145.

Lichnowsky, Prince, German Ambassador in London; 32.

Line of 1912, as agreed between Serbia and Bulgaria in 1912 before the First Balkan War, vide map; advisability of granting to Bulgaria over the head of Serbia, 12—15, 140; Grey's offer of, delayed by French, 143; by Russia, 152, 155; offer finally made by Entente 29th May, 158; British Legation still hopes to compel Serbia to grant, 209.

Lipton, Sir Thomas; 112, 113.

Lloyd George, Mr.; 144, 243, 273.

Loan to Bulgaria; 109, 111, 115, 252, 257, 258, et seq.

Macedonia; 102, 114; suggested occupation by Allies, 171.

McMahon, Sir Henry; 231.

Mahon, General Sir Bryan; 218.

Malinoff, M., Bulgarian Statesman; 133, 198, 207, 284, 285.

Marghiloman, M., Roumanian Statesman; 75.

Maritza Valley, 251, 257.

Markoff, General, Bulgarian Army.

Matharel, Colonel Count de, French M.A. at Sofia; 23, 137, 205, 212.

Maxwell, Gen. Sir John; 231.

Mecklenburg, Duke of; 196.

Morris, Lieut. R.N.; 136.

Mombelli, General Italian Army; 224, 242.

Morphoff, M., Bulgarian Director of Railways; 137, 151, 152, 159, 197, 199, 200.

Motte, M.; 49.

Napier, Field-Marshal Lord, of Magdala; 77.

Napier, Lt.-Col. Hon. H. D.; appointed M.A. at Sofia, 17; first views of situation, 28; visits Roumania, 29; suggests proposals to Bulgaria should emanate from London, 56; writes to Crown

Prince of Serbia, 58; audiences with King and Queen of Roumania, 75, 77, 82, 83; suggests despatch of Russian troops up Danube, 78; advises visit of Sir A. Paget to King of Bulgaria, 106; hands over duties of M.A. in Roumania to Col. Thompson and returns to Sofia, 126, 131; Farewell audiences, 126, 127, 129; visits Sir I. Hamilton at Lemnos, 147; suggests landing in Gulf of Saros, 148—150; urges that definite offer be made to Bulgaria, 151, 155; suggests time limit to offer made to Bulgaria, 157, 159; opposes occupation of Macedonia by Allies, except in force, via Salonika, 174; visits Bulgarian manoeuvres, 192; revisits Sir I. Hamilton, 200; Gallipoli, 201, 202; returns Sofia, 204; leaves Bulgaria with Legation, 212; appointed temporarily to Athens, 213; interview with General Dusmanis, 221, 222; suggests ultimatum to Greece, 228, 229; accompanies Sir F. Elliot to Mudros; meeting with Lord Kitchener, 231; it is proposed that he return to Roumania; ordered home; captured by German submarine, 232; two years a prisoner in Austria; return to Bulgaria as British Representative, 241; demobilised, 242; sees Mr. Balfour and Mr. P. Kerr, 243; letter to *Times* on death of Mr. Bourchier, 267; correspondence with newspapers regarding Balkans, Dardanelles and Russian Foreign policy, 268 et seq :; with M. Stambolisky, 274, 275, 284, 285, 286.

Nicolas, Grand Duke of Russia; 62.
O'Beirne, Mr., British Minister at Sofia; 12, 171, 172, 174, 190, 192, 200, 203, 207.
O'Mahony, Mr., Philanthropist; 93, 99.
Ostoitch, Colonel, Serbian Army; 113, 115.
O'Reilly; 136, 139.
Paget, General Sir Arthur; 106, 120, 122, 128, 129, 131; audience with King of Bulgaria, 133, 134.
Paléologue, M., French Ambassador at Petrograd; 14.
Panafiew, M., French Minister at Sofia; 120.
Papodopoff, General, Bulgarian Army; 26, 27, 194.
Pashitch, M., 21; threatens to make peace with Austria, 113, 114; the most moderate Serbian Statesman, 117; 175, 177.
Pau, General, French Army; 120, 136.
Pecheff, M., 256.
Petroff, General Radjko; 22.
Petroff, Madame; 23.
Philipopolis, town; 47.
Pichon, Captain, French M.A. Bukarest; 31, 53.
Plunkett, Colonel, M.A. in Serbia; 33.
Poklewsky, M., Russian Minister at Bukarest; 53, 69, 70, 71, 77, 81, 124, 128, 129.
Popoff, M., 252.
Pordim, village in Bulgaria. Relics of Russo-Turkish war; 50.
Population of Balkan States; in 1912—13, 25; in 1923, 245.
Porumbaru, M., Roumanian Minister of Foreign Affairs; 52.
Propaganda, British, 197; German, 10, 46, 82.

INDEX.

Protogaroff, M., Macedonian Leader; 207.
Psycha, M., Greek Minister at Bukarest; 128.
Radeff, M., Bulgarian Minister at Bukarest; 32, 57, 58, 67, 102, 158.
Radoslavoff, M., Bulgarian Prime Minister; 22, 68, 92, 97; conceals our offers from opposition, 111; 132, 248, 251, 252, 253, 254, 255, 256, 259, 260, 261.
Rascano, Colonel, Roumanian Army, 62.
Robeck, Admiral de; 146, 147, 230, 231.
Robertson, Field-Marshal Sir W.; 203.
Rodd, Sir Rennell, British Ambassador at Rome; 18, 243.
Roumania; enthusiasm for war; 30, 36, 43; politics of, 55; pressure from Germany, 179.
Roumania, Queen of; 62, 82.
Roumanian Army, soldier; 62, 63, 64—66, 74, 100, 101, 102, 105.
Royaards, M., Dutch Minister at Sofia; 49, 109, 110.
Russi, M. de, Roumanian Minister at Sofia; 87, 99, 150, 158, 189.
Russian Army; 97, 155; want of ammunition, 160, 164.
Salonika; O'Beirne advises occupation in force, 194; 195, 200, 207, 224.
Samardjiew, Captain, Bulgarian M.A. at Bukarest; 57, 70, 102.
Samson, Major, British Intelligence Officer at Athens; 213.
San Stefano, Treaty of; 23, 97, v. map.
Sarrail, General, French Army; 218.
Savinsky, M., Russian Minister at Sofia; 143, 175, 207.

Savoff, General, ex-Commander-in-Chief Bulgarian Army, 47, 48, 93, 227, 259.
Sazonoff, M., Russian Minister of Foreign Affairs; 69, 70, 93, 174, 175.
Scouloudis, M., Greek Prime Minister; 225, 228.
Second Balkan War; 9, 41, 42, 48.
Sells, Captain R.N., Naval Attaché at Athens; 216, 228.
Semenoff, Colonel, Russian M.A. at Bukarest; 77, 78, 80, 81, 100, 123, 124.
Serbia, political views of; 35, 38, 108; receives identic note from Entente Rulers, 177; reply, 190, 192—193.
Serbian Army; strength in 1914, 39, 40; desperate position, 79; victory 92; Macedonians in Serbian Army, 108, 116.
Seton-Watson, Mr.; 103.
Shields, bullet-proof; 124, 125, 138, 139.
Shipkov, M.; 159, 160.
Slatin (Pasha), General, Austrian Army; 240, 241.
Spalaikovitch, M., Serbian Minister at Petrograd; 15.
Stambolisky; 198, 246, 247, 258.
Stancioff, Colonel, Bulgarian Army; 42.
Stancioff, M., Bulgarian Minister in London; 15, 16.
Strandtmann, M., Russian First Secretary in Serbia; 177.
Submarines, German; 49, 73, 109, 154, 158.
Sykes, Sir Mark, M.P.; 163.
Theodoroff M., Bulgarian Prime Minister; 242, 244.
Thomson, Col., C.B., 123, 126, 128, 129, 187, 188.
Tirnovo, town; 46.

INDEX.

Tontcheff, M., Bulgarian Minister of Finance; 23, 163; his trial, 248.
Toshkoff, M., 251.
Trevelyan, Mr.; 103.
Troubetzkoy, Prince, Russian Minister in Serbia; 80, 114, 115, 175.
Turkey, Goeben-Breslau incident, 16; about to go to war, 45; fortifies against Bulgaria, 136; fear of Bulgars, 142, 182; cession of Maritza Valley, 251.
Turkish Army; 96, 171.
Turkish-Egyptian Expedition; 92, 96, 123, 153.
Tyrrell, Colonel; 200.
Tzanoff, M., Bulgarian Statesman, 198.
Union Club; 23.

Usupoff, Prince, Russian Army; 100.
Venizelos, M., confidence in Great Britain; 20; 91, 216, 217, 223, 225, 227.
Ward, Colonel; 147.
Wemyss, Admiral; 212.
Whitehead, Sir Beethom; 200.
Wilson, Captain Stanley, M.P.; 233, 234, 235, 236.
Yakovaki, M., Roumanian Diplomat; 57.
Yanakitzas, General, Greek Minister of War; 220, 224.
Young, Colonel; 201.
Zaimis, M., Greek Prime Minister; 225.
Zenoff, M.; 23.
Zotto, General, Roumanian Chief of Staff; 105.

www.ingramcontent.com/pod-product-compliance
Lightning Source LLC
Chambersburg PA
CBHW051037160426
43193CB00010B/977